To

Hugo Uyterhoeven
with many thanks

George King

26 July 82

Barriers to Entry

Barriers to Entry

A Corporate-Strategy Perspective

George S. Yip
Harvard University

LexingtonBooks
D.C. Heath and Company
Lexington, Massachusetts
Toronto

Library of Congress Cataloging in Publication Data

Yip, George S.
    Barriers to entry.

    Bibliography: p.
    Includes index.
    1. Industrial organization (Economic theory) 2. Conglomerate
corporations—Planning. I. Title. II. Title: Corporate-strategy perspective.
HD2326.Y37   658.8′02   81-47993
ISBN 0-669-05225-6   AACR2

Published simultaneously in Canada

Printed in the United States of America

International Standard Book Number: 0-669-05225-6

Library of Congress Catalog Card Number: 81-47993

*To my father and mother,
and Moira and Andrew*

Contents

List of Figures
and Tables

Foreword

Entry is one of the principal forces of competition that shapes the performance of firms and industries in any economy. It is an engine of challenge for complacent market leaders, and the tangible manifestation of many diversification strategies. It is an eventuality for which incumbents plan defensive strategies, and a subtle and difficult course of action for which potential entrants plan offensive strategies.

Since the research of Joe Bain and in bits and pieces before, scholars have known something that is second nature to managers—it is not always easy to enter an industry.[1] Bain's research began to catalog the major entry barriers, and subsequent work by economists has developed the theory of barriers and how they can be influenced by firms.[2] However, the work by economists has largely focused on identifying barriers without regard to the nature of the firm attempting entry into the industry, and the ultimate position the entrant seeks to achieve.

During the late 1970s, however, a new perspective began to be introduced into research on entry. With its roots in the business-policy field, a thread of research in industrial organization began to emphasize the heterogeneity among firm strategies for competing in an industry.[3] This work, much of which has been done at Harvard University, led to the generalization of entry barriers to mobility barriers and increasing stress on established firms as potential entrants who possess skills and resources drawn from their other businesses.[4] The focus of this work has been as much on informing the formulation of competitive strategies as it has been on improving public policy.[5]

George Yip's book is an important contribution to knowledge about entry viewed in this way. It aims to combine the perspective and tools of the economist with an awareness of the operation of real-life markets to yield a study that will at the same time be of interest to practitioners and scholars.

The conceptual contribution of the book is to advance our understanding of the role of established firms as entrants, how entry strategies differ in ways that importantly affect barriers, and how we can explain the type of entry strategy chosen and its ultimate success. A particularly interesting finding is that entrants may in some cases be *better off* than incumbents because of their stock of skills and resources and the possible existence of what Yip terms entry "gateways."

The book is perhaps even more notable for its empirical work. Yip has employed the rich PIMS data base to construct a unique test of the occurrence of entry across industries. He has also compiled a unique data base of his own that provides a detailed view of entry patterns, entry strategies, and outcomes in a sample of industries. This data base is employed to test models of the choice of entry strategy and the success of different types of entry strategies, among other things.

This book will make interesting reading for both scholars and practitioners. It also represents what I hope will be a growing stream of work about the behavior of firms and industries that aims to combine theory and careful research methods with attention to the practical concerns of actual companies. If Yip's book stimulates more work of this type by business-administration scholars and economists, then it will be an even more important new entrant into the library of economics and management than it is based on its interesting findings.

Michael E. Porter
Harvard Graduate School of
Business Administration

Notes

1. Joe S. Bain, *Barriers to New Competition,* (Cambridge, Mass.: Harvard University Press, 1956).

2. For a survey, see the collection of papers in S. Salop, ed., "Strategic Entry Deterrence," *American Economic Review* (May 1970), pp. 335-338.

3. See M.E. Porter, *Interbrand Choice, Strategy and Bilateral Market Power,* (Cambridge, Mass.: Harvard University Press, 1976); M.S. Hunt, "Competition in the Major Home Appliance Industry, 1960-1970," Ph.D. dissertation, Business Economics Committee, Harvard University, May 1972; H.H. Newman, "Strategic Groups and the Structure-Performance Relationship: A Study With Respect To The Chemical Process Industries," Ph.D. dissertation, Harvard University, December 1973.

4. See R.E. Caves and M.E. Porter, "From Entry Barriers to Mobility Barriers: Conjectural Decisions and Contrived Deterrence to New Competition," *Quarterly Journal of Economics* (May 1977), pp. 241-262.

5. See M.E. Porter, *Competitive Strategy: Techniques for Analyzing Industries and Competitors* (The Free Press, 1980).

Acknowledgments

Many people helped me to complete this book. Thanks are due to all, but only some can be acknowledged here. My first thanks go to Michael Porter, who guided me through the territory between industrial-organization economics and corporate strategy. William Fruhan helped on all aspects of the work, as well as providing his special expertise on financial strategy. Hugo Uyterhoeven was invaluable in his continuing emphasis on significance and communicability to the practitioner. Extensive assistance was also given by Richard Caves, Robert Buzzell, and David Reibstein. Norman Berg, Joseph Bower, William Hall, and Malcolm Salter have made valuable contributions. Victoria Alexander edited and improved the presentation of this entire book.

This book would not have been possible without the participation of the Strategic Planning Institute (SPI). Sidney Schoeffler generously made SPI's resources, data, and membership available. Bradley Gale steered my project through the organization as well as making many substantive contributions. Many others at SPI helped. Extensive computer-related assistance was given by Reed Sturtevant, Larry Crowson, Paul Chussil, and Roberta Bauer. The PIMS Program member companies and executives who contributed data must remain anonymous, but their cooperation is greatly appreciated.

Funding was received from the Harvard Business School's Doctoral Admissions Fellowship and Division of Research Fellowship, the Bowne & Company's thesis-proposal prize, and the Harvard Business School's Division of Research support for faculty. I thank all those who made these funds possible. Marie Castro and Mary Armistead typed tirelessly and cheerfully for three years.

Selected data, quotations, and data forms are reproduced here with permission of The Strategic Planning Institute.

1 Entry as a Strategic Issue

Entry of new competitors changes the entered market. Entry, by definition, adds a player to the competitive game, another sharer of the pie. The efforts of new competitors to establish themselves frequently render the market less profitable for all. Even worse for incumbents (the existing participants in the market), entrants can bring superior skills, greater resources, new ways to compete, or all of the above.

Procter & Gamble's entry into the tampon market with Rely was disastrous for existing competitors. The latter were saved only by an event outside their control—the toxic-shock crisis that prompted Procter's reluctant retreat. Entrants who have been able to establish beachheads have frequently gone on to assault the entire market. Japanese entrants excel at this strategy. To cite only one example, Japanese motorcycle manufacturers entered both the American and British motorcycle markets via the small-engine segment, only to work their way up through all the size segments.

On the other hand, many entrants have suffered costly failures or even more costly successes. Eastman Kodak entered the instant camera market in 1976 against Polaroid, an opponent one-sixth its size. Five years later and still in the market, Kodak harvested a meager one-third market share, a bitter price-war, and, as of late 1981, a patent-infringement suit. Anheuser-Busch has failed twice in attempting to enter the soft-drink market, once with a differentiated product and once with a me-too product.

What attracts or discourages new competitors from entering markets? What determines their success or disaster? What can entrants and incumbents do to bring about the result they desire? This book will address all these questions.

Entry also changes the entrant. For companies with no previous existence, successful entry gives their first, and often most important, market. For companies with other existing businesses, entry into a new market is one of the four ways in which their corporate mix changes; the others are differential growth and shrinkage of businesses in existing markets, and exit from a market. Thus, entry begins the strategic sequence of *entry* ⟶ *growth* ⟶ *shrinkage* ⟶ *exit*, which is the building block of the multibusiness corporation. Today, few American, European, or Japanese managers need reminding that the corporate sectors of their economies are dominated by multibusiness companies, or that the portfolio mix of such companies needs continuing adjustment.

1

How do the corporate characteristics of multibusiness companies affect their choice of markets to enter? How do these characteristics affect their choice of entry strategy and their chances of success? This book will address these questions too.

Heightened Interest in Entry

For too many American and European, if not Japanese, companies the 1970s brought slower growth, even shrinkage, of much of their existing businesses. Growth through acquisition also lost its luster of the 1960s, as companies struggled to manage their newly adopted, fully grown, and intractable children. Growth through internal development, by building businesses to enter new markets, received renewed attention.

Selecting markets for entry, and the development of entry strategies also drew increased attention as tools of strategic planning. Although definitions vary, some of the characteristics of strategic planning are[1]

1. A multifunctional focus on the total strategy of a business;
2. Emphasis on a proactive approach to planning: strategic planning should result in actions to change the corporation's strategic situation (This emphasis contrasts with the more purely forecasting philosophy of *corporate planning*, the planning concept of the 1960s);[2]
3. Frequent use in multibusiness corporations for corporate-level integrated comparisons of businesses, and for decisions on resource allocation among businesses;
4. A preference for generally applicable rules of strategy that can be used to quantify comparisons of performance and prospects of a diversified corporation's businesses.

These aspects certainly apply to entry strategy. The former chairman of General Electric, the company which is the acknowledged pioneer in strategic planning, has described one of the aims of that function as the direction of the company into growing industries.[3]

Entry should be distinguished from *diversification*. Entry is best viewed as the act of beginning activities in a market new to the entrant; diversification refers to the degree of newness. There is also not a perfect overlap between the two concepts. Expansion of an existing product into a new geographic market is usually considered entry but not diversification. At the other extreme, a conglomerate acquisition is certainly diversification, but does not usually involve market entry. Entry can also be made by companies that are new, and therefore have no existing business from which to diversify.

New Conceptual Tools

Recent innovations in theories of competition and strategy also make this a propitious time to study entry as an issue of corporate strategy. The well-developed theory of *barriers to entry* has long existed as an issue for economists. Originated by Joe S. Bain[4] and extended by other industrial-organization economists, this economic theory has greatly influenced U.S. public policy toward antitrust, yet it has had no discernible impact on the practice of corporate and competitive strategy. Only the term itself, barriers to entry, has passed into business usage and, as I will argue, the term may well be deluding, rather than illuminating, strategic practice. A major purpose of this book is to articulate and translate, for the benefit of managers, a potent strategic concept while incorporating recent innovations in theory in both economics and corporate strategy.

Industrial Organization and Competitive Heterogeneity

The traditional heart of industrial organization economics was the structure → conduct → performance paradigm,[5] which assumed that an industry could be fully described by a few structural elements, such as degree of concentration, growth rate, degree of product differentiation, extent of economies of scale, and barriers to entry.[6] According to this paradigm, structure determines the conduct of all firms in the industry, in regard to pricing, product policy, research, and advertising activities. Conduct, in turn, determines a common industry performance, in terms of both firm profitability and such broader societal dimensions as the allocation of productive resources, the efficiency of production, and the share of benefits between producers and consumers.

The industrial organization (IO) paradigm has two obvious points of anathema for business strategists. First, managers can scarcely accept that industry-wide factors determine their conduct. In the millenia-old debate on free will versus determinism, managers have to believe in the former or deny their title. Second, the IO paradigm assumes that firms are identical in all important economic aspects except size, such homogeneity applying even to management skills. Such an assumption has also not been acceptable to managers who daily seek to exploit or defend against the differences between themselves and their competitors. The assumption also directly contradicts the creed of "distinctive competence" etched in the hearts and minds of generations of MBA graduates.[7]

In the last decade, however, economists, particularly at Harvard,[8] have adapted the IO paradigm to the assumptions and requirements of corporate strategy.[9] In particular the recent IO literature recognizes the heterogeneity of competitors and their strategies. This perspective has been applied to many strategic issues, including that of barriers to entry. Michael E. Porter's well-known scheme of the five competitive forces shaping strategy (that converts IO concepts into a framework for competitive analysis) includes "threat of new entrants."[10] Kathryn Harrigan has applied the IO framework to the opposite end of the strategic sequence—exit.[11]

Corporate Strategy and Structural Homogeneity

As IO economists were exploring the possibilities of uniqueness in corporate strategy, corporate strategists were moving in the opposite direction, toward industry-wide forces and generalizable rules of strategy. The thrust in this direction was provided by the rise of diversified companies, and the resultant phenomenon of corporate-level managers trying to control diverse businesses with which they were unfamiliar or had lost familiarity. These managers hungered for concepts and rules that would allow them to analyze and evaluate business-level strategies and performances without the detailed knowledge available to business-level managers.

The General Electric Company, perhaps the world's largest diversified corporation, attempted to solve this problem of managing diversity partly by developing a cross-sectional-strategy model, which, in 1972, sired the PIMS (Profit Impact of Market Strategies) Program.[12] Like IO, the PIMS models assume that market structure has universal effects. Today at least half of the *Fortune* 500, as well as many Canadian and European companies, have joined the effort to find rules of strategy and laws of the marketplace.

The other major thrust toward structural homogeneity and rules of strategy has been led by the Boston Consulting Group (BCG). Their famous product-portfolio matrix assumes a universal rule that one element of market structure, growth rate, and one measure of competitive position, relative market share, together determine the appropriate overall strategy for a business. BCG's other famous concept, the experience curve, is also posed as a universal rule.[13] My study of entry draws on the PIMS work on market structure and the BCG work on the dynamics of competition.

Corporate-Level and Business-Level Strategies

The third conceptual development aiding a study of entry is the research distinguishing corporate- from business-level strategy. Hofer has provided a useful dichotomy of corporate- and business-level concerns.[14] The corporate-level concern is "What types and mixes of business should the firm be in?'' The business-level one is "What are the determinants of success in the XYZ business?''

The relevance to entry is obvious. Typically, a corporate-level entity creates a business to compete in the new market. Again, this conceptual development has been spurred by the rise of diversified companies. A long line of research has developed the conceptual measures to describe diversified corporations and the relationships among their differing businesses. Crowning these efforts, Rumelt elucidates the relationship between the parent company and its entrant offspring.[15]

Corporate- and business-level strategies are reasonably distinct, particularly because of the usual organizational split between them. Business strategy is composed of various functional strategies: financial, marketing, production, research and development (R&D), and so forth. Thus there is a straightforward organizational hierarchy of corporate, business, and functional strategies. These three classes of strategy can be further characterized as competitive or noncompetitive. Competitive strategy is the way in which a business organizes its activities to optimize its position *vis-à-vis* its competitors. While the two types represent a continuum rather than a clear dichotomy, noncompetitive strategy can be usefully considered as not directly focused on competitors. Examples are corporate-level strategy concerning the long-term mix of the company's businesses, business-level strategy with regard to environmental concerns, and a functional strategy for hiring the appropriate personnel. Although entry strategy is only one element of competitive strategy, for both entrants and incumbents, it is the strategic issue with the most far-reaching ramifications for all three levels of strategy.

New Statistical Sources

In addition to a growing business interest in entry and the development of new conceptual scalpels, there is a third basis for study of this issue—the availability of new statistical sources. Both IO economists and corporate/ business-strategy researchers have suffered, and continue to suffer, from the problem of data. I speak of the United States only; the problem is even worse elsewhere. Corporate and business strategies are complex; their competitive aspects are, per se, confidential. Only the broadest corporate-level issues can be tackled using data from public corporate reports. Those studying competitive and business-level issues have had to choose between the inadequacy of generalizable, large-sample, public data, and the ungeneralizability of adequate, small-sample, private data. IO economists have taken the first path, using primarily Standard Industrial Classification (SIC) data. The drawbacks of such data are well known: the broad, production-based industry definitions often group together firms that do not compete with each other and exclude those that do; the limited number of strategic variables hides the complexity of competition; the industry-wide base of measurement masks the heterogeneity of competitors. The other path, taken primarily by corporate-strategy researchers, has been to forego the generalizability of the large sample in favor of case studies based on private data.

The PIMS Data Base

The substance of the PIMS Program and its data base is now well-known, but less well known is the validity of the data as a base for research. The appendix of this book addresses that issue in some depth. I shall summarize here why the PIMS data base goes a long way toward solving the problems of sample size, confidentiality, strategic complexity, and competitor heterogeneity.

The key feature of the PIMS data base is that it comprises observations reported by managers of incumbent businesses in narrowly defined markets. The market definition avoids the usual problem of diversification noise when industry definitions are used. Market competitors are observed at the level of the business units serving the market, not at the level of the entire company. Some further advantages of the data base are that it comprises a large number of measures of dimensions of competition and performance. The sample size is both large (1,500) and representative: the data base's markets are classed in at least 60 percent of the four-digit-level industries in the manufacturing division of the Standard Industrial Classification system in the United States. However, the data base is limited to the extent that both the identity and size of the markets and their competitors are disguised.

In addition to the extant data on markets and incumbents, the PIMS Program allowed me to collect original, in-depth data on entrants, their strategies and performance. Thus, in this book I apply new theory to new data. These data are from the viewpoint of incumbents, in contrast to the data collected and analyzed by Biggadike from the viewpoint of entrants.[16]

Current Theory on Entry

There is extensive economic theory on barriers to entry, postulating how various elements of industry structure (for example, advertising intensity) can impose disadvantages on entrants relative to incumbents. Overall, the theory predicts that the existence of barriers to entry results in fewer entries and, therefore, allows incumbents to enjoy above average profitability.

Entry is, therefore, also important in economic theory as a means of promoting competition, and thereby improving the allocation of economic resources.

For the reasons discussed above, however, economic theory on entry barriers has focused on industry-wide variables as determinants of entry behavior. In most of their empirical studies on entry, IO researchers have used large-sample, cross-sectional data bases with a limited number of industry-wide variables. Most of these studies have sought to explain the level of industry profitability in terms of industry structure, inferring that this level is primarily determined by the size of entry barriers. Few studies have tried to explain the number of entrants. Corporate and business strategy researchers have not focused extensively on entry, but, rather, have addressed the broader and somewhat different issue of diversification. In addition to this difference in focus, their theory and evidence tend to emphasize the uniqueness of individual competitors and the relevance of a wide range of variables.

The differences in perspective between the industrial-organization and corporate-strategy approaches have been very salient in the theory of barriers to entry. As originally formulated, that concept fully incorporated the assumptions of the structure $\rightarrow$ conduct $\rightarrow$ performance paradigm: that the size of entry barriers was fully determined by industry structure. Only recently have additions to the theory added components drawn from corporate strategy—particularly the role of competitor- and strategy-heterogeneity.

Objective and Focus of this Study

Existing research on entry (and other strategic issues), reviewed in chapter 2, reveals a gap in both theory and evidence between economics and corporate strategy. The study described in this book attempts to bridge that gap by revising the theory of entry barriers to integrate the industry-wide perspective of economics and the competitor-specific perspective of corporate strategy. I have tested the revised theory against data with both industry-wide and competitor-specific characteristics.

Existing research began to recognize that industry structure alone was an incomplete determinant of entry barriers. Bain's original formulation identified only newborn firms as the potential entrants to be deterred by barriers. Once existing firms were included as potential entrants,[17] the assets and skills of such firms were also relevant to the theory of entry barriers: barriers could be reduced by the potential entrant's existing assets. A focus on the heterogeneous characteristics of firms is a key feature of corporate strategy. This study has drawn on that perspective to further develop the role of the assets of existing firms in reducing barriers.

Economic theory on entry has also largely neglected the heterogeneity of competitive strategies. This study uses the heterogeneity of competitive strategy to argue that in some situations barriers can be turned into "gateways" for entrants, that is, that instead of entrants facing disadvantages relative to incumbents, there are advantages to being entrants.

Thus this study seeks to add a third stage in the development of entry theory. In the first stage the concept was formulated in relation to newborn firms. In the second stage, existing firms were recognized as potential entrants, resulting in a prediction of the reduced impact of barriers. The third stage, proposed here, examines the role of particular competitive strategies in providing negative barriers or gateways. This third stage thus seeks to bring entry theory closer to a corporate-strategy perspective.

A corporate-strategy perspective of heterogeneity in markets, competitors, and competitive strategies, is used to derive a further modification of entry theory: the inclusion of acquisition entrants. According to Bain's original definition, an entrant must be a new legal entity that introduces new production capacity. This emphasis on the introduction of capacity reflects the traditional economic view of competitors as identical except in terms of size. This traditional approach suggests that entry makes its impact on an industry through the addition of capacity and increase in the number of competitors.

A more heterogeneous view of competitors and competitive strategy suggests that industries can experience entry-like impacts in other ways. A change in ownership of an existing competitor, via acquisition, does not add a new competitor; but if the acquiring firm seeks to use the acquisition as a base for expansion, such an acquisition entrant can affect the industry as if it were a traditionally defined entrant. An acquirer may have more ambitious plans than the previous owners of the acquired business, as well as the resources to back those plans. This new competitor may also play the competitive game differently.

A classic example of the dangers to incumbents of acquisition entry is Philip Morris's acquisition of the Miller Brewing Company. Philip Morris entered the beer market with the intention to convert Miller from a minor competitor with a 4-percent market share to a major one. Ten years later, Miller was second in the market with over 20-percent share. Philip Morris had both the financial resources and the competitive skills to so successfully exploit their entry base. Incumbents should therefore be aware of the threat of acquisition entry as a potential Trojan Horse; dangerous new competitors may be allowed in through the front gate, bypassing barriers.

Acquisition entry is thus an option to be considered by potential entrants. Acquisition of immediate share, assets, and skills allows the acquirer to avoid some or all of the barriers. The uncertainty of new ventures is also avoided. Even Procter & Gamble deemed it wiser to enter the soft-drink business via acquisition (of most of Crush International, Limited, in 1980). Procter & Gamble commented that the acquisition would give them "initial exposure—to a large and highly competitive business—different from any of the other categories" in which it competed.[18]

Thus, there are two types of entries. A *direct entry* occurs when a firm, whether newborn or already existing, begins selling in an existing market from which it was previously absent. An *acquisition entry* occurs when an existing competitor in an existing market is acquired by a firm not previously competing in that market. The acquisition is made with the intention of using the acquired business as a base for expansion, and not merely holding it as a portfolio investment.

It should be clear that what constitutes entry depends a great deal on the definition of the entered market. Entrants seldom come from markets so unrelated to the entered one that there is no question that a market boundary has been crossed. Entrants into U.S. markets from overseas are already in the same global market as are domestic manufacturers. Procter & Gamble was already in the consumer-products market before it entered the tampon market. Yet both types of entry involve some crossing of boundaries and barriers. Indeed, the height of the barriers depends on the strategic distance between the entrant's home markets and the entered one. It is, therefore, more useful to accept the fact that entry, like market boundaries, represents a continuum rather than one sharply defined type of activity. Some points along this continuum will be identified and discussed in chapter 4.

Research Issues

My revised view of entry results in the selection of three specific research issues central to entry barriers:

1. Whether and how barriers restrict the occurrence of entry;
2. How barriers affect the strategy of entrants—particularly the use of acquisition as a way of avoiding barriers;
3. How barriers affect the market success of entrants.

Existing data are used to examine the first issue. Original data are analyzed for the second and third issues. These empirical analyses each contribute something new. Most previous studies have investigated the impact of barriers on industry profitability rather than on the occurrence of entry. None have linked direct and acquisition entry in one framework, and none have systematically linked entrant market-share performance to entry barriers.

Outline of Study

The chapters that follow address these research issues. In chapter 2, I review existing theory and evidence on barriers to entry. The original formulation of the theory by Bain and Sylos is also the strongest prediction of how market structure poses barriers to entry. Subsequent theorists have predicted a weaker ability of market structure to create high barriers. These developments consist of the inclusion of existing firms as potential entrants, and the increasing recognition in economic theory of the heterogeneity of competitive strategies. Existing firms possess assets that can allow them to face effectively lower barriers. The heterogeneity of competitive strategies can allow entrants to avoid full confrontation with barriers.

In chapter 3, I use these modifications to develop a revised framework of how barriers affect the occurrence of entry into a given market (from the viewpoint of a market, not an entrant). This theory is formulated at the level of the market structure variables (for example, degree of advertising intensity) which give rise to barriers and inducements to entry, and the theory predicts the association between these variables and the occurrence of entry.

I argue that the variables traditionally predicted to act as inducements to entry (for example, high market growth rate) continue to do so in the revised theory, applying to all markets. In contrast, few of the variables traditionally predicted to act as barriers (such as high-R&D intensity) can be uniformly predicted, for most markets, to be negatively associated with the occurrence of entry. One reason is the weakening of barriers by two factors: the role of existing firms as potential entrants, and the heterogeneity of competitive strategies. An additional reason is that the same variables giving rise to barriers can give rise to gateways to entry. While barriers create disadvantages for entrants relative to incumbents, gateways confer potential advantages. I argue that in some cases entrants can be better off than incumbents: they may be able to invest in superior production or selling techniques, or use competitive strategies that exploit the commitments of incumbents to their strategies.

I argue that previous tests of the height of barriers have not tested this different role of barriers. Most previous studies have used industry profitability as a measure of the height of barriers. Several arguments are made as to why, in practice, this is probably not a fully appropriate measure, and the actual occurrence of entry may be more appropriate.

Chapter 3 presents a test of barriers using the occurrence of entry as the dependent variable, and a large number of market-structure and incumbent-business characteristics as explanatory variables. The sample is a cross-sectional one of 793 U.S. and Canadian manufactured-products markets, selected from the PIMS Program research data base and observed for various four-year periods during the 1970s. This sample has easily the largest number of observations and variables ever used in a study of entry. The variables are also more competitor-specific than those available to previous studies. A special feature of this sample is that the market definition is very narrow and demand-oriented, in contrast to previous studies' broad and supply-oriented definitions. In general, the results of this test support my view that market structure provides a good indication of inducements to entry but an incomplete indication of barriers. Knowledge of the characteristics of entrants and the strategies available to them appear to be necessary to complete the specification of barriers.

Chapter 3 also presents subsidiary tests explaining the number of entrants-per-market and the combined achieved-market-share of all entrants per market. These tests are conducted on special data collected for thirty-one markets. These special data are also used to compare managers' estimates of the heights of various types of barriers, and the heights as indicated by market structure.

Chapter 4 develops a theory to include acquisition entry in the entry framework, since acquisition entry can be used to avoid barriers. Acquisitions for purely portfolio purposes are distinguished from acquisition entries. The differences between traditional (direct) entry and acquisition entry are discussed, the primary one being that acquisition entry has to be effected via the financial market, while direct entry is a process internal to the entrant. These differences involve financial, managerial, and legal issues, as well as the issue of whether, and at what price, acquisition candidates are available.

I argue that barriers to entry represent an additional dimension on which the two entry modes can be evaluated. I discuss the concept of an entrant's relatedness to the entered market, and how increased relatedness reduces the impact of barriers on the cost of entry. The key impact of barriers and relatedness on the direct versus acquisition choice is that relatedness reduces barriers much more for direct than for acquisition entrants. The reason for this is that relatedness reduces the cost of breaching entry barriers for direct entrants, but does not reduce the acquisition price to be paid by an acquisition entrant. The acquisition price typically capitalizes some average barrier height, rather than the height for specific would-be entrants. Relatedness therefore has a differential impact on the expected returns on investment under the two entry modes. This holds even if the two modes would result in different entry scales and strategies.

This argument is used to develop the prediction that market-structure variables posing barriers to entry will, other things being equal, encourage acquisition rather than direct entry. I also argue that certain entrant characteristics, such as the size and diversification category of the parent company, will affect the entrant's choice of entry mode.

While the existing PIMS Program data were adequate for analysis of the occurrence of entry, additional data were required for analysis of the direct versus acquisition choice and the market-share performance of entrants. New data on entrants were obtained by recruiting thirty-one of the 793 businesses that had supplied the PIMS data on themselves and their markets. Appendix A evaluates the representativeness of this sample and argues that it is reasonably generalizable to U.S. manufactured-products markets in growth, maturity, and decline stages of the product life-cycle (that is, excluding the introductory stage). The thirty-one businesses provided data via a questionnaire designed for this study, the Entry Project Data Forms and Data Manual (see appendixes D and E). This questionnaire includes several data concepts developed for the study. Each of the businesses were incumbents in markets that had experienced entry during the previous seven years (1972 to 1979) by at least one direct or acquisition entrant.

Data on entrants into their markets were provided by a sample of incumbents. Incumbents were used as the source of information because they, not entrants, were in the best position to provide a census report of all entries within the selected time period. A census of all entrants into the market was deemed a better base for evaluating each market's barriers than data on one entrant per market. One disadvantage of my data-gathering approach is that incumbents have incomplete knowledge about entrants. I did attempt, however, to restrict the reported data to information believed to be readily available to incumbents; for example, market share was part of the data, but profitability was not. (The validity of the new data and of the existing PIMS data is discussed in detail in appendix A.)

The thirty-one incumbents (respondents) were asked to supply data on all entrants into their markets for the period 1972 to 1979. Data on a total of ninety entrants were reported, and detailed data were obtained for sixty-nine entrants, including:

Parent-company characteristics;

Relationship of the entry move to the parent company's existing businesses, for example, unrelated diversification;

Degree of sharing between entrant and other parent businesses for several types of activities and customers;

Whether the entry was direct or via acquisition;

Perceived motivation for the entry;

Entry strategy in terms of the entrant's position relative to incumbents on various dimensions of competition;

Incumbent response;

Market share achieved by the entrants.

Some of the new data are analyzed and reported descriptively in chapter 4, since these data have not been available to previous researchers: the census aspect; the comparison of direct and acquisition entry; and the integration of market-level, business-level, and corporate-level data.

The new data are then used to test my theory on the direct versus acquisition choice of entry mode. First, I attempt to explain the proportion of entries per market that was direct rather than acquisition. The explanatory variables are market structure and incumbent characteristics. The unit of analysis is the market.

Second, I analyze the direct or acquisition choice of fifty-nine individual entrants into twenty-eight of the thirty-one markets in the sample. The entrants' characteristics and strategies are now added to the market structure and incumbent-characteristic variables as explanatory variables. The unit of analysis is thus the individual entrant.

The results of the analyses are generally consistent with the predictions of how barriers affect the direct versus acquisition choice. Also the combination of market structure and entrant characteristics appears to have a great determining effect on the direct versus acquisition choice.

Chapter 5 addresses the third research issue—the market-share performance of entrants. I argue that the share gain after entry should be a function of the market structure variables posing barriers to entry, entrants' characteristics, strategies for overcoming barriers, incumbent reactions, and time elapsed since entry. Share gain is defined as the greatest share, at any time, since entry (but net of the acquired share for acquisition entrants).

The model is tested on the data base described. The dependent variable is entrant-share gain, and the explanatory variables are market structure, entrant characteristics and strategies, and the time since entry. The sample consists of sixty-nine entrants in thirty-one different markets. The sample is also split into forty-five direct and twenty-four acquisition entrants to test whether the share gain of the two types of entrants is differentially explained by the independent variables. Thus this is also a test of the extent to which acquisition entrants are true entrants.

Chapter 6 concludes by summarizing the theoretical and empirical analyses of the entire study, and drawing implications for researchers, public policymakers, and business managers.

The most important implication is for entry theory: the role of barriers is more complex than can be captured by market structure alone and depends also on the assets of entrants and the competitive strategies available to them. In fact, market-structure sources of barriers can offer gateways that confer advantages on entrants.

The implications for researchers cover both the issues for further research on entry and the broader implications for strategy research in general.

The implications for public policymakers concern the appropriate degree of intervention to preserve easy entry, and particularly, the appropriate regulation of acquisition entry. A further implication is drawn for the intermittent proposals for anti-merger legislation.

The implications for managers concern both incumbents and entrants. Incumbents must reassess the extent to which barriers to entry really protect markets. For entrants, the issue is how to overcome barriers successfully.

Notes

1. From George S. Yip, "Market Selection and Direction: The Role of Product Portfolio Planning," *Harvard Case Services,* No. 9-581-107 (Cambridge, Mass.: Harvard University, 1981).

2. A McKinsey Staff Paper elaborates four phases in the evolution of strategic decision making: Phase I—Financial Planning, Phase 2—Forecast-based Planning, Phase 3—Externally Oriented Planning, and Phase 4—Strategic Management. [See Frederick Gluck, Stephen P. Kaufman, and A. Steven Wallech, "The Evolution of Strategic Management," *McKinsey Staff Paper* (New York: McKinsey & Co., October 1978)].

3. Reported by John D.C. Roach in "From Strategic Planning to Strategic Performance: Closing the Achievement Gap," *Outlook* (New York: Booz-Allen & Hamilton, Inc., Spring 1981).

4. Joe S. Bain, *Barriers to New Competition* (Cambridge, Mass.: Harvard University Press, 1956).

5. See Scherer's summary of this "Bain/Mason" paradigm in F.M. Scherer, *Industrial Market Structure and Economic Performance* (Chicago: Rand McNally & Co., 1970):3-6.

6. For the most complete list see William B. Shepherd, "The Elements of Market Structure," *Review of Economics and Statistics* 54, no. 1 (February 1972):25-37.

7. The uniqueness of the strategic position of individual companies has been well expressed and developed by the business-policy group at the Harvard Business School. See Edmund P. Learned, C. Roland Christensen, Kenneth R. Andrews, and William Guth, *Business Policy* (Homewood, Ill.: Irwin, 1969); and Kenneth R. Andrews, *The Concept of Corporate Strategy,* rev. ed., (Homewood, Ill.: Irwin 1980).

8. Led by Richard E. Caves and Michael E. Porter, culminating in Porter's seminal work written for managers, *Competitive Strategy: Techniques for Analyzing Industries and Competitors* (New York: The Free Press, 1980).

9. For a full description of this rapprochement see Michael E. Porter, "The Contributions of Industrial Organization to Strategic Management," *Academy of Management Review* 6, no. 4 (October 1981):609-620.

10. See Porter, *Competitive Strategy;* and Michael E. Porter, "How Competitive Forces Shape Strategy," *Harvard Business Review,* (March-April 1979):137-145.

11. Kathryn Rudie Harrigan, *Strategies for Declining Businesses,* (Lexington, Mass.: Lexington Books D.C. Heath and Company, 1980).

12. See Sidney Schoeffler, Robert D. Buzzell and Donald F. Heany, "Impact of Strategic Planning on Profit Performance," *Harvard Business Review* 52, no. 2, (March-April 1974):137-145.

13. See "Perspectives on Experience," The Boston Consulting Group, 1968; and "The Experience Curve—Reviewed, I, II, III, IV," The Boston Consulting Group 1973 to 1974; and Bruce D. Henderson, *Henderson on Corporate Strategy* (Cambridge, Mass.: Abt Books, 1979).

14. Charles W. Hofer, "Toward a Contingency Theory of Business Strategy," *Academy of Management Journal,* 18, no. 4 (December 1975): 784-810.

15. See Richard P. Rumelt, *Strategy, Structure, and Economic Performance,* (Boston: Division of Research, Harvard Business School), 1974, and Bruce R. Scott, "The Industrial State: Old Myths and New Realities," *Harvard Business Review* (March-April 1973):133-148.

16. E. Ralph Biggadike *Corporate Diversification: Entry, Strategy and Performance,* (Boston: Division of Research, Harvard Business School, 1979), and also in "The Risky Business of Diversification," *Harvard Business Review* 57, no. 3, (May-June 1979):103-111.

17. Initially in Howard H. Hines, "Effectiveness of 'Entry' by Already Established Firms," *Quarterly Journal of Economics* 71, no. 1 (February 1957): pp. 131-150, but not really developed until the work of Richard E. Caves and Michael E. Porter in "From Entry Barriers to Mobility Barriers: Conjectural Decisions and Continued Deterrence to New Competition," *Quarterly Journal of Economics* 91 (May 1977):241-262.

18. "Procter & Gamble, via Takeover, to Enter Highly Competitive Soft Drink Industry," *Wall Street Journal* (New York: May 21, 1980).

2 The Concept of Barriers to Entry

Bain formulated the concept that each market can be characterized by a "condition of entry" equivalent to the state of potential competition from possible new competitors.[1] This condition of entry should be evaluated roughly:

> By the advantages of established sellers in an industry over potential entrant sellers, these advantages being reflected in the extent to which established sellers can persistently raise their prices above a competitive level without attracting new firms to enter the industry.

The highest level at which established sellers can set price without attracting entry is the *limit price*. The nature of the advantages that allow such elevated prices depend in turn on structural industry-wide characteristics.

Bain's condition of entry has passed into the language of business as *barriers to entry*. One purpose of this study is to ensure that managers understand and correctly use this concept. Barriers to entry are the disadvantages that entrants face relative to incumbents. These disadvantages arise from the fact of entry and are separate from the disadvantages of size or inferior resources and skills. Of course, entrants are often smaller companies than incumbents and face the usual size, resource, and skill disadvantages that most established small competitors also face. It is important to think of barriers as disadvantages arising from the fact of entry against established incumbents. Barriers are an inherent feature of the market, and potentially exact a cost from all entrants crossing them.

Sources of Entry Barriers

Bain attributed the condition of entry to three types of sources: absolute cost advantages, product differentiation advantages, and economies of scale.

Absolute Cost Advantages

Bain suggested that firms already in the industry may have lower costs than those achievable by an entrant because of:

1. the existence of patents and similar legal restrictions;
2. limits on the availability of raw materials, skilled personnel, techno-
    logical expertise, or other factors of production, and incumbents hav-
    ing preferential access to these scarce factors;
3. the higher cost of capital for entrants.

The effect of patents and legal restrictions is obvious. Preferential access to
scarce factors of production gives a cost advantage, independent of scale.
For example, an increasing number of global industries, such as electronics,
are today shifting their production operations to countries offering high-
skill, low-cost labor, including South Korea, Taiwan, Hong Kong, and
Singapore. Access to such work forces is an advantage for competitors
already in the market.

The third source of absolute cost advantage is often cited as a barrier in
its own right—the capital barrier. Both new firms and new ventures of existing firms can usually expect to be charged a higher risk premium in their
cost of capital. The presence of other barriers, particularly economies of
scale, exacerbates the capital barrier. Entering the automobile manufacturing industry required so much capital that John Z. DeLorean, the former
General Motors executive, had to get almost all his funding from the United
Kingdom government, in return for locating his new company in Northern
Ireland.

Fruhan demonstrated that in some markets, such as main-frame computer manufacturing, the capital required for entry has been too great for
even the largest firms.[2] He found that the market-share targets of two entrants, RCA and General Electric, implied capital needs beyond their ability
to retain earnings and generate debt.

Product Differentiation

Entrants encounter a second type of barrier if buyers prefer the brands of
incumbent firms. Bain cited high levels of advertising-to-sales ratios as a
major source of product-differentiation barriers. To overcome these barriers, entrants must either charge a lower price for an equivalent product
offering or invest heavily in remedial advertising or other promotional activities to establish their name. There is an obvious definitional problem
with differentiation. Bain applied it to markets in which the product or service offerings of incumbents and entrants are identical. This is obviously an
extreme and rare case. It is arguable that all products or services, even so-
called commodities, can be differentiated beyond psychological differences.[3]

Bain also included under product differentiation advantages (a) control
of superior product designs, and (b) ownership of favored distributive

outlets. The latter source of advantage has been generalized into a barrier class of its own.[4] Access to distribution is critical for products sold through convenience outlets—retail outlets offering little or no sales assistance. Furthermore, consumers are unwilling to travel great distances to buy the type of products sold in convenience outlets. To overcome these barriers, an entrant must rapidly achieve dense coverage of an area and the economies of scale associated with serving convenience outlets (for example, local sales-and-distribution offices). Barriers in gaining distribution are therefore particularly acute for such products.

In contrast, products sold through nonconvenience outlets have lower turnover rates and require less coverage of a market area; thus the distribution barrier is smaller for these products. An entrant can start with selective distribution coverage without jeopardizing its consumer franchise or sacrificing sales and distribution economies of scale. On the other hand, even nonconvenience products can exhibit high distribution barriers, particularly where after-sales service is important. In the U.S. earth-moving-equipment market, the Japanese entrant, Komatsu, is currently limited to a 10-percent-segment share and a 3-percent-total-market share, primarily because American incumbents have tied up the best dealers. Caterpillar, the market leader, has twice as many, mostly exclusive, highly capitalized dealers compared to Komatsu's nonexclusive, low-capitalized dealers. Thus the distribution barrier really includes all three of Bain's classes of barriers: absolute cost, product differentiation, and economies of scale.

Economies of Scale

Probably the most common barrier springs from economies of scale, that exist in almost every industry. Where scale economies exist, the sales level, needed to achieve cost parity with incumbents, may be sufficiently high that the extra capacity introduced by the entrant will have the effect of depressing prices for everyone in the market. While the previous price level would have been profitable for the entrant, the new price level is not.

Economies of scale can exist at both the production-plant level and the firm level. At the plant level, scale economies are possible because of the simple fact that production machines have definite capacities. In some industries the most efficient machines in terms of per-unit cost may have very large capacities. Other scale economies at the plant level relate to warehousing and maintenance services. The scale needed to achieve these economies is the "minimum efficient scale" (in sales).

Another scale economy depends not on current output but on accumulated output. The theory of the *experience curve* effect posits that costs decline at a constant rate as accumulated production experience increases.[5] This decrease in costs arises from five main sources: learning effects, scale effects, substitution, redesign, and technology. Porter suggests that whether the experience curve acts as an entry barrier depends on the reason for falling costs.[6] If economies of scale are the primary reason, then a new entrant can become the lowest-cost producer by buying the latest and largest facility, thereby avoiding the experience barrier.

Advertising intensity contributes to the scale economy barrier as well as to the differentiation barrier. Comanor and Wilson have described the ways in which advertising intensity can pose scale-economy barriers.[7] First, there may be a threshold effect. Second, there are usually media volume-discounts. A special case of the latter is the cost-per-audience-member difference between national-network advertising and local stations. A third scale factor, not mentioned by Comanor and Wilson, is that advertising behaves as a fixed cost—as sales increase, the advertising cost-per-unit decreases, while the effectiveness remains constant. A related effect is that the quality of the advertising message is also a fixed factor that applies across all messages. Larger advertising budgets generally produce more effective messages because of the greater company and advertising-agency resources that can be devoted to this task. There are also major learning effects in managing the advertising effort. Finally, if economies of scale do exist in advertising, the entrant will have additional capital requirements. Advertising will be a particularly risky use of these funds since no tangible assets will be generated in the case of failure—a successful brand name is an invaluable property, but an unsuccessful one is valueless.

Another area in which economies of scale can act as an entry barrier is R&D. Mueller and Tilton suggest that economies of scale in R&D (and therefore a barrier effect) exist only at one stage of the technological development cycle.[8] In the early stages, when knowledge is still rudimentary, small firms may be able to compete successfully with large ones. However, economies of scale arise at the intermediate stage of technological competition, when the research becomes increasingly specialized and sophisticated, and the technology is broken down into its component parts. The standardization stage is finally reached when R&D requirements fall, and barriers now depend on economies of scale in production and marketing.

The presence of substantial economies of scale poses a dilemma for entrants. Either they enter at the large scale needed to match incumbents' costs, and thereby increase the financial and business risks of the new venture, or they enter at a lower, less risky, scale, and suffer the attendant disadvantage in unit costs.

A large-scale entry, capturing economies, may add so much capacity that the market, initially profitable enough to attract entrants, is made unprofitable by the fact of entry. This problem is exacerbated when competitors pursue an experience-curve strategy of building scale ahead of demand. Texas Instruments entered the watch market with a large-scale strategy, and captured a large market share, only to withdraw several years later. This scale strategy may have contributed to the current low levels of profitability in the market. Even incumbents may find the required scale too great for them. Recently, the Richardson-Merrell company divested its prescription-drug business, mostly because its sales could not support the minimum necessary size in R&D.

Small-scale entry poses different problems. The cost disadvantage translates into either higher prices or lower margins. Often worse is the support and credibility disadvantage. Markets in which after-sales service is important pose a particularly great disadvantage for small-scale entrants. This service barrier has dogged the European consortium trying to sell its wide-bodied Airbus to airlines in the United States.

Incumbent Reactions

Incumbents often react more severely to the fact of entry, or to moves by entrants, than to moves by existing competitors. In fact, incumbent reactions can pose the greatest barrier to entry. Recognizing the beachhead threat of an entrant, incumbents are often willing to accept severe short-term reductions in profitability to prevent the entrant from establishing itself.

Incumbent reactions are particularly effective when they exploit economies of scale. To make use of this barrier, incumbents must maintain output in the face of entry, despite the decline in prices that should accompany the introduction by entrants of capacity above the minimum efficient scale.

Sylos developed an exact prediction for what incumbent firms need to do to maximize profits while preventing entry.[9] In the special case of oligopoly with an undifferentiated product, incumbent firms would restrict their combined output so that prices would remain higher than otherwise. This restricted output would be the competitive output minus the minimum-efficient scale. The corollary is that the price premium, over the competitive level, that established firms could command, would be the ratio of the minimum scale to the competitive output:

Entry preventing output = Competitive output X_c − Minimum scale x

Price premium = x/X_c

However, for entrants to be thus deterred, they would have to believe that incumbents would maintain their output in the face of entry, and be willing to see prices and profits fall as a result. The *Sylos Postulate* specifies this as the worst policy that established firms could adopt as their response to entrants.

An incumbent may also be able to pose a large barrier if the nature of its parent company allows substantial temporary losses. Rhoades has suggested that diversified firms pose such a reaction barrier.[10] Such firms have a greater potential for resisting new entrants by engaging in "predatory" pricing—lowering prices below costs. This is the cross-subsidization hypothesis that diversified firms have the ability to subsidize temporary losses in one market through their profits in other markets. Corporate portfolio models, such as that of the Boston Consulting Group, recommend a balance between high-growth/cash-using and low-growth/cash-generating businesses. Maintaining such a balance would certainly place the diversified firm in a position where it would be able to practice cross-subsidization of profits as well as of cash.

Incumbents can communicate to potential entrants the fact that they will react—from simply making verbal threats of retaliation to actions that enable, or even require, retaliation. There are obviously game-theory aspects to such strategies.[11] Salop describes these deterrent actions as "strategic" entry barriers, "purposely erected to reduce the possibility of entry," as opposed to "innocent" entry barriers "unintentionally erected as a side effect of innocent profit maximization."[12] The wise business strategist would surely not distinguish between the two forms of barriers.

Summary of the Original Theory

In the previous section I have presented the original theory of entry barriers and have elaborated on it, because it is still essentially correct in the extreme case of perfect homogeneity. If entrants are identical to incumbents in their skills and resources, and if they use identical competitive strategies, industry structure is the only source of entry barriers, and other factors that might reduce the impact of barriers can be excluded. Before a discussion of these other factors, it may be useful to summarize the original version.

The existence of entry barriers imposes disadvantages on entrants, so that incumbents can enjoy above-average profits that are higher than those that entrants could obtain. The expected profitability for entrants is too low to make entry worthwhile. The barriers arise as follows:

1. Absolute cost barriers require entrants to obtain factors of production at a higher cost or lower quality than they would incur if they were existing competitors;
2. Differentiation barriers require entrants to invest in catch-up differentiation activities or else face less-favorable demand conditions;

3. Scale barriers require the addition of sufficient capacity that demand conditions are worsened for all competitors, including entrants;
4. Incumbents react by accepting short-term reductions in profitability, and in ways that require entrants to face an initial or longer period of more competitive, and less profitable, conditions than are normal for the market.

It is important to remember that these additional costs are conceptually different from other entry costs—those required to create the ongoing business. For example, the existence of economies of scale may require a large investment, which may deter some potential entrants; however the investment itself does not incur an entry premium. Only the worsened demand conditions, due to the additional market capacity, impose the disadvantage.

Thus the theory of barriers to entry is consistent with what every manager recognizes—that entrants usually face disadvantages relative to incumbents. The theory specifies the sources of these disadvantages.

Modifications of the Original Theory

Bain's original theory has been modified in three ways, each weakening the effect of entry barriers:

1. The inclusion of existing firms as potential and actual entrants;
2. The use of strategic groups to redefine a market into a fringe and a core, and to distinguish between fringe entry and core entry.
3. The recognition of some acquisitions as an entry mode.

I will address these modifications and also add a fourth, and arguably most important, modification: the inclusion of heterogeneity of competitive strategies.

These modifications reflect a view of markets and competition that is similar to that of corporate strategy in terms of allowing for heterogeneity and uniqueness in competitors and strategies. The modified theory results in a predicted impact for entry barriers more complex than that in the original theory.

Existing Firms as Entrants

Bain defined entry as, first, the establishment of an independent legal entity new to an industry, and second, the introduction of new production capacity by the new firm. By excluding the entry of a preexisting firm established in another market, this definition lessens the applicability of his concept. I will present original evidence in chapter 3 that the vast majority of entrants are existing rather than newborn firms.

The inclusion of existing firms as potential entrants has a straightforward effect on the impact of barriers. Existing firms entering a market already have the resources to partly or wholly overcome barriers. Indeed, even newborn entrants have abundant skills, and perhaps resources, if they are founded by executives breaking away from incumbents in the entered market. The computer industry has spawned many such breakaway entrants. The airline industry is today witnessing this phenomenon: Southwest Airlines has given birth to Muse Air, and Texas International Airlines to People Express.

Obtaining Information. An existing firm probably has unusually good knowledge of profit opportunities in markets contiguous to its own.[13] However, newborn entrants are typically formed by employees leaving a company already in that market. These employees should have the best knowledge of all potential entrants.

Assets. Established firms may already possess some assets that offset the disadvantages of product differentiation and absolute cost; for example, existing distribution networks,[14] skilled management, and intangible goodwill assets.[15] Again, newborn entrants founded by former employees of incumbents should certainly possess skilled management. Examples abound:

> The *product differentiation* disadvantage may be offset if the entrant is able to use a brand name already well-known from its existing markets. For example, Texas Instruments initially succeeded in the watch market partly because it could rely on the brand identity it had established in calculators. An entrant's brand names in other markets may even be stronger than existing brands in the entered market.

> Entrants may already have access to the labor or raw material sources that give an *absolute cost advantage* to incumbents.

> Entrants may already possess *distribution* networks that can serve the new market. In fact, the preferred diversification strategy among consumer-products firms is to develop new products that are distributed through the same channels as existing ones. Distribution was no barrier to Procter & Gamble when it entered the tampon market.

Economies of Scale. These may already be breached by an existing activity of an existing firm.[16] Thus, entry need not be at such a scale as to depress price. For example, there may be huge economies of scale in R&D, but entrants can develop many products from one set of laboratories.

Capital Requirements. Existing firms may be able to use internally generated funds to finance entry, or be able to raise capital at a lower cost than newborn entrants, or be able to raise sufficient capital.[17] Indeed, existing firms often enter markets in order to reinvest surplus funds. IBM and Xerox currently dominate the market for electronic office equipment, which requires a great deal of capital for basic R&D and product development. Exxon, a recent entrant, has not found capital to be a barrier.

Among established firms, larger ones should find capital less costly than should smaller ones. One reason is that the cost of capital is affected by risk. Stonebraker found that small firms face higher risks than large ones, and that this higher risk is a barrier to entry since entrants usually have to start on a small scale.[18] Risk was defined as "the probability of earning less than the competitive return (or of taking an economic loss), and the size of such possible losses." Stonebraker also found that for the smaller firm risk was more closely correlated with high advertising and R&D costs than with large economies of scale.

Existing firms with surplus funds may also seek out markets with high barriers, so that they can invest those funds to get behind the barriers and enjoy a return from this investment when the original source of the funds has diminished. Companies with threatened markets, such as cigarette companies, may be particularly attracted to such high-barrier markets.

Risk Reduction. For an established firm, a new activity will have imperfect covariance of performance with existing activities.[19] Thus the risk-return mix of its portfolio of activities can be improved by entering the new market.

Incumbent Reactions. Incumbents may react less severely to entry by existing firms with skills or resources that threaten superiority in a competitive war. Thus, established firms have many advantages in entering new markets, although there is little systematic empirical evidence of these advantages. Furthermore, all arguments for the advantages of established firms should apply even more to large established firms. Berry suggests that large firms are less deterred by barriers than are small firms.[20] As evidence he cites data on entry (net of exit) into SIC-four-digit manufacturing industries by 460 *Fortune* 500 companies between 1960 and 1965. Berry notes that "many of the conventional barriers to entry—risk, high initial capital requirements, the need for extensive marketing networks, and so forth—are less applicable to the large corporation than to the smaller firm."

The Higher Platform. As cited above, previous writers have argued that the existing skills and resources of entrants can reduce barriers. I wish to go beyond that and argue that entrants may have advantages over incumbents and face, in effect, negative barriers.

Entrants with greater skills and resources than incumbents face a negative barrier in that they have an advantage over incumbents on the same strategic dimensions that give rise to barriers. If barriers are a wall, existing skills and resources are a platform. A platform higher than the wall affords the entrant an advantage over incumbents. If, for example, the barrier is product differentiation created or maintained by high advertising expenditures, an entrant more adept at advertising or with more money to spend can turn this particular barrier against incumbents. Advertising becomes a quick way to get into the market. The product differentiation barrier to entry becomes a gateway to entry.

Often, entrants need not even have greater skills and resources to benefit from a higher platform. There can be many advantages simply in being a latecomer to a market. Entrants can take advantage of improvements in technology, while incumbents are committed to their existing investments. Entrants can achieve greater economies of scale than can incumbents. A common situation is that the optimal size of plant continually increases, with a corresponding continual decrease in average costs. Entrants can obtain better terms from suppliers, employees, or customers. In many markets older firms are locked into higher labor costs. For example, New York Air and People Express are latecomers that enjoy large absolute cost advantages over incumbent airlines because they employ younger, less expensive crews and are generally less encumbered by contracts, union agreements, and route-system obligations. Entrants can also use the price weapon, whereas incumbents find it costly to match an entrant's price reduction. An entrant offering lower prices to part of the market poses a dilemma for incumbents: should they forego all of the margin on some of their customers by not matching the entrant's cut, or should they forego some of the margin on all of their customers by matching the cut? In markets where lateness offers these advantages, incumbents' positions are continually deteriorating relative to that of future entrants.

Redefinition of the Entered Market

A major bridge between the homogeneity of industrial organization and the heterogeneity of corporate strategy is the concept of *strategic groups*.[21] Essentially this concept breaks up markets into groups of competitors somewhat analogous to the way segmentation theory in marketing groups customers.

Caves and Porter argue that the existence of strategic groups means that entry barriers do not protect all industry incumbents equally.[22] The size of the barrier differs according to the particular strategic group. Furthermore, there are barriers between groups, which Caves and Porter designate "mobility barriers." Mobility barriers arise from the same set of structural characteristics that give rise to entry barriers. Their existence explains why firms in low-performance groups cannot easily move to high-performance groups. For example, narrow-line (specialist) producers may not have the capital resources to convert themselves into full-line producers. Economies of scale may also dictate that there is room for only a small number of full-line producers, as in the case of the U.S. automobile-manufacturing industry.

Entry into some groups will be easier than entry into others. Typically the more easily entered groups will be those composed of small specialist producers—the fringe. In some industries entrants may be able to migrate from group to group and perhaps end up in what is often the most profitable group—the full-line, large-share producers. The costs and difficulty of migration will depend on the height of the mobility barriers. Easy entry into the fringe group does not necessarily mean easy entry into the oligopolistic core of an industry.

Thus frequent entry of minor competitors does not indicate low barriers for firms wishing to become major competitors. There is also the public-policy implication that easy entry into an industry's fringe may have little effect on the forces of competition in the core of the industry. Brock notes that large-scale entrants have failed in the core main-frame segment of the computer industry, while small-scale entrants in the fringe segments, such as peripherals, have succeeded.[23] He also documents how IBM erected mobility barriers to insulate the main-frame segment from the rest of the industry. Caves and Porter suggest that existing firms tend to enter the oligopolistic core, whereas new firms are more likely to enter the competitive fringe.

Acquisition Entry

A third modification of the concept of barriers to entry is the inclusion of acquisition as an entry mode. This aspect of entry has been little addressed, although Hines argued that a merger qualifies as entry where it "enables a firm to leave the atomistic periphery of a group and to take a place amidst the oligopolistic portion . . . the number of active decision makers increases."[24] Caves and Porter have argued that acquisition allows the vaulting of the industry barrier and provides a base for breaching internal-mobility barriers.

Acquisition entry is obviously important since it allows entrants to avoid barriers. Although such entrants are not additional competitors, they can be new in terms of objectives and resources. I have cited in chapter 1 the examples of Philip Morris's acquisition entry into the beer industry and Procter & Gamble's into the soft-drink industry.

Heterogeneity of Competitive Strategies

Perhaps the most important way in which entrants can overcome barriers is to use a competitive strategy different from that of the incumbents. Competitive strategies are different, or heterogeneous, in the sense that, for a given industry or market, there are many possible configurations of product features and of the production, distribution, selling, and communications activities to deliver the product. Thus, competitors' offerings are typically differentiated along several dimensions. Competitors and entrants need not have identical strategies that compete directly. For example, a high level of product differentiation in a market does not automatically impose a disadvantage on entrants, if there are unused product-mix configurations. The incompatibility of different product strategies is a common vulnerability allowing entry with little retaliation from incumbents.

Thus, the availability of heterogeneous strategies may allow entrants to avoid direct confrontation of the differentiation barrier. A smaller initial investment is needed to achieve a differentiated position, with a product configuration somewhat diffent from that of incumbents, than would be the case with a product configuration identical to that of incumbents.

The availability of heterogeneous strategies similarly allows entrants to avoid the absolute cost and scale barriers. An entrant's strategy that is different from that of incumbents may mitigate absolute cost barriers through (a) the avoidance of patent restrictions, (b) the use of other, nonscarce factors of production, or (c) a smaller capital outlay to offset any higher cost of capital. The scale barrier may be partially avoided through a heterogeneous strategy. The new demand thus created partially offsets the large additional supply that the entrant introduces in order to achieve the minimum efficient scale.

The availability of heterogeneous strategies can also mitigate incumbent reactions. Entrant strategies that compete only indirectly with incumbents should result in indirect reactions; in particular, avoiding a price reaction. In a study of entry into the Australian cigarette market, Alemson observed that the resulting battle between incumbents and entrants was centered not on price, but on frequent redesign of the marketing mix and on brand repositioning.[25]

An entrant's strategy may be so incompatible with incumbents' strategies that incumbents would severely damage their existing businesses by reacting directly to the entrant. For example, BIC established itself in the shaving market by entering with a disposable unitized razor—a product strategy radically different from the existing one of disposable blades and durable holders. Retaliation by incumbents was greatly constrained because of the dangers of cannibalization of their existing, more expensive products. Thus, like the higher platform, a different strategy can create a negative barrier or gateway.

Heterogeneous strategies have three sources:

1. Opportunities to exploit radical technological or other environmental changes;
2. Opportunities to avoid direct competition;
3. Opportunities to negate barriers directly.

Technological Change. Radical technological or environmental change usually offers the widest gateway for the most entrants and poses the greatest threat to incumbents. It has been said that the Roman Empire was destroyed by the invention of the stirrup. This simple innovation shifted the tactical edge from infantry to cavalry and the strategic advantage from organized societies which could field disciplined cohorts, to nomadic ones fielding reckless horsemen. A more recent example is the impact of semiconductor technology on the watch industry. The ability to drive watches with electronics rather than clockwork shifted the required competitive capabilities from craftsmanship to technology and low-cost assembly labor. These changes negated the Swiss watch manufacturers' barriers to entry: access to a skilled-labor force and consumer preference for Swiss reliability.

Technology or environmental changes can also easily destroy the scale barrier to entry. Incumbents' commitments to large-scale, obsolete, facilities become their feet of clay—both fragile and immobile.

Legal and regulatory changes have frequently removed or lessened the barrier imposed by law. Such changes should not be equated with the creation of gateways. The removal of the legal-regulatory barrier merely allows entry. This can be sufficient for successful entry if the legal barrier prevented the satisfaction of demand. Where there is no great imbalance of supply and demand, however, entrants must still find gateways via superior skills and resources, the advantages of lateness, or some strategy different from that of incumbents. The recent deregulation of the airline industry provides examples of both situations. Some new airlines have simply created new routes between previously unserved destinations; a me-too strategy has been sufficient in such cases. Others, such as New York Air, have used certain advantages over incumbents to enter existing routes.

Avoiding Direct Competition. Entrants cannot rely on technological or environmental changes to create gateways, nor can incumbents rely on their absence as surety of protection. Entrants can also sidestep barriers by avoiding direct competition with incumbents, that is, by offering a product (or service) serving a different need or customer group. There is obviously a definitional issue here: a sufficiently different offering may constitute a different market. Yet incumbents should certainly be wary. American and British motorcycle manufacturers have learned to their cost that what they considered a different, contiguous market—small motorcycles—was to the Japanese a beachhead in the same market.

Such flank-attack entries pose two types of dangers for incumbents, and corresponding opportunities for entrants. The flank position can be used as a base to gain experience and credibility for invading the core market, or, often more dramatic, the flank position can become the core market. Michelin's push into the United States with radial tires greatly accelerated the shift of the core market from bias-ply to radial. Radials are now the core.

How does a flank entry avoid barriers? A product appealing to a somewhat different need or customer group obviously reduces the differentiation barrier. The hitherto monolithic toilet-soap oligopoly is now under assault by entrants selling liquid soaps. In one year the number of competitors offering liquid soap for domestic use jumped from zero to forty.

The liquid-soap example also shows how scale barriers can be reduced by the flank strategy. The entrants have not needed to build the same huge plants to achieve costs comparable to incumbents. Their differentiated entry has also reduced the distribution barrier. Obtaining shelf space has been much easier than with a me-too product.

Reduction of the scale, differentiation, and absolute cost barriers can result in a lower capital barrier. Versatec was able to make a successful low-capital entry into the market for computer peripheral-plotter machines by minimizing the scale of its operation in all facets. This reduced scale was competitively viable because Versatec focused on a narrow, previously untargeted, market segment.

Perhaps the most dramatic aspect of the indirect strategy is its impact on the retaliation barrier. An indirect entry, by definition, avoids the full rigors of direct retaliation if incumbents keep to their existing product lines. To retaliate directly, incumbents must match the entrant's product. Frequently, incumbents are constrained from such direct retaliation. Cannibalization intervenes. U.S. automobile manufacturers have faced this dilemma with small, imported cars over the last decade. The hard-soap companies are similarly constrained with respect to liquid-soap entrants. As yet, only Procter & Gamble has decided, reluctantly, to copy the entrants. Facing the same situation in the United Kingdom, neither Lever Brothers nor Procter & Gamble, which dominate the market, has responded.

Directly Negating Barriers. The third way to create a gateway is to negate barriers directly. The entrant structures its business in a different way from incumbents and in a way that simply avoids barriers, while still offering directly competitive products. The soft-drink industry poses huge distribution barriers because of the limited number of bottlers, most of which have highly lucrative contracts with Coca-Cola or Pepsi-Cola. Shasta negated this barrier not by offering a different product, but by distributing it in a different way—directly to supermarkets. Japanese manufacturers of many consumer durables have negated service-network barriers by making more reliable products.

Entrants that change the accepted business structure probably benefit most in terms of the retaliation barrier. Incumbents have built barriers via their existing business structure; these commitments become their barriers to response.

Sleepy Incumbents. All three differentiated strategies—exploiting technological and environmental change, avoiding competition, directly negating barriers—rely on incumbents' responses being constrained by their commitments. However, even in the absense of incumbent commitments and constraints, entrants, even me-too's, can benefit from simple incumbent lethargy.

Bevan documents this phenomenon for Imperial Tobacco's acquisition entry into the British potato-crisps (chips) market.[26] The dominant incumbent, Smiths Crisps, ignored the entry for several years because Golden Wonder created a new market segment by selling through supermarkets for home consumption rather than in bars for consumption on the premises. Smiths was content to lose market share as long as its absolute-sales level was increasing. Not until five years after the entry, when its absolute sales started to fall, did Smiths attempt to retaliate.

Need for a Revised Theory

The four modifications of the theory of entry barriers need to be integrated into one revised theory:

1. The theory should recognize existing firms, with their skills and resources, as potential entrants.
2. The recognition of strategic groups with their own mobility barriers requires that the theory be specified for entrants seeking admittance to specific groups, not simply to an industry aggregate. In practice this issue can be dealt with in the definition of the entered market.

3. The addition of acquisition as an alternative to direct entry requires that the revised theory explain the choice between direct and acquisition entry.
4. The acceptance of heterogeneity in competitive strategy requires a major restructuring of the current theory of direct entry.

For the benefit of managers, the revised theory should focus on the direct impact of barriers on entry behavior rather than on its indirect impact on average industry profitability. While entry behavior should be of concern to economists, it is particularly important to business strategists. For entrants, entry is a key strategic option in building the activities of a firm. For incumbents of entered markets, entry typically initiates strenuous competitive struggles.

I suggest that the key components of entry behavior are

1. Whether and how barriers discourage the occurrence of entry;
2. when acquisition entry is or should be used to avoid barriers;
3. how barriers affect the market performance of entrants.

These three components of entry behavior are based on the recognition of acquisition entry and mobility barriers, as well as the recognition of existing firms and their resources, and of strategic heterogeneity.

Notes

1. Joe S. Bain, *Barriers to New Competition,* (Cambridge, Mass.: Harvard University Press, 1956), p. 3.

2. William E. Fruhan, Jr., "Pyrrhic Victories in Fights for Market Share," *Harvard Business Review* 50, no. 5 (September-October 1972): 100-107.

3. Theodore Levitt, "Marketing Success through Differentiation—of Anything," *Harvard Business Review* 58, no. 1 (January-February 1980):83-91.

4. Michael E. Porter, *Retailer Power, Manufacturer Strategy and Performance in Consumer Goods Industries,* Ph.D. dissertation, Harvard University 1973, subsequently amended and published as *Interbrand Choice, Strategy, and Bilateral Market Power,* (Cambridge, Mass.: Harvard University Press, 1976).

5. Boston Consulting Group, "Perspectives on Experience," (Boston: 1968).

6. Michael E. Porter, "How Competitive Forces Shape Strategy," *Harvard Business Review* 57, no. 2, (March-April):137-145.

7. William S. Comanor and Thomas A. Wilson, "Advertising, Market Structure and Performance," *Review of Economics and Statistics* 49, no. 4 (November 1967):423-440.

8. D. Mueller and J. Tilton, "Research and Development Costs as a Barrier to Entry," *Canadian Journal of Economics* 2 (November 1969): 570-579.

9. See Franco Modigliani, "New Developments on the Oligopoly Front," *Journal of Political Economy* 66 (June 1958):215-232.

10. Stephen A. Rhoades, "The Effect of Diversification on Industry Profit Performance in 241 Manufacturing Industries: 1963," *Review of Economics and Statistics* 50, no. 2 (May 1973):146-155, and "Notes," *Review of Economics and Statistics* 51, no. 4 (November 1974):557-559.

11. Thomas C. Schelling, *The Strategy of Conflict,* (Cambridge, Mass.: Harvard University Press, 1960).

12. Steven C. Salop, "Strategic Entry Deterrence," *American Economic Review* 69, no. 2 (May 1979):335-338.

13. Howard H. Hines, "Effectiveness of 'Entry' by Already Established Firms," *Quarterly Journal of Economics* 71, no. 1 (February 1957): 132-150.

14. Hines, *Effectiveness.*

15. Richard E. Caves and Michael E. Porter, "From Entry Barriers to Mobility Barriers: Conjectural Decisions and Continued Deterrence to New Competition," *Quarterly Journal of Economics* 99 (May 1977):241-262.

16. Caves and Porter, "From Entry Barriers."

17. Ibid.

18. Robert J. Stonebraker, "Corporate Profits and the Risk of Entry," *Review of Economics and Statistics* 58, no. 1 (February 1976):534-544.

19. Caves and Porter, "From Entry Barriers."

20. Charles H. Berry, *Corporate Growth and Diversification,* (Princeton, N.J.: Princeton University Press, 1975) p. 125.

21. In its most general form, the theory of strategic groups hypothesizes that the firms in an industry can be grouped such that the within-group variance along certain key dimensions is significantly less than the between-group variance. These key dimensions include performance, range of viable strategic choices; and actual choices made on such variables as degree of vertical integration, breadth of product-line coverage of customer groups, degree of product differentiation and their strategic variables. The concept was first stated in Michael D. Hunt, *Competition in the Major Home Appliance Industry.* Unpublished Ph.D. dissertation (Cambridge, Mass.: Harvard University, 1972), and fully developed in Michael E. Porter, *Retailer Power, Manufacturer Strategy and Performance in Consumer Goods Industries.* Unpublished Ph.D. dissertation (Cambridge, Mass.: Harvard University, 1973), subsequently amended and

published as *Interbrand Choice, Strategy, and Bilateral Market Power,* (Cambridge, Mass.: Harvard University Press, 1976). See also Richard E. Caves and Michael E. Porter, "From Entry Barriers to Mobility Barriers: Conjectural Decisions and Continued Deterrence to New Competition," pp. 241-262.

22. Caves and Porter, "From Entry Barriers."

23. Gerald W. Brock, *The U.S. Computer Industry: A Study of Market Power,* (Cambridge, Mass.: Ballinger), 1974.

24. Hines, "Effectiveness."

25. M.A. Alemson, "Demand, Entry, and the Game of Conflict of Oligopoly Over Time: Recent Australian Experience," *Oxford Economic Papers,* (July 1969).

26. Alan Bevan, "The U.K. Potato Crisp Industry, 1960-72: A Study of New Entry Competition," *Journal of Industrial Economics* 22, no. 4 (June 1974):281-197. See also "Smith's Potato Crisps Ltd." IMEDE teaching case 1968 (distributed by Harvard Case Services, Boston, no. 9-513-099).

3 The Occurrence of Entry

The previous chapter drew a distinction between the impact of barriers on industry profitability and their impact on entry behavior. Existing theory has not adequately addressed this difference; essentially it assumes that above-average industry profitability is maintained through the restriction of entry, and that the same models of entry barriers should explain both profitability and entry behavior. In this chapter I argue otherwise.

I have reviewed and extended the arguments for incorporating into entry theory existing firms and their resources as potential entrants, and the heterogeneity of competitive strategies. These two factors are particularly relevant in explaining entry behavior rather than the level of profitability protected by barriers. In this chapter I argue that entrant resources and strategic heterogeneity allow entry despite high barriers, and that previous studies have not considered this possibility because of their methodological focus on profitability and because of their data limitations. The methodology and data base used here circumvent these problems.

The Difference between Industry Profitability and Entry Behavior

Previous Studies of Profitability

Previous studies of entry barriers have focused on models and evidence explaining profitability. In the initial study, Bain evaluated twenty industries with respect to each of his classes of entry barriers and concluded that the industries formed three groups: industries with "very high" barriers, industries with "substantial" barriers, and those with "moderate to low" barriers.[1] When comparing these subjectively evaluated barriers to price-cost margins, he observed a correspondence between the two. The industries with very high barriers had prices that were 10 percent or more above what was judged to be the competitive level. The industries with substantial entry barriers had prices about 7 percent above the competitive level. The moderate-to-low barrier group had prices from 1 to 4 percent above the competitive level. Bain concluded that barriers to entry exist and can be measured.

Bain's results and conclusions were replicated by Mann for the decade 1950-1960,[2] a period when the Great Depression or rapid postwar inflation would not affect the results as they might have done for the period studied by Bain. Mann evaluated thirty industries, seventeen of which were also on Bain's list. Numerous subsequent studies have used profitability as the dependent variable,[3] all accepting Bain's assumption that the level of profitability corresponds to the height of barriers.

Why Barrier Theory Should Focus on Entry Behavior

There are three compelling reasons for shifting the focus of barrier theory away from industry profitability. First, as already argued, entry behavior, not average industry profitability, should be of interest to business strategists. Second, only in completely undifferentiated markets can the level of profitability be primarily determined by the number of competitors. Most economists now recognize that the number of competitors is only one of the factors determining profitability. These factors include the severity of rivalry among existing competitors (little affected by their number), bargaining power with customers and suppliers, competition from substitutes, and the threat of entry, which is just one, though an important, factor.[4] Theories of barriers should, therefore, be confined to the proximate issue of entry behavior, rather than the second-order issue of profitability. Third, even if the number of competitors is the primary determinant of industry profitability, a high level of profitability need not correlate with an absence of entries. Strategic-group theory and its concept of mobility barriers suggest that there can be frequent entry into an industry's fringe of small competitors without affecting the profitability of the oligopolistic core. Also, the occurrence of entry is not an instantaneous process, and the pool of potential entrants is finite. Thus, even with low barriers and high profitability, it may take many years for entries to drive down industry profit levels.

Previous Studies of Entry Behavior

Recognizing the limitation of profitability, Orr and Duetsch have provided the only extensive tests using a direct measure of entry as the dependent variable.[5] Orr observed a sample of 71 Canadian industries, defined at the three-digit level, over the years 1963 to 1967. His dependent variable was the annual change in the number of corporations in each industry. Duetsch used a similar measure of entry, the percentage change in the number of firms in the industry. He observed a sample of 134 four-digit U.S. industries from 1958 to 1963 and 307 industries from 1963 to 1967.

Orr found that capital requirements, advertising intensity, and concentration were high barriers to entry; R&D intensity and risk (standard deviation of industry profit rates) were modest barriers; industry size was a positive inducement to entry; and past industry profit and growth rates were weak inducements. Duetsch found that industry growth rate and concentration level were both positively associated with entry; diversification outside the industry and product-promotion expenditures were negatively associated with entry. There are some reservations about the validity of Orr's and Duetsch's dependent measures. Their measure of entry, the annual change in an industry's number of corporations, was net of both exit and intra-industry mergers.

These studies provide an empirical precedent for focusing on entry behavior. What is needed is a more complete model.

A Model of Entry Occurrence

This chapter deals with the first component of entry behavior—the occurrence of entry. A model of this phenomenon should include as explanatory measures both barriers and inducements to entry, as did Orr's model. A model that can be empirically tested must also recognize that barriers themselves cannot be observed; only the elements of market structure that give rise to them can be seen. Such recognition makes clear how barriers can be reduced by the resources of entrants and by their exploitation of heterogeneity in competitive strategies. This is because structural variables contribute to both the height of barriers and the strategic heterogeneity mitigating them. For example, high expenses relative to sales in activities such as advertising and R&D allow greater scale, differentiation, and absolute cost barriers. Simultaneously, however, such high expenses also allow greater strategic heterogeneity, because complexity, and therefore heterogeneity, usually increase as more is spent on a class of activity. Two effects result. First, greater heterogeneity increases the chances that a potential entrant's existing activities create assets and skills overlapping those suitable for a potential market to be entered. Second, greater heterogeneity increases the chances that incumbents cannot collectively utilize all viable strategies, given contradictions among different strategies. Thus as the industry spending on an activity increases, there are two conflicting effects: heightened barriers and increased strategic heterogeneity mitigating those barriers. That is, structure gives rise to both barrier and heterogeneity effects. Finally, the model should separately identify the general, market-wide conditions of disequilibrium that prevent barriers having their full effect. Disequilibrium effects are also indicated by elements of market structure.

The overall model can be specified as

p_{it} (the probability of the ith

market being entered in period t)

$= f(B_{it}$ barrier effects, H_{it} heterogeneity effects, I_{it} disequilibrium effects)

$= f$(Market Structure)

The key feature of this model is that the impact of structure on entry behavior is decomposed into four separate effects. The dependent variable can also be a count of the number of entrants in a given time period. I will report on empirical tests using both forms of the dependent variable, but the focus here is on P_{it} because a larger data base was available for testing that version of the model.

Barrier Effects

The usual classes of barriers apply. *Absolute cost* barriers exist in the form of patents and other restrictions in the supply of factors of production.

Production-differentiation barriers take the form of high levels of advertising or selling intensity.[6] According to Porter, advertising has a more powerful influence on the rate of return for consumer products sold through convenience outlets than those sold through nonconvenience outlets.[7] There should be an analogous difference for advertising's impact on entry behavior. This effect should also hold for the industrial versus consumer distinction.

Scale barriers exist in the form of scale economies available at the single and multiplant levels: in advertising, in R&D,[8] and in distribution.[9] Dynamic scale barriers in the form of accumulated experience should also be included.

Reaction barriers are posed by high levels of concentration because of the threat of oligopolistic coordination in the face of entry. Certain incumbent characteristics may also contribute to reaction barriers: diversified firms are capable of cross-subsidization defense of the business in the entered market.[10] Furthermore, the size of incumbents' parent companies relative to that of potential entrants should affect the expected severity of reaction. Deeper pockets should allow longer and more vigorous defense of oligopoly profits.

Inducement Effects

The expectation of above-average rates of return induces entry. With the occurrence of entry used as the model's dependent variable, industry profitability is only one predictor of expected returns. Expected industry sales growth rate is arguably a better indicator. A heterogenous view of competitors and strategies clearly supports this argument: present high incumbent profitability is little guarantee that entrants can achieve similar results, given heterogeneity. In contrast, a high expected industry growth rate offers not just a growing return but a greater expectation that entrants can extract their share.

It is often argued that the stage of the product life-cycle (PLC) captures growth effects not entirely represented by a simple measure of annual change in market sales. Such effects include the degree of fluidity of product design and the production process. The market-growth rate should have a different effect on entry occurrence at different stages of the product life-cycle.

Seller concentration should also be included as an inducement. If an entrant can survive the reaction barrier posed by high concentration, it too can enjoy the less rivalrous condition of such an industry. Thus seller concentration has two opposite effects on the likelihood of entry: reaction barrier and inducement. These effects also interact with the potential entrant's resources relative to those of incumbents: weaker entrants are likely to find the reaction aspect of high concentration outweighing its inducement aspect, while the opposite should hold for stronger entrants. A common observation is that large or resourceful companies appear to prefer entry into concentrated markets, as in the earlier cited example of Exxon entering the office-equipment market.

While concentration is one indicator of the severity of rivalry, another is the importance of price as the basis of competition. Industries in which price is not the major basis of competition should be more attractive, since they usually offer greater stability in profit levels. In addition, entrants probably perceive such industries as posing less risk of a reaction barrier.

Disequilibrium Effects

Apart from long-run inducements, short-run factors contributing to market-disequilibrium conditions of temporary excess-demand should ease the occurrence of entry. Rapid industry-growth rate, high-capacity utilization, recent technological change, and recent exit should all qualify. Exit is included as a source of disequilibrium in recognition of a turnover mechanism: despite high barriers, a steady stream of entrants can replace less-well-qualified incumbents.

A heterogeneous view of strategy suggests the inclusion of high levels of new product activity. Markets in which new product introductions are prominent, and therefore presumably also relatively easy, thereby have sectors of disequilibrium. Old products are made partially obsolete by the existence of the new and better, or promoted-as-better, products.

Heterogeneity Effects

I argued earlier that heterogeneity effects are made possible by high values of intensity measures (such as investment, advertising, R&D, selling). The mitigating effects of heterogeneity are therefore specific to classes of activity; for example, high advertising intensity creates offsetting opportunities for heterogeneous advertising strategies.

Summary

Structural variables can, therefore, have more than one effect, and sometimes conflicting effects, on the likelihood that a given market will be entered. The structural variables that give rise to each effect and their predicted direction of impact on P_{it} are summarized in table 3-1. Some variables have their traditional unidirectional impact. Others are indeterminate. Their net direction of impact on P_{it} depends on the composition of the pool of active potential entrants.

A Data Base for Testing the Model

In addition to a large, cross-sectional sample, the model requires a direct measure of entry and variables representing as many dimensions of competition as possible. The qualifying data base has some unconventional aspects that should be briefly noted here. The appendix provides a more detailed discussion.

The PIMS Program data base of the Strategic Planning Institute includes a subsample of 793 consumer and industrial, U.S. and Canadian manufactured-products markets observed over four-year periods from 1972 to 1979. The key feature of this data base is that it comprises observations on narrowly defined markets reported by managers of incumbent businesses. The market definition avoids the usual problems of diversification noise in industry definitions. In addition, the narrow market-definition helps ensure that the unit of analysis is a single strategic group. Market competitors are observed at the level of the entire company. Another advantage of the data base is that it has numerous measures of dimensions of competition and performance. The data base's markets are also classed in at least 60 percent of the four-digit-level industries in the manufacturing division of the Standard Industrial Classification system in the United States.

Table 3-1
Summary of the Hypothesized Impact on Entry Occurrence of Structural and Incumbent Variables

Variable	Heterogeneity/ Barrier Effect[a]	Inducement Effect	Disequilibrium Effect	Net Hypothesized Impact
Patents/other absolute cost advantages	−			−
Growth		+	+	+
Profitability		+		+
Concentration	−	+		?
Price spread		+		+
Exit			+	+
Capacity utilization			+	+
Technological change			+	+
New-product activity			+	+
MES plant	−			−
Experience effects	−			−
Investment intensity	+/−	+		?
Advertising intensity	+/−			?
R&D intensity	+/−			?
Selling intensity	+/−			?
Incumbent-parent size	−			−
Incumbent-parent diversity	−			−

[a]Barrier effects are indicated by minus signs, heterogeneity by plus.

The data base is limited in that the markets and competitors are disguised in terms of both identity and measures of absolute size. The lack of identity is mitigated by the broad representativeness of the sample. The lack of absolute size is a more serious limitation, because it precludes, as an explanatory variable, the capital requirement for a minimum-efficient-scale (MES) plant or firm. Another limitation is that some variables that should represent all competitors are reported by one business only. Most reporting businesses, however, are market leaders, whose characteristics are the more relevant ones in determining the height of barriers. Indeed, the reporting businesses, on average, rank second in share of their respective markets.

The Dependent Measure

An ideal measure of entry into a given market would be the number of new firms attaining some minimum size each year. The PIMS questionnaire records the following measure of entry:

> During the past five years, have any competitors with at least 5 percent market share entered the served market? (No/Yes)

Thus the measure, ENTRY, is a 0,1 variable that provides a direct measure of the occurrence of entry; but it is not a perfect direct measure, because it does not record the number of entrants. Nevertheless, this measure does indicate whether barriers are sufficiently low to allow at least one entry of significant size. A share of 5 percent is, of course, small relative to the entire market, but it is greater than the minimum used in many other studies. For example, Orr effectively excluded firms with less than a 2 percent market share.

The Explanatory Variables

To match the five-year observation period of the dependent measure, the explanatory variables are either four-year averages for the most recent four of the five observed years, or constant categorizations, such as Stage of the Product Life Cycle (see the summary of time dimensions in table 3-2). This matching of observation periods means that structural variables are measured just before or soon after the occurrence of entry, and, therefore,

Table 3-2
Summary of Time Dimensions of Variables

Four-Year Averages		Constants	
MG	NPAC	ENTRY	EXIT
ROI	INVST	PATS	TECH CHG
CONC	ADVT	LIMS	DUR, NON-DUR, IND
PR SPR	R&D	CAPC ADD	PRN SZE
CAPC	SELL	PLC1, PLC2, PLC3, PLC4	PRN DIV

should offer a good indication of the barriers faced by the entrant. The contruction of the variables is explained later and also summarized in appendix C. The relevant portions of the PIMS questionnaire are reproduced in appendix F.

Absolute Cost Measures (Barrier Effect)

While Bain proposed as sources of absolute cost barriers the presence of patents or limitations in factor availability, few formal statistical studies have had measures of these variables.

PATS is a 0,1,2 variable indicating whether the reporting business benefited "to a significant degree from patents, trade secrets or other proprietary methods of production or operation." The 1 value is for either product or process patents, the 2 value for both.

LIMS is a 0,1,2,3,4, variable indicating whether the reporting business was constrained by any scarcity in materials, fuel, personnel, or plant capacity. A 1 value indicates constraint in one factor, a 2 in two, and so forth. Constraints should indicate that entrants may incur higher costs in obtaining these factors.

Economies of Scale (Barrier Effect)

As already mentioned, no absolute measure of scale is available. A relative measure is CAPC ADD, the minimum-efficient-scale (MES) addition to the standard capacity of the reporting business, expressed as a percentage of that capacity. A further limitation is that this measure is for additions to existing capacity rather than for introduction *ab initio*. Of course, the intensity measures described later provide other indications of scale barriers (for example, the advertising-intensity variable indicates the possibility of scale as well as of differentiation barriers). No measure is available for the experience-curve effect.

Market-Growth Rate (Inducement Effect)

The market-growth rate is represented by MG, the four-year-average annual change in market sales. To allow for differing growth-rate effects at different stages of the product life-cycle, four interaction variables are used: MG*PLC1, MG*PLC2, MG*PLC3, MG*PLC4. PLC1, PLC2, PLC3, and PLC4 are dummy variables that respectively represent the introductory, growth, maturity, and decline stages of the product life-cycle for that market, as estimated by the reporting managers using criteria including market-growth rate.

Incumbent Profitability (Inducement Effect)

Return on Investment (ROI), the profitability of the reporting incumbent, is the four-year average of pretax income/investment. Pretax income refers to annual revenues, less depreciation, general and administrative expenses, and corporate-overhead assessments, except for charges for corporate debt and nonrecurring costs not incurred by the reporting business. Investment is defined as working capital plus net plant and equipment plus other assets. This measure of investment is superior to the more usual one of total assets because it excludes current liabilities to obtain working-capital and uses net, not gross, plant and equipment.

Seller Concentration (Barrier and Inducement Effects)

CONC, the measure of seller concentration, is the four-year-average share of the reporting business and its three leading competitors in the market. The reporting business is among the largest four in over 80 percent of cases; when it is not, CONC is less than the four-firm-concentration ratio.

Price Spread (Inducement Effect)

PR SPR, price spread, is constructed as an index of the prices of the reporting business relative to its three leading competitors. The annual relative price, RP, was estimated directly by the reporting manager as an index based on 100.

$$PR \; SPR \; = \sqrt{(RP - 100)^2}$$

Thus *PR SPR* is an absolute measure of price spread in either direction. It measures the extent to which at least one competitor, the reporting business, has average prices divergent from its competition. A composite measure for all competitors would, of course, be preferable.

Exit of Competitors (Disequilibrium Effect)

EXIT is reported in exactly the same way as ENTRY and is also a 0,1 variable.

Capacity Utilization (Disequilibrium Effect)

CAPC is reported as the annual percentage of standard capacity utilized (averaged over four years). Standard capacity is defined in relation to normal work practices (for instance, two-shift, five-day weeks).

Technological Change (Disequilibrium Effect)

TECH CHG is a 0,1 variable recording major technological changes in the products offered by the reporting business or its major competitors or in methods of production during the previous eight years.

New-Product Activity (Disequilibrium Effect)

NPAC is the percentage of a given year's sales (of the reporting business) accounted for by products introduced during the three preceding years. This percentage is reported for and averaged over each of four years.

Investment Intensity (Barrier, Heterogeneity and
Inducement Effects)

INVST is the average annual investment (defined under Incumbent Profitability) divided by revenues.

Advertising Intensity (Barrier and
Heterogeneity Effects)

ADVT is the average annual expenditure on media-advertising expenses, divided by revenues, of the reporting business. An advantage of this PIMS measure is that it allows the exclusion of sales-promotion expenses. High levels of such expenses often indicate weakness in brand differentiation, in contrast to high levels of advertising indicating strong differentiation.

To test for differential effects by type of industry, dummy interaction terms were created for consumer-durable markets, ADVT*DUR, consumer-nondurable markets, ADVT*NON, and industrial markets, ADVT*IND. These three categories cover all the industries in the sample.

R&D Intensity (Barrier and Heterogeneity Effects)

R&D is the average of the annual sum of both product and process R&D expenditures, divided by revenues.

Selling Intensity (Barrier and Heterogeneity)

SELL is the average annual expense of the sum of compensation and expenses incurred by salespersons, commissions paid to brokers or agents, and cost-of-sales-force administration, divided by revenues.

Incumbent-Parent Size (Barrier Effect)

PRN SZE is the absolute size, in dollars of revenue, of the parent company of the reporting business. PIMS businesses have, on average, very large parent companies, with a mean value of $1,500 million for PRN SZE and a median of about $750 million. For the sample's median observation year, 1976, this median-sized parent would have ranked 275th in the *Fortune* list of U.S. manufacturing companies.

Incumbent-Parent Diversification (Barrier Effect)

PRN DIV is a subjective measure of diversification, made by PIMS staff, on a continuous scale from 0 to 3, indicating increasing diversification among each parent's total activities. PIMS parent companies are, on average, much more diversified than are companies in, for instance, the *Fortune* 500 list (the latter's diversification as estimated by Rumelt[11]).

Empirical Results

Statistical Methodology

The 0,1 nature of the dependent variable and the probabilistic specification of the model together dictated the use of binary regression as the estimation technique. Maximum-likelihood estimation and the logit transformation of the probability function were used. Binary regression was performed rather than discriminant analysis because the dependent variable is a direct function of the values of the explanatory variables, not a prior classification from which the values of the dependent variables derive.[12] Equations were specified in additive, not log, form because of the estimation and interpretation problems of using the log of a 0,1 dependent variable. Various theoretically supportable functional forms of each variable were tested if the linear form was not statistically significant.

Overall Results

Table 3-3 presents the equation with the largest number of statistically significant variables, dropping several nonsignificant ones (PATS, LIMS, TECH CHG, PRN DIV). It also shows the hypothesized directions of association suggested by (a) traditional entry-barrier theory, and (b) this paper's entry-occurrence theory (from table 3-1). Comparison of the actual signs and their significance (column 4), with the hypothesized signs (column 5) shows that most of the variables hypothesized to have a positive association with entry occurrence did have significant and positive coefficients. In contrast, there were many fewer significant and negative coefficients. Table 3-4 prevents the correlation matrix of variables.

Figure 3-1 presents column 2 of table 3-3 visually. The base probability is .28 (or 28 percent), this being the proportion of all markets entered. For each variable, figure 3-1 shows the increase or decrease, in the base probability, associated with the variable being above or below average in value. Above average is defined as being in the top third of the range for this variable among all the markets analyzed (one standard deviation above the mean); below average is defined as the bottom third of the range. The contribution to the probability of entry cannot be added across variables, but should be viewed as the impact of each variable when the other variables are held constant. For example, a market-profitability (ROI) level that was above average compared to other markets had a probability of entry higher by .08 (or 8 percent) above the average level of .28 (or 28 percent), if all other variables were at their average level.

Individual Results

Absolute Cost Factors. Since neither *PATS* nor *LIMS*, the two absolute cost measures, had statistically significant coefficients, they were dropped from the final equation. A heterogeneous view of competitive strategies would expect patent and factor limitations to be particularly ineffective as barriers to entry. They are entirely static barriers that might easily be avoided through alternate product designs or modes of production and distribution.

Table 3-3
Regression on Occurrence of Entry

Variable Code		(1) P-Standardized Coefficient (for unit chge.)	(2) U-Standardized Coefficient (for 1 s.d. chge)	(3) Probability of Significance (two-tail)	(4) Actual Sign and Significance	(5) Hypothesized Sign Entry Barrier Theory	Entry Occurrence Theory
MG*PLC1	Mkt Grwth*PLC1	.005	.007	.62		+	+
MG*PLC2	Mkt Grwth*PLC2	.010	.059	1.00	+++	+	+
MG*PLC3	Mkt Grwth*PLC3	.006	.047	.99	+++	+	+
MG*PLC4	Mkt Grwth*PLC4	.023	.035	.94	++	+	+
ROI	ROI	.004	.083	1.00	+++	+	+
CONC	Four Firm Share −93% SQD	.000	.027	.89		−	?
PR SPR	Price Spread	.000	.030	.92	+	+	+
EXIT	Exit of Competitors	.342	.130	1.00	+++	+	+
CAPC	Capacity Utilization	−.003	−.049	.98	− −	+	?
INVST	Investment/Revenues	.001	.015	.73		−	−
MES	% Capacity Addition	.001	.025	.89		−	−
NPAC	New Products as % Sales	.003	.046	.99	+++	+	+
ADVT*DUR	Advertising* Durables	−.065	−.048	.92	−	−	?
ADVT*NONDUR	Advertising* NonDurables	.013	.017	.79		−	?
ADVT*IND	Advertising* Industrial	.152	.048	.98	++	−	?
R&D	R&D/Revenues	.007	.018	.77		−	?
SELL	Sales Force/Revenues	−.015	−.057	.99	− −	−	?
PRN SZE	Incumbent Parent Size	.000	−.033	.89		−	−

$R^2 = .146$

Observations misclassified by model is 25 percent.

Mean of $Y = 1$ is .28

$N = 793$ consumer and industrial U.S./Canadian markets.

1. The P-standardized coefficient is the contribution to the estimated probability that $Y = 1$, for one unit change in the independent variable, at the point where $f(Pr\ Y = 1) = .5$. This latter restriction is a result of the nonlinear relationship between independent variables and the estimated $Pr(Y = 1)$ inherent in binary regression.

2. The U-standardized coefficient is as (1), for one standard deviation change in the independent variable.

4. Number of $+/-$ signs indicates p-value above .90, .95, .99 respectively.

5. Hypothesized signs from table 3-1.

The R^2 of .146 is quite high for a 0, 1 dependent variable, as evidenced by the fact that only 25 percent of observations were misclassified by the model.

Table 3-4
Correlation Matrix: Regression on Occurrence of Entry

	(1)	(2)	(3)	(4)	(5)	(6)	(7)	(8)	(9)	(10)	(11)	(12)	(13)	(14)	(15)	(16)	(17)	(18)	(19)
(1) Entry of Competitors	1.00																		
(2) Mkt. Growth * PLC1	.04	1.00																	
(3) Mkt. Growth * PLC2	.14	-.01	1.00																
(4) Mkt. Growth * PLC3	.11	-.00	-.02	1.00															
(5) Mkt. Growth * PLC4	.06	.00	.01	-.01	1.00														
(6) ROI	.12	-.00	-.09	-.00	.07	1.00													
(7) Four Firm Share - 93% Sqd.	.01	-.01	-.06	-.06	.05	-.11	1.00												
(8) Price Spread	.12	.09	.04	.07	.06	.05	-.00	1.00											
(9) Exit of Competitors	.26	.06	.04	.05	-.06	-.02	.04	.06	1.00										
(10) Investment/Revenues	-.02	.01	-.01	-.00	-.00	-.31	-.06	-.04	-.03	1.00									
(11) Capacity Utilization	-.07	.00	.02	-.04	-.00	.18	-.03	-.08	-.03	.05	1.00								
(12) % Capacity Addition	-.07	-.03	.03	-.00	-.07	.02	.03	-.02	.08	.10	-.01	1.00							
(13) New Products as % of Sales	.18	-.11	.13	.03	.03	-.01	.03	.09	.00	.04	-.11	-.03	1.00						
(14) Advertising * Durables	-.05	-.01	.02	-.10	.02	.00	.01	.10	-.01	-.01	.00	-.02	-.00	1.00					
(15) Advertising * Nondurables	.04	-.01	.02	-.11	.01	.05	.01	.07	-.03	-.05	.00	-.05	-.00	-.04	1.00				
(16) Advertising * Industrial	.10	.05	.00	.12	.02	-.04	-.04	.21	-.06	.12	-.10	.08	.09	-.10	-.09	1.00			
(17) R&D/Revenues	.06	.11	.10	.02	-.03	-.03	-.19	.02	-.04	.23	-.17	-.00	.28	-.02	-.08	.27	1.00		
(18) Sales Force/Revenues	-.02	.01	-.02	.08	.07	-.04	.03	.19	-.04	.03	-.25	-.02	.11	-.08	.12	.26	.07	1.00	
(19) Incumbent Parent Size	-.09	.00	-.01	-.13	-.01	.02	-.06	-.09	-.09	-.09	.15	-.11	.00	.04	-.06	-.09	.08	-.06	1.00

n = 793 markets

Correlations above |.07| are statistically significant at the 95 percent level, two-tail.

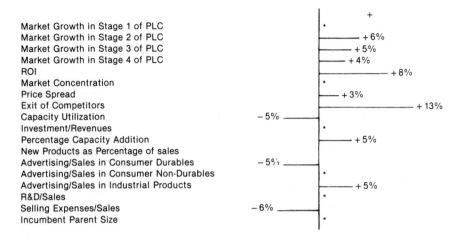

Market Growth in Stage 1 of PLC

Market Growth in Stage 2 of PLC ── +6%

Market Growth in Stage 3 of PLC ── +5%

Market Growth in Stage 4 of PLC ── +4%

ROI ── +8%

Market Concentration

Price Spread ── +3%

Exit of Competitors ── +13%

Capacity Utilization −5%

Investment/Revenues

Percentage Capacity Addition ── +5%

New Products as Percentage of sales

Advertising/Sales in Consumer Durables −5%

Advertising/Sales in Consumer Non-Durables

Advertising/Sales in Industrial Products ── +5%

R&D/Sales

Selling Expenses/Sales −6%

Incumbent Parent Size

*Not statistically significant at the 95 percent level.

Figure 3-1. Contributions of Above-Average Values of Market-Structure Variables to Probability of Entry

MES Plant Addition. In view of the inadequacy of *CAP ADD* as a measure of MES, it is not surprising that this variable did not have the predicted significant negative association with *ENTRY*. Indeed, the significant coefficients were positive in all specifications tested.

Market Growth (*MG*). MG had a significant positive coefficient of .08 (standardized, at .99 significance level, in an equation not shown here). Interaction terms (MG*PLC1, and so forth) revealed that market growth had the largest (standardized) positive coefficient in the second (growth) stage of the product life-cycle. The coefficients were also positive and significant in the third (maturity) and fourth (decline) stages but not in the first (introductory) stage. This lack of significance in the introductory stage is not surprising, since the market-growth rate is already very rapid. The significant growth variables had some of the largest standardized coefficients in the equation.

Most previous studies, including Orr's, have found growth to be an inducement to entry, although Orr found it to be only a weak inducement. In the revised model that I present here, market growth is very important because it has both a disequilibrium and an inducement effect and is one of the few variables with an unambiguous predicted direction of association with the occurrence of entry. The results here support this view of market growth.

Profitability. ROI (of the reporting incumbent business unit) had the second largest significant standardized coefficient (after EXIT), and positive as expected.

Concentration. Market concentration was hypothesized to be ambiguous in its impact on entry occurrence, because the barrier of high concentration could be offset by entrants' expectations of higher market share and profitability after entry. This hypothesis was not rejectable, since in no regressions did the significance level of the coefficient for CONC rise above .76. Contrary to expectations, CONC had very low correlations with other explanatory variables. The only one with which it had a significant correlation-coefficient was EXIT (.085, while the 95 percent two-tail-significance level was .070 for this sample size).

It was possible that the barrier effect might offset the inducement effect only at very high levels of concentration, but even the squared form of CONC did not have a significant coefficient. U-shape and inverse U-shape relationships were also tested, since there might have been a turning point value of concentration in relationship to the probability of entry. Tested turning points were the mean (72 percent for CONC) and one standard deviation beyond the mean (93 percent). The functional form with the turning point at 93 percent was almost significant at the 10 percent level, with a significance level of .89. However, the sign indicated a U-shape rather than an inverse U-shape relationship; this is, the probability of entry decreased as concentration increased to about the 93 percent level, then increased as concentration increased above 93 percent. This seems an improbable relationship.

Disequilibrium Measures. High market-growth rate is obviously a source of disequilibrium as well as an inducement to entry—its highly positive association with the dependent variable has already been noted. The exit of competitors indicates both disequilibrium and low exit and entry barriers. (Porter has observed a close, though not perfect, match between entry and exit barriers.[13]) Low exit barriers also reduce the risk of entry. EXIT had a highly significant and positive coefficient as hypothesized (significance level of 1.00). It also had the largest standardized coefficient of any variable.

CAPC (capacity utilization) had a highly significant but negative coefficient, contrary to both traditional theory and my hypothesis of its role in creating disequilibrium. There may be some cause-and-effect problem between this variable and the dependent variable. The measurement of the dependent and independent variables over the same time period probably causes the greatest problem for this variable.

The coefficient for TECH CHG was positive and significant at the .91 level, but only in the absence of NPAC (new products as percentage of sales), with which it was positively correlated (.25). The latter variable had higher significance levels (.99 in the best overall equation), which remained above .90 even in the presence of TECH CHG.

Intensity Measures. As hypothesized, all these measures were ambiguous in their net impact on the occurrence of entry. Only the measure of sales-expense intensity, SELL, had a significant and negative coefficient as predicted by traditional theory. It is not surprising that sales-expense intensity appears to be such a strong barrier to entry. A very large national scale is often needed to achieve economies at the fragmented regional level at which selling typically occurs. (Porter has made a similar argument for barriers to distribution.[14]) In contrast, production economies of scale can usually be achieved at the plant level, which is almost always a higher level of aggregration than the sales region.

The results for the linear form of INVST (investment intensity) did not achieve a significance level above .73, even in the absence of all collinear variables, including ROI (correlation of $-.31$). The squared form was also not significant (significance level of .82 and negative).

Also tested was whether INVST might pose more of a barrier when interacted with measures of incumbent-reaction strength, PRN SZE and CONC; that is, high investment relative to revenues, and, by implication, high fixed costs, might be a greater deterrent when incumbents have large parents or large market shares. However, neither interaction term was significant (when tested separately and in the absence of the linear form of each component of the interaction term, and other collinear terms).

It was also possible that investment intensity would pose more of a barrier later in the product life-cycle. However, the interaction term, INVST*PLC, did not have a significant coefficient.

None of the functional forms of ADVT achieved statistical significance. These tested forms were the linear; the square; interactions with PRN SZE, CONC, PLC; and U-shapes with the turning points at the mean (0.5 percent) and one standard deviation beyond the mean (2.0 percent). The results of splitting the advertising effect by industry, via interaction terms for consumer durables, consumer nondurables, and industrial products (ADVT*DUR, ADVT*NON-DUR, ADVT*IND) suggest that advertising plays a different role in each product class. The coefficient was significant and negative for durables, insignificant for nondurables, and positive and significant for industrial products. Thus only for consumer durables does advertising appear to act as a barrier to entry. This is a surprising result, indirectly contradicting Porter, since advertising should play a lesser role in product differentiation in durables.

Price Competition. The model hypothesized that price competition would act as both a barrier, by facilitating price responses to entry (for example, the Sylos Postulate), and as a disincentive, by threatening the stability of profit levels. The measure used here should represent the degree of price competition, not just the presence of product differentiation. First, the usual measure of differentiation, advertising intensity (ADVT), is included in the estimated equation. Second, the narrowness of PIMS markets reduces the degree to which the price spread variable might reflect the presence of multiple price segments rather than the degree of price competition within a segment. As hypothesized, PR SPR was positively associated with entry at a significance level of .92.

Incumbent-Parent Characteristics. The size and diversity (degree of corporate diversification) of incumbents' parent companies were hypothesized to have unambiguous negative impacts on the probability of entry. Large incumbent parents and diversified incumbent parents should both pose greater reaction barriers. The two measures, PRN SZE and PRN DIV, had relatively low correlations (.21), allowing their use in the same equation. However, both in the presence and absence of PRN SZE, the diversity measure's coefficient had extremely low significance levels (barely above .51). In contrast, the size measure had significant coefficients (significance level above .90 in most equations and .89 in the equation presented here). However, it had one of the smaller significant coefficients. The sign was negative as predicted.

Overview of Results and Implications for Theory

Many variables hypothesized to be positively associated with the occurrence of entry were found to be significant and positive: market-growth rate in all except the introductory stages of the product life-cycle, incumbent profitability, price spread, exit of competitors, and new-product activity. Capacity utilization was the only variable which did not reveal the hypothesized positive association, and its actual significant negative association may well have been due to simultaneity with the dependent variable.

In contrast, few of the variables traditionally viewed as barriers to entry revealed significant negative coefficients against entry occurrence. The few significant variables were incumbent-parent size, advertising intensity in consumer-durables markets, and selling intensity. Nonsignificant variables included concentration, investment intensity, advertising intensity in consumer nondurables and in industrial markets, R&D intensity, and incumbent-parent diversity.

The model hypothesized that market structure alone would not completely determine barriers to entry occurrence, given that barriers may be lowered by the assets of entrants and may be avoided or reversed by heterogeneous competitive strategies. The results of these tests, using a direct measure of entry on a narrowly defined set of markets, appear to be consistent with this hypothesis.

Other Measures of Entry

The measure of entry used in these tests has two limitations. First, as a 0,1 (no/yes) variable, it distinguishes only between no entries and one or more entries. Second, it reports only entries that achieved 5 percent or more market share. The tests of explanatory variables were therefore limited to whether the variables could explain this one measure of the occurrence of entry. Other direct measures of entry are also relevant to the theory of entry barriers, particularly the number of entrants and their entry scale.

Both the traditional theory and my revised version postulate, in Bain's words, a "queue of potential entrants" outside each market. Those at the head of the queue have the assets and motivations that make them the most probable entrants. More favorable market-conditions should elicit more entries. Market variables should therefore be able to explain the number of entries, as well as whether any entries occurred at all.

The number of entries is not a complete measure of the ease of entry. A large number of entries may indicate only that minor competitors can easily enter the specialist fringe of a market, while entry into the oligopolistic core is virtually impossible. Strategic-group theory suggests that "mobility barriers" may prevent these fringe entrants from ever becoming major competitors.

The Original Data Collected

To allow the analysis of these other measures of entry, the original data collected for the special sample of thirty-one PIMS markets included (a) the number of direct entries into those markets over the eight-year period 1972 to 1979; and (b) the maximum market share achieved by each entrant. These additional data allowed the measures of entry number and scale to be tested against the same market structure/incumbent variables as were used for the 0,1 measure of entry on the total PIMS sample of 793 markets. Other explanatory variables not available in the total sample were also collected for the special sample of thirty one markets.

The far smaller number of observations in the special sample compared with the total sample (31 versus 793), of course, greatly reduced the likelihood of finding statistically significant coefficients, because of the great increase in multicollinearity among explanatory variables. Accordingly, the regression analyses presented below should be viewed as supportive and illustrative of those for the larger sample. Also, the special sample of thirty-one was recruited on the basis that all had experienced at least one direct or ac-quisition entry achieving a 1 percent market share or greater, over an eight-year period. Seventy-one percent had experienced at least one direct entry. The total sample had a 28 percent incidence of direct entry, of entrants with over 5 percent market share, over a five-year period. Thus the special sam-ple is not directly comparable to the total sample.

The Number of Entrants

NUMBER OF DIRECT ENTRANTS was used as the dependent variable in cross-sectional regression on the thirty-one markets. The mean number of direct entrants was 2.7 per market over the total eight-year period, for the 71 percent of the sample that experienced one or more direct entries. The total sample of thirty-one markets experienced sixty direct entries and thirty acquisition entries. The high degree of collinearity among explantory vari-ables limited the number that could be tested in the same equation. The best overall equations (table 3-5) could not expand beyond five independent variables before one or more variables lost their statistical significance. These five variables were measures of growth, exit, capacity utilization, in-vestment intensity, and either concentration or incumbent company size. The latter two could not be used in the same equation without both losing their statistical significance—see equation 1,table 3-5.)

Growth. As for the regressions on the occurrence of entry, market-growth rate was positively and significantly associated with this dependent variable, NUMBER OF DIRECT ENTRANTS. In these regressions the LIFE CY-CLE STAGE variable was a better measure of growth than REAL MAR-KET GROWTH RATE, in that its significance levels were slightly higher. More important, it was less collinear with other explanatory variables. It was also the single largest contributor to R^2

The results for growth rate were predictable since NUMBER OF DIRECT ENTRANTS included smaller entrants (1 percent versus 5 percent minimum market share) than did the occurrence measure. High market-growth rate should be a more important inducement for small entrants who need the easiest entry environment. It has also been suggested that larger scale entrants prefer to enter later in the product life-cycle, when product design and technology are more stable, so that their larger scale investment will be less subject to obsolescence (for example, see Hayes and Wheelwright[15]).

Profitability. This was an important explanatory variable in the regressions on the occurrence of entry, and its sign was positive as hypothesized. Unfor-

Table 3-5
Regressions on the Number of Direct Entrants

	Equation 1		Equation 2		Equation 3		Equation 4	
	Standardized Coefficient	Significance	Standardized Coefficient	Significance	Standardized Coefficient	Significance	Standardized Coefficient	Significance
Life-cycle stage	-.680	(1.00)	-.764	(1.00)	-.365	(.96)	-.481	(.99)
Four-firm share -93 percent SQD			-.167	(.89)			-.175	(.87)
Exit of competitors	-.354	(.99)	-.414	(.99)				
Total exits closed					.289	(.96)	.248	(.93)
Capacity utilization	-.425	(.99)	-.415	(.99)	-.380	(.99)	-.333	(.98)
Investment/ revenues	-.285	(.94)	-.407	(.99)	-.053	(.61)	-.243	(.90)
Incumbent-parent size	-.170	(.87)			-.331	(.98)		
R^2	.58		.59		.54		.48	

Table 3-6
Correlation Matrix: Thirty-One Entered Markets

		(1)	(2)	(3)	(4)	(5)	(6)	(7)	(8)
Number of direct entrants	(1)	1.00							
Life-cycle stage	(2)	−.55	1.00						
Four-firm share − 93 percent squared	(3)	−.03	−.07	1.00					
Exit of competitors	(4)	−.11	−.30	−.01	1.00				
Total exits—closed	(5)	.44	−.39	.25	.33	1.00			
Capacity utilization	(6)	−.44	.35	−.04	−.23	−.12	1.00		
Investment/revenues	(7)	.16	−.56	−.14	.06	−.02	−.36	1.00	
Incumbent-parent size	(8)	−.18	−.10	.34	.25	.12	−.26	.36	1.00

n = 31 markets

Correlations above |.36| are statistically significant at the 95 percent level, two-tail.

tunately profitability could not be satisfactorily tested against the number of direct entrants because of the very high correlation between ROI and IN-VESTMENT/REVENUES (− .54).

Concentration. The concentration variable did not have significant coefficients except in a U-shape form, and the turning point was as before—at one standard deviation beyond the mean. However, contrary to the occurrence regressions, the sign was negative, indicating an inverse U-shape relationship between concentration and the dependent variable, NUMBER OF DIRECT ENTRANTS; that is, the number of entrants increased with concentration to about the 93 percent concentration level, then decreased with concentration. This relationship is far more understandable than the reverse one found for the occurrence of entry. If, as I have suggested, concentration has an incentive effect that can offset its barrier effect, it seems likely that, at a very high level of concentration, the barrier effect will assume greater weight relative to the incentive effect.

Incumbent-Parent Size. This variable had a negative coefficient, and almost significant at .87. The significance level fell when the concentration measure was included, presumably because of their very high correlation (.34).

Disequilibrium Measures. Two of the disequilibrium measures found to be significant for the occurrence of entry were also significant in explaining the NUMBER OF DIRECT ENTRANTS. These two were EXIT OF COMPETITORS and CAPACITY UTILIZATION. TECHNOLOGICAL CHANGE and NEW PRODUCTS AS PERCENTAGE OF SALES were insignificant. This reduction in the number of significant variables is not surprising in view of the much smaller sample size. What is surprising is that the sign for the exit measure was negative, contrary to both theory and the result for the occurrence of entry. The explanation of this contrary result may be that EXIT OF COMPETITORS applies only to competitors with over 5 percent market share, while NUMBER OF DIRECT ENTRANTS applies starting at 1 percent of market share. An additional measure of exit was used for the special sample of thirty-one markets. This measure, TOTAL EXITS CLOSED, reported the number of exits of competitors with 1 percent or more share that closed down (as opposed to selling out). When this measure of exit was used the coefficients were significant and positive, as for the occurrence regressions (equations 3 and 4, table 3-5). However, despite their opposite regression signs for explaining the number of entrants, the two measures of exit were positively correlated (.33).

The CAPACITY UTILIZATION variable had the same negative sign in these regressions on the number of entrants as it had for the occurrence regressions.

Intensity Measures. The only intensity measure that was statistically significant was INVESTMENT/REVENUES. However, unlike the occurrence regressions, this measure of investment intensity was significant in the simple linear form and with a negative sign, as predicted.

Price Competition. The PRICE SPREAD variable was not significant in these regressions on the number of direct entrants.

Overview of Results. Three of the key variables explaining the occurrence of entry had the same sign and approximate level of significance for explaining the number of direct entrants in the special sample of thirty-one markets. These variables were the measures of growth, capacity utilization, and incumbent company size. A fourth variable, exit, had the same sign for an alternative measure with the same market share cutoff as the dependent measure. The measure of investment intensity behaved more according to the traditional theory, as purely a barrier to entry, than it did in the occurrence regressions. Only the concentration measure had a completely opposite sign from that in the occurrence regressions, and one that fit my revised theory. Several other variables were significant in the occurrence regressions but not here. Unfortunately, the disparity in sample size, and hence much greater collinearity among variables, makes it difficult to draw conclusions from differences in results between the two sets of analyses.

The Scale of Entrants

Data were also collected on the maximum market share achieved by forty-five of the sixty direct entrants, the forty-five representing the first, second, or third largest entrants per market (on the basis of market share). The sum of the market share of the three largest entrants should be close to the total achieved by all entrants combined. This sum was used as an alternative measure of entry to the number of entrants.

Following the arguments concerning strategic groups and mobility barriers, I expected that market-share sum used as the dependent measure of entry would result in more statistically significant explanatory variables than the number of entrants as the dependent measure. Also, the total explained variance should be higher.

Summary Statistics. The market share sum averaged 9.8 points per market for all 31 markets. Obviously the amount of time since each entry affects share gain. However, this time factor is really relevant only when evaluating entry performance from the viewpoint of entrants, and it is taken into account in such an analysis in chapter 5. From the viewpoint of the markets, time since each entry is less relevant. Over an eight-year period these thirty-one markets lost an average of 9.8 share points to all direct entrants. The median loss was smaller: 6.0 share points lost. Thus, we have a measure of the extent to which these markets were disturbed by entries over that time period.

Regression Results. The same equations were estimated for TOTAL DIRECT ENTRANT MARKET SHARE as had been estimated for NUMBER OF DIRECT ENTRANTS. While the regressions on the number of direct entrants had six significant variables and R^2 of about .59, the regressions on the total share of direct entrants had only four significant variables of about .32 (table 3-7).

The four significant variables, each with the predicted sign, were:

TOTAL EXITS CLOSED (+)

ROI (+)

NEW PRODUCTS AS PERCENTAGE OF SALES (+)

INCUMBENT-PARENT SIZE (-)

Table 3-7
Regressions on Total Direct-Entrant Market Share

	Equation 1		Equation 2	
	Standardized Coefficient	Significance	Standardized Coefficient	Significance
Total exits closed	.186	(.87)	.072	(.65)
ROI	.303	(.95)	.377	(.98)
New products as percentage of sales	.264	(.93)	.275	(.94)
Incumbent-parent size	-.333	(.97)	-.261	(.92)
Number of direct entrants			.242	(.89)
R^2	.32		.36	

Inclusion of the number of direct entrants improved R^2 to only .36, although the NUMBER OF DIRECT ENTRANTS variable did have the predicted positive sign and had a significance level of .89.

Implications of Regression Results. The relative inability to find significant coefficients or high R^2 suggests that the alternative measure of entry, share achieved by entrants, is much less explainable by market structure than is the number of entrants. The implication is that market structure has a much larger influence on the number of entry attempts than on their success. Success presumably depends significantly on entrant characteristics and entry strategy. This is indeed the case when the market share achieved by each entrant (in contrast to the combined share of all entrants) is analyzed in chapter 5.

Managers' Estimates of Barriers

These tests reflect the statistical approach to estimating the height of entry barriers—searching for associations between the values of market structure variables and the occurrence or absence of entry, then inferring that barriers exist. One problem with this approach is that, as argued above, some structure variables give rise to both barrier and inducement effects not separable in statistical analysis. Another problem applies to any statistical approach to complex business phenomena: the observed associations may be due to causes other than those hypothesized.

In view of these problems, it seemed useful to question managers directly about how they perceived the various hypothesized barriers to entry. Accordingly, the thirty-one special-sample respondents were asked about the barrier effect of eleven aspects of market structure. The question used is reproduced here from line 106 of the Entry Data Manual (see appendix E):

Difficulties in Entering This Market

For a new competitor that is an established company but that has not previously competed in this served market or industry, estimate the level of difficulty in meeting the requirements in this served market for

(a) Sufficient Financial Capital
(b) Competitive Product Design
(c) Adequate Production Quality/Efficiency
(d) Successful R&D
(e) Extensive enough Distribution Network
(f) Competitive Sales Force
(g) Advertising and Promotion to develop Product Image/Identity
(h) Sales Volume necessary to support overhead costs
(i) Getting Raw Materials or Labor

(j) Getting penetration of Distribution Outlets, e.g. wholesalers or retailers

(k) Obtaining Patents/Licenses

In each box for this question, write one of the following:

"1" (if your estimate is "Little Difficulty")
"2" (if your estimate is "Moderate Difficulty")
"3" (if your estimate is "High Difficulty")

This question does have two potential weaknesses. First, it concerns the difficulties for a hypothetical new competitor rather than an actual one. Second, the trichotomous classification of potential difficulty is subjective. However, a manager with a minimum understanding of his or her business ought to have fairly definite views about these difficulties. Bain also used a trichotomous subjective classification.

The results are summarized in table 3-8. The overall mean of 1.8 is less than 2, the value for moderate difficulty, a result that is not too surprising since this is a sample of entered markets. However, the range of mean values for individual barriers is wide:

2.4 for sales volume to support overhead costs;

1.4 for patents/licenses;

Table 3-8
Estimated Difficulties in Entry

		Number of Markets		
	Mean	*1 = Low*	*2 = Moderate*	*3 = High*
(a) Capital	1.9	11	11	9
(b) Product Design	1.9	11	13	7
(c) Production	1.9	10	14	7
(d) R&D	1.8	12	12	7
(e) Distribution Network	1.9	12	11	8
(f) Sales Force	1.8	11	14	6
(g) Advertising & Promotion	1.2	26	4	1
(h) Sales Volume	2.4	4	10	17
(i) Raw Materials	1.3	23	7	1
(j) Retail/Wholesale Outlets	1.9	12	9	10
(k) Patents/Licenses	1.4	22	5	4

Average	Mean 1.8
(a) to (k)	Min 1.0
	Max 2.4

n = 31 markets

1.3 for raw materials/labor;

1.2 for advertising and promotion.

The low value for advertising and promotion reflects the sample's relatively low representation of consumer businesses (six out of thirty-one). The very high value for sales volume is in dramatic contrast to the other potential-barriers. Despite each of ten individual potential-barriers rating, on average, less than moderate, there is this very high overall volume barrier. This finding is reinforced by the relatively high values for the minimum-viable-share question (see chapter 5). In discussing economies of scale, I hypothesized that economies arising from fixed costs should increase with sales indefinitely. These results certainly support that hypothesis. The result for the sales volume barrier also suggests that even the most advantaged entrants will have to incur short-term losses while building up volume.

The estimated barriers appear to be closely related to the actual market structures. Table 3-9 compares estimated difficulties with the level of invest-ment intensity for each set of markets estimated to present low, moderate,

Table 3-9
Estimated Entry Difficulties versus Intensity Values
(percentage)

Difficulty	Structural Variable[a]	*Mean Value of Structural Variable for Each Level of Difficulty*		
		1 = Low	*2 = Moderate*	*3 = High*
(a) Capital	Investment revenues	47	49	60
(b) Product design	Percentage new products	1	10	24
(c) Production	Manufacturing and distribution/revenues	19	27	29
(d) R&D	R&D/revenues	1.3	3.6	4.0
(e) Distribution network	Manufacturing and distribution/revenues	2	21	30
(f) Sales force	Sales force/revenues	3.4	6.3	7.9
(g) Advertising and promotion	Advertising and promotion/revenues	2.1	3.4	5.5
(h) Sales volume	n.a.			
(i) Raw materials	RM and work in progress/revenues	7.3	8.6	9.1
(j) Retail/wholesale outlets	Marketing expenditure/ revenues	8.8	11.7	11.3
(k) Patents/licenses	(i) Product patents	27	80	50
	(ii) Process patents	23	60	0

[a]Structural variables are annual average of latest two years of data available, that is, as current as possible relative to when the levels of difficulty were estimated (second half 1979).

and high levels of entry difficulty. The level of estimated entry difficulty is indeed highly positively correlated with the equivalent intensity measure (true for all difficulties except patents/licenses). Thus, it appears that a market-structure theory of entry barriers has a correspondence with managers' thinking.

Summary

The model described in this chapter explains the occurrence of entry in terms of the market structure variables that give rise to barrier, inducement, disequilibrium, and heterogeneity effects. The model emphasizes that market structure alone is an incomplete determinant of the ability of barriers to prevent entry. Other factors are (a) the assets of established firms offsetting barriers, and (b) the availability of competitive strategies that avoid barriers or even give the entrant an advantage over incumbents.

This model has been tested against a large cross-sectional sample of markets, with the occurrence of entry as the dependent measure. The results appear consistent with the revised theory. Supporting evidence has been provided in tests on a much smaller sample with two other measures of entry: the number of entrants, and the combined market share of entrants. Managers were also asked to estimate the difficulties of entering their markets, and their estimates were compared with actual market structures. The results of this comparison suggest that the market-structure approach to barriers is consistent with managerial thinking.

Notes

1. Joe S. Bain, *Barriers to New Competition*, (Cambridge, Mass.: Harvard University Press, 1956).

2. Michael H. Mann, "Seller Concentration, Barriers to Entry, and Rates of Return in Thirty Industries, 1950-1960," *Review of Economics and Statistics* 43, no. 3 (August 1966):296-307.

3. For example see William S. Comanor and Thomas A. Wilson, "Advertising, Market Structure and Performance," *Review of Economics and Statistics* 49, no. 4 (November 1967):423-440; and Richard A. Miller, "Market Structure and Industrial Performance: Relation of Profit Rates to Concentration, Advertising Intensity, and Diversity," *Journal of Industrial Economics* 19, no. 3 (April 1971):104-118.

4. Michael E. Porter, "How Competitive Forces Shape Strategy," *Harvard Business Review* 57, no. 2 (March-April 1979):137-145.

5. See Dale Orr, "The Determinants of Entry: A Study of the Canadian Manufacturing Industries," *Review of Economics and Statistics* 56, no. 1 (February 1974):58-66; and Larry L. Duetsch, "Structure, Performance and the Net Rate of Entry into Manufacturing Industries," *Southern Economic Journal* 41, no. 3 (January 1975):450-456. Edwin Mansfield, "Entry, Gibrat's Law, Innovation, and the Growth of Firms," *American Economic Review* 52 (December 1962):1023-1051, also used a direct measure of entry, but tested only two independent variables across only four industries—steel, petroleum refining, rubber tires, and automobiles. Paul K. Gorecki, "The Determinants of Entry by Domestic and Foreign Enterprises in Canadian Manufacturing Industries: Some Comments and Empirical Results," *Review of Economics and Statistics* 58, no. 4 (November 1976):485-488, extended Orr's study to distinguish between domestic (Canadian) and foreign firms as entrants.

6. Selling intensity is suggested by Oliver E. Williamson, "Selling Expense as a Barrier to Entry," *Quarterly Journal of Economics* 77 (February 1963):112-128.

7. Michael E. Porter, *Retailer Power, Manufacturer Strategy and Performance in Consumer Goods Industries*. Ph.D. dissertation, Harvard University, 1973; subsequently amended and published as *Interbrand Choice, Strategy, and Bilateral Market Power* (Cambridge, Mass.: Harvard University Press, 1976). See also "Consumer Behavior, Retailer Power and Market Performance in Consumer Goods Industries," *Review of Economics and Statistics*, 56, no. 4 (November 1974):419-435.

8. D. Mueller and J. Tilton, "Research and Development Costs as a Barrier to Entry," *Canadian Journal of Economics* 2 (November 1969):570-579.

9. Porter, *Retailer*.

10. Stephen A. Rhoades, "The Effect of Diversification on Industry Profit Performance in 241 Manufacturing Industries: 1963," *Review of Economics and Statistics* 50, no. 2 (May 1973):146-155; and "Notes," *Review of Economics and Statistics* 51, no. 4 (November 1974):557-559.

11. Richard P. Rumelt, *Strategy, Structure, and Economic Performance*, (Boston: Division of Research, Harvard Business School, 1974).

12. See Robert Schlaifer, *User's Guide to the AQD Collection*, seventh ed., (Boston: Harvard Business School, 1978).

13. Michael E. Porter, "Please Note Location of Nearest Exit: Exit Barriers and Planning," *California Management Review* 19, no. 2 (Winter 1976):21-33.

14. Porter, *Retailer*.

15. Robert H. Hayes and Steven G. Wheelwright, "The Dynamics of Process-Product Life Cycles," *Harvard Business Reivew* 57, no. 2 (March-April 1979):127-136.

4 Direct versus Acquisition Entry

In the previous chapter I presented and tested a model of the occurrence of direct entry—one of the three primary components of entry behavior. Direct entry introduces a new competitor and is therefore crucial for both entrants and incumbents, as well as for the theory of entry barriers.

In this chapter I argue that change of ownership through acquisition may also be a way of introducing a new competitor into a market. A theory of entry barriers must therefore include acquisition entry as a means of avoiding barriers. The model I develop to explain the choice between direct and acquisition entry has two components: the entered market's barriers and an entrant's ability to overcome those barriers. This chapter also describes the original data collected on entrants and their entry mode and strategy, and reports the results of regression analyses performed on these data to explain the choice of entry mode.

The Theoretical Role of Acquisition in Entry

Traditionally, entry is defined as occurring when a new competitor in a market starts from zero output and expands to some positive output. Thus, entry via an initial acquisition of an existing competitor in the new market is excluded. In practice, managers probably view direct entry and acquisition entry (my terminology) as standard alternatives when deciding on entry into a new market. The theoretical implications of these two types of entry are more similar than might be expected.

Acquisition is most like direct entry when the acquired business is treated as a base for rapid expansion. Under the mobility-barriers paradigm, acquisition is used as a strategy to vault the industry barrier and provide a base for breaching internal mobility barriers. Acquisition entry is frequently followed by heavy investment for expansion. Bevan's description of Imperial Tobacco's strategy in the British potato crisps market provides an excellent example of how this type of acquisition is analogous to entry.[1]

Even when it is not followed by an ambitious expansion program, acquisition can pose new problems for incumbents. The acquirer from another industry (and we are concerned with only such acquisitions) has different notions of competition and different skills for competing. In many cases the acquirer will be unwilling or unable to follow established practices, thereby increasing the level of rivalry. Strategic-group theory suggests that heterogeneity in the backgrounds of competitors increases the degree of rivalry and reduces overall profitability.

Perhaps the classic example of acquisition entry is that of Philip Morris into the beer industry in 1970 via the purchase of Miller Brewing. Heavy investment by Philip Morris propelled Miller Brewing from seventh place, with 4 percent market share, to second place, with 22 percent market share, in ten years. Philip Morris had the motivation, the means, and the management skills for expansion. Diversification from cigarettes was an obvious spur. Money from cigarettes allowed the parent to invest over one billion dollars in the acquired company. Philip Morris's competitive skills, particularly their easily transferable expertise in marketing, turned out to be superior to those of incumbents. The combination of financial cross-subsidization and superior skills was disastrous for the incumbents—industry profitability was drastically reduced by the heightened competition that shifted eighteen market-share points to Miller. The Miller experience is also an example of how acquisition breaches mobility barriers by transforming a minor competitor into a major one.

Clearly, not all diversifying acquisitions are entries (and horizontal acquisitions are not even diversification). A distinction can be made between an acquisition made primarily for purposes of adding to an investment portfolio and acquisition for the purpose of entering a market. Some features more characteristics of entry acquisitions than portfolio ones are

1. An intention to use the acquired business as a base for expansion in the new market;
2. A desire to exploit relatedness/synergy between the acquired business and other parent businesses;
3. An interest in the market, not just in the acquired business; that is, the acquiring company would have seriously considered entering directly.

Linking direct and acquisition entry also has implications for public policy. The doctrine of potential competition has been applied to prevent or reverse conglomerate (diversifying) acquisitions on the grounds that the acquiring company would have entered directly. My model will demonstrate that there are strong reasons why acquisition entrants would seldom have taken the direct-entry route.

Since I have argued that acquisition is like direct entry when it is followed by rapid expansion, it may also be necessary to treat the choice as a continuum rather than as a dichotomy. At one extreme is direct entry or internal development. At the other is acquisition without further investment for expansion; that is, the acquirer is content with the market share of the acquired company and will run it as a status-quo operation. Between these two extremes is acquisition followed by varying levels of expansion. In terms of their disruptive effect on incumbents, direct entry and entry by acquisition can then be readily compared on the single dimension of target-share change, where

$$\text{Target-share change} = \text{Target share} - \text{Initial share.}$$

Other things being equal, direct entry with a target of 20 percent market share poses a threat to incumbents equivalent to the threat posed by acquisition of a company with a 15 percent share and planned expansion to 35 percent. Planned expansion following acquisition often poses a greater threat than an equivalent share gain by direct entrants. Acquirers may be particularly willing and able to subsidize investments in share expansion; the fact of acquisition implies surplus funds.

The Concept of Relatedness

Relatedness is crucial to the concept of entry barriers, since barriers are lower for firms with greater relatedness to the entered market. Rumelt defined relatedness in terms of the interdependency effects among businesses within one corporation.[2] The definition is equally applicable for comparing an entrant's existing businesses with an entered market. Rumelt's test of relatedness is whether a strategic change in one business would significantly affect another business in the corporation. If so, they are related. His examples of strategic change are

[A] decision to drop the product-market activity entirely or, conversely, to greatly increase its relative size;

[A] decision to employ a different production technology or process or to use a different type of raw material;

[A] decision to significantly alter the price, quality, or services associated with the product. (p. 13)

Rumelt's definition of relatedness is an extension of Ansoff's concept of synergy. Ansoff defined synergy as a joint effect measured between two product markets.[3] Such effects occur if, by competing in both product markets, the combined costs are less than the sum of their parts, the combined required investment is less than its sum, or the combined sales are greater than their sum.

Rumelt's and Ansoff's definitions can be simplified for our purposes here. In regard to entry, the degree of relatedness is *the extent to which an entrant's skills and assets (including intangible assets, such as customer relationships) are applicable to the entered market.* This definition is very similar to Biggadike's notion of shared costs and activities.[4]

The Choice between Direct and Acquisition Entry

Although direct and acquisition entry are both ways of entering a market, they involve entirely different processes. Once a market has been selected for entry, many factors might affect the entrant's choice between the modes. These factors should also affect the selection of markets for entry— a preference for one entry mode should encourage the selection of some markets over others. Analysis of the choice of entry mode has traditionally focused on financial, managerial, and legal issues, and on whether acquisition candidates are available. The height of entry barriers is an additional issue that both affects the traditional ones and has an impact of its own.

Traditional Considerations

Direct and acquisition entry have several different financial implications for the entrant, in terms of both the balance sheet and the profit-and-loss statement. First, acquisition requires greater front-end financing, and therefore depends largely on the entrant's cash reserves, ability to raise external debt or equity, or ability to persuade the seller to accept the buyer's debt or equity obligations. Direct entry is more likely to be fundable from internally generated funds, because of the typically incremental use of funds. Second, if the acquisition qualifies as a pooling of interests, it may bring substantial goodwill without incurring expenditures that flow through the profit-and-loss (P&L) statement. In contrast, a direct entry would have to achieve goodwill, such as brand identity, via advertising and other expense activities. Third, acquisition usually has more immediate impact on the level of revenues.

Direct and acquisition entry also differ in their managerial implications. For the individual manager, the two modes present different types of risks and opportunities. Direct entry is typically more risky because there is no guarantee that there will ever be an ongoing business of the required size and profitability. The typically long initial period of start-up losses imposes many strains and career risks. Biggadike found that his sample of start-up businesses required an average of eight years before reaching profitability;[5] few managers keep the same responsibilities for so long. Acquisition entry typically imposes different risks and demands on managers. The managers responsible for operating the acquisition may be expected to make rapid turnaround improvements, or to achieve synergy with the new parent quickly in order to justify the acquisition price. The two modes may therefore also require different styles of management—a more entrepreneurial approach for direct entry, and a more organizational and cost-conscious approach for acquisition entry.

Direct and acquisition entry also differ in their availability as alternatives. Acquisition candidates in a particular market are typically scarce. Restricted availability of skilled personnel can be a major hindrance to direct entry.

Legal constraints on acquisition entry may arise from the characteristics of the entrant or of the market. The Clayton Act and its amendments forbid acquisitions that lessen competition. This constraint clearly applies to horizontal acquisitions, since a direct competitor is eliminated. The act has also been applied to vertical mergers, since the acquiring firm will have advantages over competitors in the market of the acquired firm. The act has been extended to conglomerate mergers where the acquiring firm is judged to have sufficient strength to increase significantly its share, and, therefore, concentration, in the entered market. This was one of the grounds against Procter & Gamble's acquisition of Clorox[6].

An even more extreme extension of the Clayton Act is the *doctrine of potential competition,* applied by the U.S. Supreme Court to forbid acquisitions into a market when the acquirer is considered a potential (direct) entrant. This represents a direct application of Bain's theory concerning the role of potential entrants in affecting the limit price and other aspects of incumbent behavior. The doctrine of potential competition has been applied notably in *United States* v. *Penn-Olin Chemical Company*[7] (a joint venture entry by two potential entrants), as the primary ground in the Clorox case, and in *United States* v. *Falstaff Brewing Corporation*[8] (an acquirer the Court accepted as having no intention of direct entry). In 1979 the Federal Trade Commission (FTC) forced Exxon to operate partially at a distance its new acquisition, the Reliance Electric Company. The FTC argued that Exxon could and would have entered the drives industry on its own had it not acquired Reliance.

Barrier Considerations

The financial, managerial, availability, and legal considerations noted above are both separate from and affected by the impact of entry barriers on the choice between direct and acquisition entry. The existence of barriers affects financial considerations via the costs of breaching barriers in direct entry. Their existence affects managerial considerations via the risks incurred and skills required to breach barriers. Their existence affects the availability of factors of production for use in direct entry. Their existence affects whether antitrust constraints might prevent acquisition entry.

The existence of barriers to entry also affects the expected return on investment associated with each entry mode for a given company entering a given market. This effect is separate from financial considerations, such as the terms of an acquisition deal, and contributes to the expected profitability of entry, which must be weighed with all other impacts.

Efficiency of capital markets implies that expected returns under the two modes would be equal: the cost of direct breaching of entry barriers would be included in the acquisition price of a business already behind those barriers. The height of barriers would therefore have no systematic financial influence on the choice of entry mode.

But this view of barriers as neutral can be rejected even without questioning the efficiency of capital markets. First, career considerations should discourage direct entry into higher-barrier markets. Second, barriers do indeed make a difference in expected returns under the two entry modes, because the relatedness that reduces barriers has an asymmetric impact under the two modes. Thus, the cost of direct entry should vary directly with the degree of relatedness of the entering company to the new business created in the entered market. In contrast, relatedness does not reduce the price of an acquisition (and may even raise it), since the price is set by the market for acquisitions. Other parties are involved: the seller with its floor price, and other actual or potential bidders, and what they are, or might be, willing to pay. The relatedness of other bidders to the market should affect the price they are willing to pay, but that is a factor beyond the control of the final buyer.

The nature and height of barriers, therefore, result in two direct influences on the choice of entry mode. First, higher barriers favor acquisition entry. Second, greater relatedness favors direct entry. It is important, however, to note that the combination of barriers and relatedness does not determine the choice of entry mode. They are one set of factors among others to be evaluated by managers.

A Model of the Choice of Entry Mode

My arguments suggest that the choice between direct and acquisition entry is a function of two distinct sets of considerations: (1) a target market's barriers and the entrant's ability to breach those barriers; and (2) such other considerations as finance, managerial motivation, legality, and availability. A model of the choice of entry mode should therefore include as explanatory variables measures of (a) the market's barriers, (b) an entrant's ability to breach those barriers, and (c) the other considerations. Following

Bain, certain elements of market structure can represent the extent of barriers. As I have argued in earlier chapters, market structure includes some characteristics of incumbents.

An entrant's ability to breach barriers depends primarily on relatedness, but should also be affected by parent-company characteristics, such as corporate size and diversity. The competitiveness of the entrant's initial position is a further indication of the ability to breach barriers. The motive for entry should also affect the entrant's choice of entry mode.

The market structure and entrant variables will capture many of the managerial, availability, and legal effects, where correlated with market structure. Financial factors, such as whether the entrant's balance-sheet and profit-and-loss position favor one mode or the other, can be omitted from the model: they are unlikely to be correlated with sources of market barriers and entrant relatedness. The managerial factor of career risk is directly represented by the height of barriers and the entrant's ability to breach them. The likelihood of legal constraints on acquisition should also be captured by market structure and entrant characteristics, since these are the criteria for antitrust action. The availability of acquisition candidates depends on market structure in that the number and health of competitors are a function of both market concentration and market-growth rate. (A relevant factor exogenous to market structure is stock-market conditions, represented in the model by a separate variable.) In discussing each independent variable, I will show more specifically how market structure represents these managerial, legal, and availability factors.

The dependent variable can be conveniently specified as $Y_{d/a}$, the probability of an entry being direct rather than being via acquistion, and the model can be represented as follows:

$$Y_{d/a} = f \text{ (Market Structure and Incumbent Characteristics,}$$
$$\text{Entrant Parent Characteristics,}$$
$$\text{Entrant Relatedness to Entered Market,}$$
$$\text{Entrant Competitiveness,}$$
$$\text{Entrant Motivation)}$$

The Data Base

Data on fifty-nine entrants into thirty-one markets were used to test the model. Of the fifty-nine, thirty-seven entered via internal development (direct entrants) and twenty-two via acquisition (acquisition entrants). The thirty-one markets were a subsample of the PIMS data base for which PIMS had already collected market structure and incumbent data. The additional entrant data, reported by incumbents in those markets, were the number of entrants; their entry mode; and their characteristics, strategy, and performance.

The sample comprised six consumer-nondurable-product and twenty-five industrial-product markets, all in the United States. Twelve markets were in the growth state of the product life-cycle, seventeen in the maturity stage, and two in the decline stage (none in the introductory stage). (Stages were estimated directly by managers of the reporting businesses.)

Definition of Entry Mode

The two types of entry were defined as follows: A direct entry occurs when a firm, whether newborn or already existing, begins selling on an ongoing basis in an existing market from which it was previously absent. An acquisition entry occurs when an existing competitor in an existing market is acquired by a firm not previously competing in that market. The acquiring firm should intend to use the acquired business as a base for expansion, and not merely hold it as a portfolio investment.

Incumbent businesses reported on up to three each direct or acquisition entries into their markets within the previous seven years (1972 to 1978).

Explanatory Variables

Market Structure

Market-structure variables that raise barriers should favor acquisition entry, and those that reduce barriers should favor direct entry. To save degrees of freedom, the model was tested on only five key-structure variables in addition to the entrant-characteristic and strategy variables.

These key-structure variables together measure the strength of the standard set of conceptual barriers—differentiation, scale, capital requirements, and incumbent reactions (omitting absolute cost, the least prevalent barrier)—and the degree of market disequilibrium weakening barriers.

Market-Growth Rate. Rapid market growth should reduce the impact of barriers by creating disequilibrium and, thereby, encouraging direct entry.

Managerial motives should also favor acquisition in low-growth markets. Managers given a diversification charter usually face time pressures. Direct entry may allow an acceptable rate of expansion into a high-growth market, but not into a low-growth market.

More acquisition candidates should be available in more mature, low-growth markets. There has been a longer time for the number of companies to build up, and also mature markets are likely to be consolidating by squeezing out weaker competitors. Such competitors may be suitable acquisition candidates.

Barrier, managerial, and availability factors, therefore, all favor direct entry into high-growth markets and acquisition entry into low-growth markets. Market-growth rate is represented by MKT GRW, the four-year average annual change in market sales (constant dollars).

Market Concentration. This variable measures the extent of both reaction and scale barriers. The larger the share of market leaders the more likely they are to react against entrants and the greater their market power to implement resistance. Concentration also indicates the presence of scale barriers. High levels of concentration should therefore favor acquisition entry as a means of avoiding both reaction and scale barriers.

Antitrust factors yield an opposite effect. The objection that acquisitions, even conglomerate ones, can increase concentration is naturally salient in more concentrated markets. The latter markets should also, by definition, offer fewer acquisition candidates.

Thus the barrier effect of higher concentration favoring acquisition is offset by antitrust and availability factors. In empirical analysis, therefore, no direction of association can be predicted between market concentration and the choice of entry mode. Market concentration is represented by CONC, the four-year-average market share of the reporting business and its three leading competitors, as defined by the reporting business.

Investment Intensity. Investment intensity indicates the presence of scale barriers, as well as the need to commit large amounts of capital to entry. Greater capital requirements should be more problematic for direct entry, which typically uses internally generated funds. In contrast, acquisition entry often allows funding through exchange of equity, which imposes much less strain on both the balance sheet and the profit-and-loss statement. The investment intensity variable should therefore be negatively associated with direct entry and positively with acquisition. INVST is the average of each year's investment (net plant and equipment plus working capital) divided by revenues.

Advertising Intensity. The advertising/sales ratio is generally accepted as the best indicator of the height of the differentiation barrier. Previous studies have assumed that high levels of advertising intensity should create a strong barrier to entry. I propose that high advertising intensity can also encourage direct entry, because advertising campaigns can be mounted quickly regardless of scale. In contrast, R&D programs or factory investments require longer lead times, and the latter increase with scale, whereas advertising is a strategic tool with relatively rapid results for entrants. Since high levels of advertising intensity can thus attract as well as deter entrants, no hypothesis can be made about the empirical association between advertising intensity and the choice of entry mode. ADVT is the average of the reporting business's annual expenditures on media advertising expenses, divided by revenues.

Incumbent-Parent Size. The elements of market structure that determine barriers to entry should include the resources of incumbents. Incumbents with greater resources should be able to mount stronger defenses against entrants. I hypothesize that potential entrants particularly consider the absolute size of the parent companies of incumbent business. Entrants into markets with large incumbent-parent companies should be more likely to choose acquisition in order to avoid competitive battles with incumbents backed by the resources of large parents. The size of an entrant's parent company in relation to those of incumbents should also be relevant—greater size should favor the choice of direct entry. INC PRN SZE is the absolute size, in dollars of revenue, of the reporting business's (the incumbent) parent company. REL PRN SZE is the ratio of the size of the entrant's parent company to that of the reporting business.

Entrant-Parent Characteristics

Parent Size. A larger parent should favor the direct-entry mode for two reasons: greater resources available to overcome direct-entry barriers, and more potential for antitrust objections to acquisitions. On the other hand, larger parents should be more capable of making an acquisition. Therefore, the net effect of parent size is unclear. (I have already argued that greater size relative to incumbents' parents should favor direct entry.) ENT PRN SZE is the absolute size, in dollars of revenue, of the entrant business's parent company.

Parent Diversity. Diversified parent companies should be more likely to use acquisition entry because of their greater previous experience with growth through acquisition. Entrants' parent companies were classified using Rumelt's categories, and dummy variables were created to represent each category: SNGL BUS, DOM BUS, REL BUS, and UNREL BUS are 0, 1 variables respectively representing Rumelt's single-business, dominant-business, related-business, and unrelated-business/conglomerate categories.

Entrant Relatedness

Two classes of entrant relatedness to the entered market should affect the choice of entry mode: type of diversification move, and shared activities and customers.

Type of Diversification Move. The entries were classified by their overall relatedness to the existing business of the diversifier as follows: geographic expansion, segment expansion, related expansion, forward vertical integration, backward vertical integration, and unrelated diversification. No-Preexisting-Businesses was a seventh category. Entrants whose parents had no preexisting businesses were, by definition, newborn firms. Such entrants were excluded from these analyses because they would not have had the option of acquisition entry. A newborn firm cannot begin life through acquisition.

Geographic expansion is included as entry because a company introducing an existing product into a new geographic area can face many of the standard barriers to entry. Segment expansion is entry from one segment of a market into another segment of the same market. Related expansion is entry from one market into a separate, but horizontally related, market. The other categories are defined in the usual ways. I hypothesize that the more unrelated the entry move, the more likely it is that acquisition will be the entry mode. Dummy variables were created to represent each classification separately: GEOG, SEGM, REL EXP, FWD VER, BCK VER, UNREL DIV.

Shared Activities and Customers. A more detailed measure of relatedness is the degree to which parent and entrant share specific activities and customers. The degree of sharing indicates actual, rather than just potential, synergy. Greater sharing should be associated with direct entry.

Data were collected for several categories of shared activities and customers: manufacturing/production, R&D, distribution, sales, advertising and promotion, immediate customers, and end users. Entrants were classed on each type of activity/customer as sharing (1) up to 10 percent of activities with parent, (2) 10 to 50 percent, (3) 50 to 90 percent and (4) 90 to 100 percent. A composite variable, AVG SHR, average sharing, was created to use in regression estimation. It weights all seven categories equally and treats the 1, 2, 3, 4 codings as a continuous scale.

Entrant Competitiveness

Barriers and an entrant's ability to reduce them obviously affect the initial competitiveness of the entrant. Those who can achieve a strong competitive position initially should favor the choice of direct entry. The entrant who can achieve only a weak competitive position through direct entry should prefer acquisition entry. Although perhaps not entirely rational, buying a weak entry position seems more attractive than building a similarly weak one. The acquirer of a weak business may believe that its own skills and resources will transform the purchase. This was the case with Philip Morris's purchase of Miller Brewing and Imperial Tobacco's purchase of Golden Wonder, among many others. Furthermore, available acquisition candidates are far more likely to have weak rather than strong competitive positions. Thus, I hypothesize that the direct-entry mode is more closely associated with a strong competitive position on entry, and acquisition with a weaker position.

Measures were obtained for eight aspects of competitiveness: product quality, prices, costs, production effectiveness, sales-force effectiveness, distribution effectiveness, advertising-and-promotion expenditures, and reputation of company/strength of brand name. Entrant positions were rated on these dimensions relative to leading incumbents as (1) much lower, (2) somewhat lower, (3) about the same, (4) somewhat higher, and (5) much higher. Variables were constructed for each dimension using the 1, 2, 3, 4, 5 codings as a continuous scale. For regression purposes, a composite variable, AVG POSN, was constructed as an average of six variables, excluding the price and cost variables. The latter two variables, REL PRC and REL COST, were used individually in the regression analyses.

Motives for Entry. Separate from barrier considerations, an entrant's motives for entry should affect its choice of entry mode. The direct mode should be more likely where entry is made into a new market to exploit advantages or skills developed in an existing market (Motivation—Offense). The same should hold when the entry is made to defend a position in an existing market (Motivation—Defense). In both cases there is a high degree of relatedness with the entered market.

Entrants motivated by a market's growth prospects (Motivation—Market Growth) should be more willing to use direct entry since it is the future growth from market participation that motivates them, rather than the immediate growth provided by acquisition.

Data were collected for the following motives: market profitability, market growth, share costs, offense, defense, access to suppliers, access to outlets, (achievement of) counter-cyclical sales, generate cash, and use cash. Each motivation was rated as (1) little/no importance, (2) some importance, (3) major importance. Variables with values of 1, 2, or 3 were constructed for each of the ten measures above as follows: MOTV PROF, MOTV GRW, MOTV COSTS, MOTV ADVN, MOTV DEF, MOTV SUP, MOTV OUT, MOTV CYC, MOTV GEN, MOTV USE.

Active Acquisition Year

In addition to market structure and incumbent factors, stock market and other conditions affecting acquisitions in general may affect the choice of entry mode. To test for this effect, a dummy variable for active acquisition years was included, DUM ACQ YR. The measure of acquisition activity was the total number of acquisitions reported for each year by the FTC Bureau of Economics.[9] For the observation period 1972 to 1979, only 1972 and 1973 were coded 1 (highly active years). The other years were coded 0. Note that this is the only variable with a time dimension.

Summary

The probability that an entrant will choose one entry mode rather than the other has been specified in terms of variables representing the structure of the entered market (including incumbent characteristics), characteristics of the entrant's parent company, the entrant's relatedness to the entered market, its initial competitiveness relative to incumbents, and its motives for entry. These variables together also capture the financial, managerial, availability, and legal factors. I have added a variable to control for stock market and other conditions affecting the general level of acquisition activity.

Patterns in Entrant Data

To test the hypotheses concerning the choice between direct and acquisition entry (and hypotheses about market-share gain, discussed in chapter 5), original data were collected from the special sample of thirty-one PIMS markets. These data included:

1. The number of direct and acquisition entries into each market over the eight-year period 1972 to 1979;
2. detailed information for sixty-nine entrants covering their entry mode (direct or acquisition), parent-company characteristics, relatedness measures, entry strategy, and market performance.

These entrant data were then combined with the existing PIMS data on market structure/incumbent characteristics.

Number of Entrants

The thirty-one markets experienced a mixed pattern of direct and acquisition entries: eleven markets experienced direct entries only, nine markets acquisition entries only, and eleven markets both, for a total of sixty direct and thirty acquisitions.

The fact that one-third of the markets experienced both types of entry supports the view that direct and acquisition entry can be alternative routes, and that the choice depends on the entrant, as well as on the market. Two-thirds of the markets experienced only one entry mode, suggesting that market conditions do have a major impact on the direct versus acquisition choice.

Economic observers suggest that American business is currently eschewing risk-taking activity, preferring growth through acquisition to growth through internal development. These suggestions are based on publicly available data concerning only acquisition activity. As far as I know, my sample offers the only comparable data on direct entry. Obviously my sample is very limited in its generalizability, but the ratio of sixty direct to thirty acquisition entrants contradicts this emphasis on acquisition.

Might the sample be biased? It was not designed to be biased in favor of either entry mode. The criterion for inclusion was the occurrence of at least one of either type of entry. To check that my sample was one of acquisition entries, twenty-four of the thirty acquisition entrants were asked the following question [reproduced from line 308 of the Entry Data Manual (See appendix E)]:

Importance of this Market for Acquisition

Entry into this served market may have been an incidental reason for the acquisition, e.g., the business competing in this served market was acquired as part of a larger company. Indicate which one of the following best describes the importance of entry into this market as a reason for the acquisition:

Entry not relevant or incidental (write "0" in box)

Entry of minor importance (write "1" in box)

Entry of major importance (write "2" in box)

Of the twenty-four acquisition entrants, eighteen reported that entry was of major importance, four of minor importance, and two not relevant. If the same proportions are applied to all thirty acquisition entrants, and there is no reason to assume a different proportion, the sample of thirty overwhelmingly consists of entry rather than portfolio acquisitions.

The categories of entrant data are

Parent company characteristics,

Relatedness—the type of move,

Relatedness—shared activities and customers,

Motives for entry,

Competitive position relative to entrants,

Initial and maximum market share.

The summary statistics for these categories are described below (except for the market-share category, which is discussed in chapter 5).

Parent-Company Characteristics

Data were collected for three measures: whether the entrant had an existing parent, and if so, its size and diversity. The size measure was simply the revenues of all activities of the parent at the time of entry. The diversity measure was Rumelt's four-group classification: single business, dominant business, related business, and unrelated business or conglomerate (see Entry Data Manual in appendix E for definitions and examples supplied to respondents).

Of the sixty-six respondents, eight had no existing parent; that is, they were newborn firms making direct entries. Thus, only a fraction of entrants, 12 percent (eight out of sixty-nine) or 18 percent (eight out of forty-five direct entrants), was of the type favored by economic theory, public policy, and even public sentiment as a source of new competition—the new company. Percentages for the other categories were 9 percent single business, 19 percent dominant business, 36 percent related business, and 36 percent unrelated business (see table 4-1). These proportions were weighted toward

Table 4-1
Type of Parent

Type of Parent	(1) Total Entrants	(2) Direct Entrants	(3) Acquisition Entrants	(4) Acquisitions as Percentage of Total
No existing parent	8	8	0	0
Single business	5	4	1	20
Dominant business	11	8	3	27
Related business	21	11	10	48
Unrelated business	21	11	10	48
Total	66	42	24	36
n.a.	3	3	0	
Total	69	45	24	

$n = 69$

the more diversified categories, compared with Rumelt's proportions for the Fortune 500 as a whole (6, 29, 45, and 19 percent, respectively). Figure 4-1 makes this comparison usually. It is perhaps no surprise that the more diversified companies account disproportionately for a given sample of diversification moves.

More interesting is the support for my hypothesis that acquisition will be preferred by the more diversified companies. While only 20 percent of single-business-parent entrants chose acquisition rather than direct entry, this proportion increased to 27 percent for dominant-business-parent entrants, and 48 percent for both related-business-parent entrants and unrelated-business-parent entrants (also shown in figure 4-1).

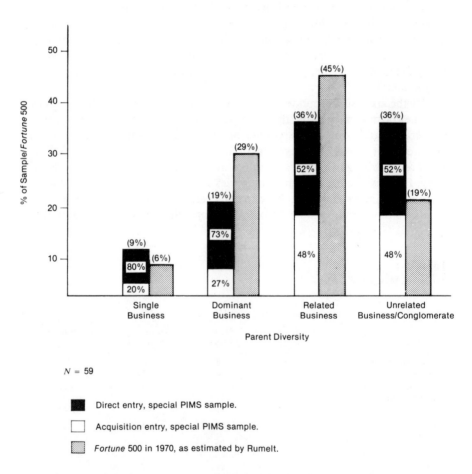

N = 59

■ Direct entry, special PIMS sample.

☐ Acquisition entry, special PIMS sample.

▨ *Fortune* 500 in 1970, as estimated by Rumelt.

Figure 4-1. Parent Diversity, Sample Distribution, and Entry Mode

The mean size of the 69 entrants' parents (measured during the 1970s) was $4,500 million, and was about the same for both direct and acquisition entrants. The median size was much smaller, $1,100 million, and was also much smaller for direct entrants than for acquisition entrants ($800 million versus $3,000 million), supporting the hypothesis that acquisition will be preferred by larger companies.

Relatedness—Type of Move

The degree of relatedness between entrant and parent can be measured in terms of the type of diversification move or in terms of shared activities. Several schemes have been proposed for classifying diversification moves. Probably the most widely used is the scheme that the Federal Trade Commission applies to acquisitions:[10] horizontal mergers, vertical mergers, product extension mergers, market extension mergers, and pure conglomerate mergers.

In the product extension merger the acquiring firm adds products in some way related to existing production processes or marketing channels. This category is similar to Ansoff's "present mission-new product," and to Kitching's "concentric marketing."[11] In the market-extension merger the acquiring firm already sells the same product as the acquired one, but in a different market. The market-extension category is very similar to Ansoff's "present product-new mission" and to Kitching's "concentric technology." The other categories are self-explanatory.

The FTC and similar classifications are not suitable for the purposes of this study of entry. The FTC classification was designed to describe mergers, irrespective of whether there is entry into a new market; horizontal mergers do not involve entry except where the acquired business is in a different geographic market. I include as entry the expansion (whether direct or via acquisition) of an existing-product category into a new geographic area. The geographic entrant faces many of the standard barriers to entry, although it is obviously one of the least disadvantaged types of entrants. Such geographic expansions can be as difficult as any entry. For example, Procter & Gamble fought a classic entry-battle when it entered the U.S. east-coast coffee market with an existing brand, Folgers. The resisting incumbent was General Foods.

The diversification classification schemes of Ansoff, Kitching, and others are also not appropriate. First, they exclude both horizontal and vertical moves. I have discussed the need to include horizontal-geographic moves. Vertical moves also need to be included as entries since new markets are involved. Second, the category variously called "product extension," "present mission-new product," and "concentric marketing" describes moves that are not necessarily entries.

My investigation required a scheme which could accommodate all types of direct and acquisition moves. The following question, reproduced from line 208 of the Entry Data Manual (see appendix E) was developed:

Nature of Direct Entry Move

Characterize each direct entry as *one* of the following in relation to the pre-existing businesses of the entering company:

Geographic Expansion (write "1" in box)
—the new entry is the expansion of an existing product or service to a previously unserved geographic area.
Segment Expansion (write "2" in box)
—the entering company was already competing in the Total Market of which this Served Market is a segment.
Related Expansion (write "3" in box)
—the entering company was not already competing in the Total Market, but the entry is closely related horizontally to its pre-existing businesses.
Forward Vertical Integration (write "4" in box)
—the new entry is related to pre-existing businesses and is at a stage closer to the end user.
Backward Vertical Integration (write in "5" in box)
—the new entry is related to pre-existing businesses and is at a stage closer to sources of supply.
Unrelated Diversification (write "6" in box)
—the new entry is not closely related to its pre-existing business.
No Pre-Existing Businesses
—if you answered "new ("0")" for Line 205, the entrant has no pre-existing businesses.

An analogous question was asked about acquisition entrants, but without the "no pre-existing businesses" option.
Apart from the inclusion of geographic expansion and two directions of vertical integration, the major difference in my classification is the use of segment expansion and related expansion, instead of the product-extension and market-extension categories. Product extension (adding a new product to a firm's existing market) does not really count as entry into a new market. The segment-expansion and related-expansion categories allow two levels of market extension. This is particularly important because of the narrow PIMS market definition and the arbitrariness of market boundaries (discussed in chapter 1). The "total market," to which the expansion moves were related, had been defined earlier in the questionnaire. The "served market" is the standard PIMS-defined market, experiencing entry.

Results (see table 4-2 and figure 4-2). Most entry moves were reported as geographic, segment, or related expansion (forty-eight out of sixty-one, excluding eight with no previous parent or activities). It is noteworthy that twenty-eight of the sixty-one entry moves (46 percent) were geographic or

Table 4-2
Type of Entry Move

Type of Entry Move	Total	Direct	Acquisition	Percent Direct
No existing parent	8	8	0	100
Geographic expansion	15	7	8	47
Segment expansion	13	8	5	62
Related expansion	20	15	5	75
Forward vertical integration	6	4	2	67
Backward vertical integration	1	1	0	100
Unrelated diversification	6	2	4	33
Total	69	45	24	65

$N = 69$

segment expansion; that is, the entries were made by companies already competing in other parts of the total market. This pattern supports the common observation that competitors in contiguous markets are the primary source of entrants. Admittedly, the narrow PIMS definition of the served

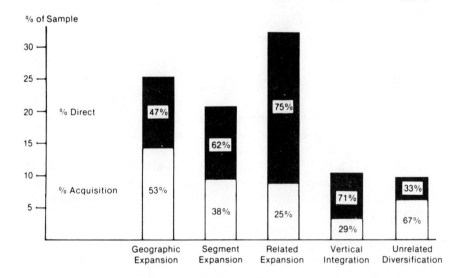

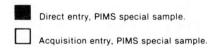

Direct entry, PIMS special sample.

Acquisition entry, PIMS special sample.

Figure 4-2. Type of Diversification Move

market results in intraindustry (or intratotal market) moves being defined as entry. However, even when these moves are exluded, thirty-three entries remain: related expansion, forward-vertical integration, backward-vertical integration, and unrelated diversification. Only six (18 percent) were basically unrelated.

The split between direct and acquisition entries does not fit the hypothesis that acquisition will increase with decreasing relatedness. If the vertical-integration moves are excluded (because of ambiguity about their degree of relatedness and the small number of observations), the remaining moves might be ranked in descending degree of relatedness:

	%Direct
Geographic Expansion	47
Segment Expansion	62
Related Expansion	75
Unrelated Diversification	33

The hypothesis would have been supported had the percentages of direct entries decreased monotonically with relatedness. They do not.

Relatedness—Shared Activities and Customers

The classification of any entry move as one of the six types discussed above can only crudely capture the nature and degree of relatedness between the entrant business and its parent. Also, the type classification indicates potential, rather than actual, synergy between parent and entrant. A more accurate measure of relatedness is the sharing of activities and customers between parent and entrant. This shared-activities measure parallels Biggadike's.[12]

Measurement. Respondents were asked to estimate the degree to which the entrant shared key activities and customers with other components of its parent company. Respondents were asked for the maximum extent of actual sharing for direct entrants and of potential sharing for acquisition entrants. The latter distinction was made because acquisitions take time to integrate with their new parents, while direct entrants probably start sharing as much as possible, and probably reduce sharing as their activities increase.

The categories of shared activities and customers were

Manufacturing/production, R&D,

Distribution/service,

Sales,

Advertising and promotion,

Immediate customers (those from whom the business receives purchase orders—a PIMS definition),

End users (individuals, households, and businesses that consume the products or incorporate them in other goods and services—a PIMS definition).

Results. The degree of sharing was surprisingly low. For most of the categories, almost half of the sixty-one entrants with pre-existing parents were reported as sharing 10 percent or less with other components of their parent. In each category the remaining twenty-eight to thirty-six entrants were divided about evenly among the 10-50 percent, 50-90 percent, and 90-100 percent categories (see table B-1 in appendix B). Manufacturing had a somewhat lower level of sharing than the other categories. (The categories were also assigned codes from 1 to 4, allowing the comparison of means.)

It was hypothesized that direct entrants would have a higher level of sharing, because entry barriers are lowered through existing activities, and acquisition is, therefore, less necessary as a way of vaulting entry barriers. This hypothesis was not supported by the univariate results (see table B-2). There was little difference in sharing between direct and acquisition entrants, although the degree of sharing was somewhat higher for manufacturing. Sharing of advertising and promotion was actually higher for acquisition entrants, but this was probably due to a number of geographic-expansion acquisitions by consumer businesses in the sample. This may also explain the higher levels of sharing of immediate customers and end users for acquisition entrants.

As expected, there were very high correlations among the different types of sharing (see table B-3). However, these correlations were generally lower for acquisition than for direct entrants. The lower correlations for acquisition entrants are consistent with the view that they have less choice in the fit between parent and (acquired) entrant. The acquired company comes as a whole; some of its activities may be suitable for sharing with the new parent and other parts may not. In contrast, a direct entrant is built from scratch, allowing a more consistent pattern of sharing with its parent.

For both direct and acquisition entrants, manufacturing/production sharing and R&D sharing were highly correlated with each other (.85 for direct entrants, .71 for acquisition entrants), but much less correlated with other categories of sharing. These others—distribution/service sharing, sales sharing, advertising-and-promotion sharing, immediate-customers sharing, and end-users sharing—were fairly highly correlated with each other, reflecting their similarity as measures of marketing activities.

Motives for Entry

Motives for entry can help explain entrants' performances after entry (discussed in chapter 5). Motives also provide another measure of relatedness, and are therefore relevant to the choice of entry mode.

Motives are obviously correlated with both market structure and shared activities. For example, the growth motive can only be satisfied in a market exhibiting a high growth rate. However, it seemed worthwhile to attempt to separate the two sets of factors. Similarly, actual shared-costs do not fully capture the synergy motives of entrants. Also, some strategic objectives of entrants are easier to capture in an overall motive such as the offensive and defensive ones described below, than in the specification of shared activities.

Measurement. Respondents were asked the following question, reproduced from line 209 of the Entry Data Manual, concerning motives:

Estimate for each entrant the importance of each of the following in motivating entry:

(a) Served market profitability at time of entry
(b) Served market growth prospects
(c) To share costs with entrant's other activities
(d) To exploit an advantage arising from entrant's other activities (basically an offensive move)
(e) To strengthen entrant's market position in other activities (basically a defensive move)
(f) To improve access to suppliers for entrant's other activities
(g) To improve access to outlets for entrant's other activities
(h) Served market sales are counter-cyclical to entrant's other sales
(i) Served market would generate surplus cash for entrant's other activities
(j) Served market would use surplus cash from entrant's other activities

In each box for this question, write one of the following:

"1" (if your estimate is "Little/No Importance")
"2" (if your estimate is "Some Importance")
"3" (if your estimate is "Major Importance")

Note that the respondents are the incumbents, not the entrants; that is, the incumbents estimated the entrants' motives. However, all the motives can be inferred mainly from the nature of the entered market, which is known to incumbents, rather than from factors internal to entrants and unobserved by incumbents.

Results. As expected, profitability and growth were the two strongest motives for entry, with mean ratings of 2.4 and 2.6 in a 1 to 3 range (see table B-4). Growth received a higher rating than profitability, suggesting the paramount importance of the investment aspect of entry. In both cases the motive was much stronger for direct than for acquisition entrants. The motive of sharing costs was surprisingly weak, with a mean of 1.5; it was somewhat stronger for direct than for acquisition entrants (see table B-5). The relatedness of entries to entrants' previous activities comes through more in the exploit-advantage (offense) and strengthen-position (defense) motives. These had the highest mean ratings, after growth and profitability, of 1.8 and 2.0, respectively (a slightly stronger strengthen-position motive was attributed to acquisition entrants).

Access to suppliers had the lowest possible mean of 1.0, which is explained by the fact that only one of the sixty-nine entries was a case of backward-vertical integration. Access to outlets was rated higher at 1.6 (twenty-nine respondents rated this motive as one of some or major importance). Improving access to retail outlets was cited as a major motive in the 1979 acquisition of the Green Giant Company by the Pillsbury Company.[13] Acquisitions did receive a higher rating for this motive. The greater importance of the outlet's motive relative to the supplier's motive also fits Pfeffer and Salancik's prediction about resource dependence—that acquisitions are made to reduce external dependence, and that customers are generally a more important source of uncontrolled dependence than are suppliers.[14]

Diversification literature and management consultants frequently advocate diversification moves to improve the sales balance (in terms of counter-cyclicality) and cash-flow balance of the corporate portfolio. Yet the respondents in the PIMS special sample reported that virtually none of the entries were motivated by the wish to achieve counter-cyclical sales (only four out of sixty-seven entrants). Similarly, very few (though more) reported that the desire to generate cash or to use cash was an important motive. Even acquisition entries rated only a mean of 1.4 for use cash. One reason why portfolio balance is not a prominent motive in this sample is because a large proportion of the entries are related in one way or another to preexisting businesses of the entrants.

The correlations among motivations differed more between direct and acquisition entrants than they did for shared activities (see table B-6). Also, it was notable that the profitability motive was negatively correlated with all others for direct, but not for acquisition, entrants. The other correlations were almost all positive. Several results should be noted:

The (market) growth motive was uncorrelated with other motives for direct entrants, but fairly highly correlated with other motives for acquisition entrants.

The exploit advantage (offensive) motive was fairly highly correlated (.40) with the strengthen position (defensive) motive for direct entrants—the two motives must frequently spring from the same relatedness source. However, the correlation for acquisition entrants was lower (.22).

The use cash motive was highly correlated with many other motives for acquisition entrants, as expected.

Shared Activities versus Motives. The various motives for entry might also be expected to be correlated with certain shared activities. Table B-7 presents the correlations between each type of motivation and each category of shared activity. Notable results are

The profitability motive tended to be negatively correlated with all shared activities of direct entrants, but was somewhat positively correlated for acquisition entrants. This was also true of the correlation between profitability and other motives. The possible interpretation in both cases is that direct entrants have to make a short-term trade-off between profitability and other goals of entry.

The motivation to share costs was, as expected, positively correlated with all categories of sharing for direct and acquisition entrants. However, the correlations were higher in all categories for acquisition than for direct entrants. Again, this suggests that direct entrants have to make some short-term trade-offs, while acquisition entrants can immediately enjoy whatever relatedness benefits are available to them.

The access to outlets motive had moderately positive correlations with each category of shared activities. Surprisingly, these correlations were highest for manufacturing/production sharing and R&D sharing, rather than for the marketing/sales categories of sharing. The other motives—access to suppliers, counter-cyclical sales, generate cash, and use cash—all had very low correlations with the categories of sharing, reflecting the low variance in perceived intensity of these motives.

Entrant Competitiveness

In developing a model of the direct-versus-acquisition choice, I argued that the better the competitive position an entrant could achieve through direct entry, the more likely that the entrant would choose that mode. The initial position of direct entrants (along such dimensions as product quality) is obviously an excellent proxy for the potential position they had in mind when evaluating the direct versus acquisition choice.

The potential position of aquisition entrants, had they entered directly, is more difficult to measure. However, the position actually achieved through acquisition is seldom likely to be worse than the position that could have been achieved through direct entry, since acquisition entry is usually chosen because direct entry does not offer good competitive prospects. Indeed, the acquired position may more often be much better than that available through direct entry. There is, however, likely to be a constraint on the selling side. The majority of acquired businesses are not in the best of competitive positions. The strongest competitors usually are, or appear to be, too expensive. Thus, there seem to be adequate grounds for using the initial position of both direct and acquisition entrants as a proxy for their potential position as direct entrants.

Measurement of Initial Position. Respondents were asked to rank the entrant's starting position on eight dimensions relative to leading incumbents (reproduced from line 211 of the Entry Data Manual):

For each direct entrant, estimate the level relative to leading incumbents at the time of entry, for:

(a) Product Quality (include after sales service)
(b) Prices
(c) Costs
(d) Production Effectiveness
(e) Sales Force Effectiveness
(f) Distribution Effectiveness
(g) Advertising and Promotion Expenditures
(h) Reputation of Company/Strength of Brand Name

In each box for this question, write one of the following:

"1" (if your estimate is "much lower")
"2" (if your estimate is "somewhat lower")
"3" (if your estimate is "about the same")
"4" (if your estimate is "somewhat higher")
"5" (if your estimate is "much higher")

Results. Excluding prices and costs, the overall-average-performance rating (of the 1 to 5 codes) was 2.6 for all entrants (see table B-8). Thus, incumbents viewed the performance of entrants as somewhat less than equal to incumbent performance (an average of 3.0 would be equivalent to equality). This overall, somewhat inferior, position held for each of the six performance dimensions, with the individual means ranging from 2.5 to 2.7. However forty-four entrants were viewed as having some advantage over incumbents: twenty-one entrants had an advantage on at least one of the six performance dimensions, twenty-three had a cost or price advantage, and twelve had advantages on at least one performance dimension and on prices or costs. This left twenty-five entrants with no advantages whatsoever.

As expected, direct entrants scored as well as or better than acquisition entrants on all six dimensions (see table B-9). This supports my hypothesis that direct entrants would have positions superior to acquisition entrants. The average entrant position was not considered greatly inferior to incumbents, but was reported as about halfway between about-the-same and somewhat-lower. Thus potential entrants appear to enter only if their relative position will not be too inferior, whether they enter directly or via acquisition.

Entrants also seem to accept a slight cost disadvantage relative to incumbents (mean of 3.2; a higher score is worse for costs), and again the position is the same for both direct and acquisition entrants.

Entrants were reported to offer an equivalently lower selling price to offset their competitive disadvantages (mean of 2.6, which matches the mean on performance dimensions.) The combination of higher costs and lower prices must reduce profit margins and, by inference, return on investment. (No direct data were collected about entrants' financial performances, which would have been difficult for incumbents to evaluate.)

Correlations among Position Dimensions. As expected, these correlations were all positive, except for those between relative costs and other dimensions. This latter set of correlations should also be positive, since high costs tend to be incurred in achieving high quality, reputation, and so forth. The patterns of correlation appeared to be the same for direct and acquisition entrants (see table B-10).

The price, product quality, and reputation/brand-name ratings were all highly correlated with each other, as might be expected. Ratings of sales-force effectiveness and distribution effectiveness were also very highly correlated.

Correlations between Shared Activities and Relative Position. These correlations were expected to be positive, since a high level of shared activities ought to result in a better competitive position. Except for relative costs, the correlations were positive for direct entrants, but they were mostly negative for acquisition entrants (see table B-11). This latter pattern supports the view that entrants choose the acquisition mode to obtain an acceptable competitive position, because there is insufficient synergy between their existing activities and the new market to provide such a position through direct entry.

The correlations reported in table B-11 also permit more specific comparisons between a specific shared activity and the equivalent dimension of competition. For example, how was the degree of manufacturing/production sharing correlated with the entrant's initial production effectiveness? These correlations were surprisingly low for direct entrants—sharing did not correlate with strong relative positions. The correlations for acquisition entrants were negative, as they were for most of the correlations for acquisition entrants.

Correlations between Motives and Relative Position. These were generally not very high, reflecting the low variance in levels of motivation (see table B-12). Several results are noteworthy:

1. The profitability motive was negatively correlated with most of the competitive dimensions for both direct and acquisition entrants.
2. The share costs motive was negatively correlated with most of the competitive dimensions for acquisition entrants. This suggests that acquisition entrants may be willing to acquire businesses with relatively weak positions in order to share costs. Also, a parent company that can share costs with the acquired business can probably improve its relative position. A direct entrant can ill afford a weak entry position since it has to confront entry barriers directly.
3. The use-cash motive had a high positive correlation with product quality for direct entrants, suggesting that direct entrants like to invest in a competitively strong product.

Summary of Entrant Characteristics

Ninety entrants were reported for the thirty-one markets over the period 1972-1979, with twice as many direct as acquisition entrants. Detailed data were collected for the sixty-nine entrants that made the greatest gains in market share. These data included parent-company characteristics, two measures of relatedness (the overall type of move, and shared activities and customers), entry motives, and the entrant's position relative to incumbents on various dimensions of competition.

The parent companies were more diversified on average than the *Fortune* 500. Their median size was over $1 billion. Acquisition entrants' parents were both much more diversified and larger than those of direct entrants.

Only eight of the sixty-nine entrants were new companies with no preexisting parent. Of the remainder, most entries were related to existing parent businesses as geographic expansion (same business, new geographic market), segment expansion (entry from another part of the total market), or related expansion (entry from another related market). There was no particular difference between direct and acquisition entrants on this dimension.

There was a surprisingly low degree of sharing of activities and customers between entrants and their parents, and there was also little difference between direct and acquisition entrants in the degree of sharing. There were very high correlations between the different types of sharing, particularly for direct entrants.

Entered-market profitability and growth were easily the two strongest perceived motives for entry, and both were stronger for direct than for acquisition entrants. Offensive and defensive motives were also important. The motives of using or generating cash were unimportant, even for acquisition entrants.

Entrants had slightly inferior competitive positions relative to incumbents. However, two-thirds of the entrants had a better position than incumbents on at least one dimension. Direct and acquisition entrants did not differ in their average competitive position.

Market-Regression Results

The choice between direct and acquisitions entry can be analyzed from two viewpoints—that of the market and that of the entrant. For a given market, the proportion of direct or acquisition entries is a measure of the extent to which the market's barriers to entry affect the choices of all entrants. An entrant's choice between the two modes can be analyzed in relation to both the barriers of the entered market and the entrant's ability to overcome barriers. In this section I report regression results using the market as the unit of observation. The next section reports results using the individual entrant. Using the thirty-one special sample markets as the units of observation, the dependent variable was the percentage of direct, as opposed to acquisition, entrants in each market (PERCENTAGE DIRECT ENTRANTS). The variable's values ranged from 0 for markets with acquisition entrants only to 100 for those with direct entrants only. The independent variables were the market structure and incumbent characteristics hypothesized as posing barriers to entry.

One issue was whether the equations explaining the number of direct entrants would also apply to this dependent variable. The regressions on NUMBER OF DIRECT ENTRANTS, reported in chapter 3, were run to test the barrier effects of structure-incumbent variables on that measure of the occurrence of direct entry. My theory on the direct versus acquisition choice suggests that structural sources of barriers will also discourage direct entry relative to acquisition entry. The predicted signs for the coefficients of explanatory variables should therefore be the same when regressing on % DIRECT ENTRANTS as on NUMBER OF DIRECT ENTRANTS. (The two variables are closely but not perfectly correlated: + .61.).

Table 4-3 presents the same regression equations for % DIRECT ENTRANTS as did Table 3-5 for NUMBER OF DIRECT ENTRANTS. The results here are almost identical to those for the number of direct entrants, with one major exception. In the regressions on the number of direct entrants one measure of exit, EXIT OF COMPETITORS, had a negative sign contrary to theory, while another measure, TOTAL EXITS CLOSED, had the predicted positive sign. Here both measures had negative signs, contrary to the theory that exits should facilitate direct entry. An explanation for these results is that sellouts are usually made by weak competitors, and markets with weak competitors that sell out will also have weak competitors that close down altogether and exit. This is corroborated by the high positive correlation (.44) between TOTAL EXITS CLOSED and TOTAL EXITS-SOLD TO OUTSIDER (that is, business sold to entrants). TOTAL EXITS CLOSED was also highly positively correlated (.36) with TOTAL EXITS-SOLD TO COMPETITOR) (that is, a horizontal merger not counting as entry).

The other variables had the same signs and about the same levels of significance as in the regressions on the number of direct entrants:

LIFE CYCLE STAGE had a negative association with % DIRECT ENTRANTS, as hypothesized.

FOUR FIRM SHARE—93% SQD, the U-shape measure of concentration, had an inverse U-shape association, suggesting that direct entry is preferred to acquisition except at very high levels of concentration.

CAPACITY UTILIZATION had the same negative sign, counter to traditional theory. In this context, relative to the alternative of acquisition, the negative sign also implies that acquirers tend to avoid buying into markets with low-capacity utilization (the utilization measure is for the reporting business, not for the acquired business).

INVESTMENT/REVENUES had the same negative sign as predicted—entrants find high investment intensity a barrier to direct entry and resort to acquisition entry.

INCUMBENT PARENT SIZE had the same negative sign as predicted—again a barrier to direct entry.

The R^2 values were also approximately the same as for the regressions on the number of direct entrants, with a maximum value of .56.

Table 4-3
Regressions on Percentage of Direct Entrants

	Equation 1		Equation 2		Equation 3		Equation 4	
	Standardized Coefficient	Significance	Standardized Coefficient	Significance	Standardized Coefficient	Significance	Standardized Coefficient	Significance
Life-cycle Stage	-.478	(.99)	-.668	(.99)	-.501	(.99)	-.673	(.99)
Four-Firm Share –93% SQD			-.233	(.88)			-.186	(.86)
Exit of Competitors	-.224	(.94)	-.395	(.99)				
Total Exits Closed					-.199	(.89)	-.278	(.93)
Capacity Utilization	-.294	(.97)	-.248	(.93)	-.267	(.96)	-.188	(.86)
Investment/Revenues	.053	(.62)	-.233	(.99)	.040	(.58)	-.235	(.86)
Incumbent-Parent Size	-.481	(.99)			-.508	(.99)		
R^2	.56		.45		.54		.37	

Same Equations as for Regressions on Number of Direct Entrants.

Entrant-Regression Results

I turn now to regressions on the individual entrants as the units of observation. Entrant characteristics and strategy can now be added to market structure as explanatory variables. This provides a full test of the model developed earlier in the chapter:

$$Y_{d/a} = f \text{ (Market Structure and Incumbent}$$
$$\text{Characteristics, Entrant-Parent}$$
$$\text{Characteristics, Entrant Relatedness to}$$
$$\text{Entered Market, Entrant Competitiveness,}$$
$$\text{Entrant Motivation)}$$

Methodology

Given the 0,1 dependent variable and the probabilistic specification of the model, binary regression seemed the most appropriate estimation method. Since the dependent variable is coded 0 for direct entry and 1 for acquisition, the regressions estimated the probability that the acquisition mode of entry would be chosen rather than the direct mode.

The sample was fifty-nine entrants, excluding ten entrants that would not have faced an entry choice. These latter included eight entrants with no preexisting parent, direct by definition, and acquisition entrants for whom entry into the market was not a relevant motive for the acquisition—direct entry would not, therefore, have been considered as an alternative. The reduced sample consisted of thirty-seven direct and twenty-two acquisition entrants.

With only fifty-nine observations and a potentially large number of independent variables, it was necessary to select a small subset of explanatory variables in order to minimize correlation and maximize the number of degrees of freedom. The five market-structure/incumbent variables were selected from a larger set of variables regressed on the dependent variable. The variables were selected for their theoretical importance and stability of coefficients in the absence and presence of correlated variables. This procedure was also followed for each set of entrant characteristics: type of parent, type of move, relatedness, motivation, sharing, relative position. The entire set within each category was regressed twice on the dependent variable; first, using only that set's variables and, second, in conjunction with market-structure/incumbent variables and other sets' variables. This procedure resulted in the selection of individual variables in each set (for instance, unrelated-business parent within the set, type of parent) or composite variables representing the entire set (for example, average sharing and average competitive position). All the variables in the final equation presented here are single variables or single composite variables, and all showed stability in the signs of their coefficients in many different formulations of the equation. The end result was fourteen independent variables. Table 4-4 presents the regression results, and table 4-5 the correlation matrix. Figure 4-3 summarizes the impact of each independent variable on the probability of choosing the acquisition mode of entry.

Market Structure and Incumbent Characteristics

Two of the five variables tested had significant coefficients of the predicted sign. Faster market growth (MKT GRW) was indeed more closely associated with direct entry, and larger incumbent parent companies (INC PRN SZE) were more closely associated with acquisition entry. Concentration (CONC) and advertising intensity (ADVT), the two variables for which no directional hypothesis could be drawn, did not have significant coefficients.

Table 4-4
Regression on Direct versus Acquisition Choice

Variable	(1) P-Standardized Coefficient	(2) U-Standardized Coefficient	Probability of Significance	Predicted Sign	Significant* Actual Sign	Significant** Association with
MKT GRW	-.03	-.35	.96	-	-	Direct
CONC	-.01	-.16	.81	?		
INVST	-.01	-.35	.96	+	-	Direct
ADVT	-.21	-.23	.84	?		
INC PRN SZE	.00	.51	.98	+	+	Acquisition
REL PRN SZE	-.00	-.16	.71	-		
ENT PRN SZE	.00	.18	.86	?		
UNREL BUS	.66	.31	.97	+	+	Acquisition
UNREL DIV	.04	.01	.54	+		
MOTV GRW	-.00	-.64	.99	-	-	Direct
MOTV DEF	.11	.09	.73	-		
AVG SHR	.04	.03	.59	-		
AVG POSN	-.79	-.53	.99	-	-	Direct
DUM ACQ YR	.11	.05	.63	+		

*At 90 percent level or above.

**negative sign represents association with direct entry (Y = O), positive with acquisition entry (Y = 1).

(1) The P-standardized coefficient is the contribution to the estimated probability that $Y = 1$, for one unit change in the independent variable, at the point where $f(PR\ Y = 1) = .5$. This latter restriction is a result of the nonlinear relationship between independent variables and the estimated $PR(Y = 1)$ inherent in binary regression.

(2) The U-standardized coefficient is as (1), for one standard deviation change in the independent variable.

$R^2 = .62$

Observations misclassified by model = 8.5 percent

Mean of Y = 1 is .37

$N = 59$

Table 4-5
Correlation Matrix: Direct versus Acquisition Choice

	(1)	(2)	(3)	(4)	(5)	(6)	(7)	(8)	(9)	(10)	(11)	(12)	(13)	(14)	(15)
Direct or acquisition (1)	1.00														
Real-market growth (2)	-.14	1.00													
Four-firm share (3)	-.15	.04	1.00												
Investment/revenues (4)	-.19	.49	-.04	1.00											
Advertising/revenues (5)	-.13	-.00	.34	.34	1.00										
Incumbent-parent size (6)	.11	.36	-.28	-.28	.09	1.00									
Entrant size/incumbent size (7)	-.13	-.14	.12	-.20	-.12	-.18	1.00								
Entrant-parent size (8)	.02	.25	-.07	.15	-.13	.23	.16	1.00							
Unrelated-business parent (9)	.11	.12	-.01	.13	-.10	.04	-.13	.04	1.00						
Unrelated diversification (10)	.07	-.00	-.19	-.14	.03	-.04	-.05	.19	.23	1.00					
Motivation—growth (11)	-.52	.12	.10	.19	-.03	-.12	.06	-.13	.13	-.12	1.00				
Motivation—defense (12)	.19	.24	-.38	.18	-.26	.31	-.28	.18	-.13	-.05	-.23	1.00			
Average sharing (13)	-.13	.12	-.00	.20	-.20	.10	-.23	.01	-.28	-.27	.24	.31	1.00		
Average relative position (14)	-.21	-.00	-.43	.01	.08	.17	-.13	.25	.09	.15	.18	.38	.19	1.00	
Active-acquisition year (15)	.07	.08	-.01	.12	.01	.13	-.33	.04	-.14	-.02	-.24	.24	.21	-.00	1.00

N = 59
Correlations above |.26| are statistically significant at the 95 percent level, two-tail.

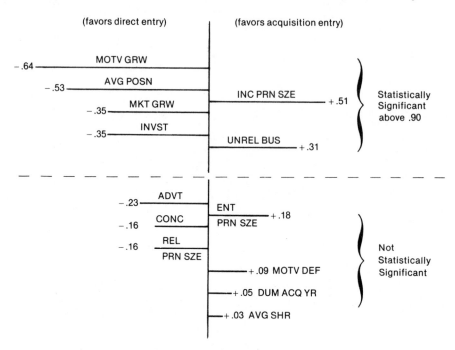

This figure depicts the contribution of one standard deviation change in each independent variable to the probability that the entry mode will be acquisition. The base probability is .37. Coefficients are taken from column 2 of table 4-4.

Figure 4-3. Contributions of Above-Average Values of Variables to Probability of Entry Mode

The last structure variable, investment intensity (INVST) was predicted to be positively associated with acquisition but actually had a significant negative coefficient, representing association with direct entry.

Entrant-Parent Characteristics

Parent Size. In view of the conflicting effects of entrant-parent size, I made no definite hypothesis about the direction of association between this variable and the entry mode. The regression estimations do not contradict this assumption: the coefficient for ENT PRN SZE was not significant.

I did, however, hypothesize that the size of an entrant's parent relative to that of an incumbent's parent would be negatively associated with the acquisition choice. The results were inconclusive as the coefficient for REL PRN SZE was not significant. The significance level did not increase in the absence of the two absolute measures of parent size, INC PRN SZE and ENT PRN SZE.

Parent Diversity. The dummy variables representing all four of the parent-diversity categories were tested. In support of my hypothesis that more diversified parents would favor acquisition, the dummy for unrelated business, UNREL BUS, had a positive and significant coefficient in the presence and absence of the dummy variables for dominant business and related business. UNREL BUS also had a very low correlation (.04) with ENT PRN SZE. Thus the diversity effect was quite separate from that of parent size.

Entrant Relatedness

Type of Diversification Move. This overall measure of relatedness did not discriminate between the two entry modes. None of the dummy variables representing each type of move (geographic expansion, segment expansion, related expansion, forward and backward vertical integration, and unrelated diversification) had statistically significant variables. To save degrees of freedom, the final equation in table 4-4 contained only the variable for unrelated diversification, UNREL DIV.

Shared Activities and Customers. These more specific measures of relatedness were also statistically insignificant, both as individual variables and combined in the composite measure, AVG SHR.

Entrant Competitiveness

Three measures of entrant competitiveness relative to incumbents were tested in regression estimations: average prices, average costs, and average relative position (the composite of the competitive dimensions other than prices and costs). The price and cost variables were insignificant and therefore dropped from the final equation. However, the composite variable, AVG POSN, was highly significant and of the expected sign. Thus, even if the relatedness variables were not significant, the end result of relatedness—an entrant's competitive position—did show the predicted preference for direct entry. A further explanation of AVG POSN's significance could be that direct entry is the more effective way to exploit a competitive innovation. Why acquire a business already made obsolete by your own innovation?

It is also notable that acquisition seems to center on the weaker members of the competitive structure. The frail competitor is obviously more likely to be up for sale. In addition it should offer more scope for improvement by a strong acquiring company, or so it might seem.

Motives for Entry

The coefficients for market growth as a motive, MOTV GRW, did indeed have a highly significant positive association with the direct mode. This effect was separate from the actual past growth rate of the market; the MKT GRW and MOTV GRW variables had a very low correlation of .12, and the direction and significance of MOTV GRW's coefficient was unchanged when MKT GRW was dropped from the regression. The motives of exploiting an advantage, MOTV ADVN, and defending a position, MOTV DEF, were not statistically significant. This lack of significance might be attributed to the respondents' inability to judge such motives.

Active Acquisition

The variable DUM YR did not have a significant coefficient.

Summary of Results

The regression results are consistent with my model of how the choice between direct and acquisition entry is affected by market structure and entrant characteristics. The overall explanatory power is very high: the R^2 of .62 is high for a 0,1 dependent variable. Furthermore, when the coefficients generated by the regression model were used to predict whether each entry was direct or via acquisition, only 8.5 percent of the observations (five of the fifty-nine entries) were misclassified. Ideally, this measure of misclassification should have been obtained on a sample other than the one on which the model's parameters were estimated. The small sample available did not allow for the usual split-sample approach. Nevertheless, the 8.5 percent error compares very favorably with the 37 or 46 percent errors of a naive model (thirty-seven percent if the naive model classifies all observations as direct, given that 37 percent of the entries were made via acquisition; 46 percent if the naive model assigns observations randomly between 63 percent direct and 37 percent acquisition, as recommended by Morrison.[15]

Only one variable had a significant sign opposite from that predicted: investment intensity. Five variables had significant signs in the predicted direction. Those negatively associated with the acquisition choice (and positively with direct entry) were market-growth rate, investment intensity, market growth as an entrant motive, and the average position of the entrant relative to incumbents. Those positively associated with the acquisition choice (and negatively with direct entry) were incumbent-parent size and entrants with diversified parents (unrelated business category).

Independent of the structure of the entered market and other variables, entrant-parent characteristics appear, therefore, to be major determinants of the choice of entry mode. However, the degree of relatedness between entrant and parent does not appear to be important, in contradiction of my model. The unimportance of relatedness is offset by the importance of the entrant's average competitive position relative to incumbents. A strong competitive position is largely the result of a high degree of relatedness. Entrants thus appear to be more influenced by what relatedness delivers in terms of a competitive position than by the promise of relatedness per se.

It should be restated that the model is limited. First, it deals only with the choice of entry mode given that a particular entrant has already selected a particular market into which to diversify. Second, it is not complete in predicting the actual choice of mode. It deals only with the influence of barrier-related factors, apart from the traditional financial and managerial factors affecting this choice. The model's contribution is the hypothesis that barrier-related factors have their own predictable influence.

Notes

1. Alan Bevan, "The U.K. Potato Crisp Industry, 1960-72: A Study of New Entry Competition," *Journal of Industrial Economics* 22, no. 4 (June 1974):281-297. See also "Smith's Potato Crisps Ltd." IMEDE teaching case 1968 (distributed by Harvard Case Services, Boston, No. 9-513-099).

2. Richard P. Rumelt, *Strategy, Structure, and Economic Performance*, (Boston: Division of Research, Harvard Business School, 1974).

3. H. Igor Ansoff, *Corporate Strategy*, (New York: McGraw-Hill, 1965).

4. E. Ralph Biggadike, *Corporate Diversification: Entry, Strategy and Performance*, (Boston: Division of Research, Harvard Business School, 1979), and also in "The Risky Business of Diversification," *Harvard Business Review* 55, no. 3 (May-June 1979):103-111.

5. Biggadike, *Corporate Diversification*.

6. *Federal Trade Commission v. Procter & Gamble Co., 386 U.S. 568 (1967).*

7. *United States v. Penn-Olin Chemical Co., 378 U.S. 158 (1964).*

8. *United States v. Falstaff Brewing Corporation, 410 U.S. 526 (1973).*

9. Source: Malcolm S. Salter and Wolf A. Weinhold, "Introduction to Corporate Diversification" (Harvard Business School note 1-377-135 6/77) and latest editions of *Mergers and Acquisitions*.

10. U.S. Federal Trade Commission, *Statistical Report on Mergers and Acquisitions*, Washington, D.C.: Bureau of Economics (November 1976).

11. H. Igor Ansoff, *Corporate Strategy*, (New York: McGraw-Hill, 1965); and John Kitching, "Why do Mergers Miscarry?" *Harvard Business Review* 45, no. 6 (November-December 1967):84-101.

12. Biggadike, *Corporate Diversification*.

13. *Business Week*, "Pillsbury's ambitious plans to use Green Giant," (July 9, 1978).

14. Jeffrey Pfeffer and Gerald R. Salancik, *The External Control of Organizations: A Resource Dependence Perspective*, (New York: Harper & Row, 1978).

15. Donald G. Morrison, "On the Interpretation of Discriminant Analysis," *Journal of Marketing Research* 6, no. 2 (May 1969):156-163.

5 Market Performance and the Impact of Entrants

In discussing how barriers might affect the occurrence of (direct) entry and how acquisition can be an entry mode that bypasses barriers, I analyzed only the number of entrants. Another, in some ways more important, measure of entry is the market share gained by entrants: total share gain for direct entrants and change in share for acquisition entrants. Markets in which many entrants achieve low shares probably have lower barriers than those in which there are fewer entrants that achieve high shares. Frequent entry and low shares are typical of markets in which the entrant can easily enter as a fringe, specialist competitor, but encounter high barriers to the oligopolistic core of full-line competitors. The ease of entry into the oligopolistic core is the issue of interest to entrants, incumbents, and public policymakers.

The cost of entry is also a relevant measure of the strength of entry barriers. However, my data do not include entrant financial-performance because my respondents were incumbents, not entrants. Also, the entrant's financial performance is not of interest to incumbents or public policymakers except as it affects the entrant's ability to affect the market in terms of share gained or altered incumbent behavior, for example, price reductions. For these reasons, I focus here on the market-share aspect of entrant performance.

Existing theories of entry say little about the market share that entrants will achieve. In this chapter I develop a model to explain the share gain of entrants, report on the data concerning this issue, and present the results of a regression analysis testing the model.

Predicting Entrant Market Share

It is difficult to specify a complete model of market-share change for entrants (or competitors in general), because many more variables are involved than in the case of occurrence and choice of entry mode. These two cases involve decisions made by potential entrants in the light of their own characteristics, the structure of the markets considered for entry, and the strategy of incumbents in those markets. While the anticipated, uncontrollable reaction of incumbents is also a factor, the decisions are made in an essentially static and closed context.

The context is static because both the entry and entry mode decisions are one-time events (even though there may be many points in time at which the entry decision is considered). In contrast, the outcome of entry in terms of market performance is the result of a dynamic process—the ongoing struggle between entrants and incumbents. Such dynamic processes involve all the usual associated modeling problems, especially time-lag effects.

The entry-decision context is also largely closed in that all the relevant variables are in the control of the decision makers (entrant characteristics), are known to the decision maker (market structure and incumbent characteristics/strategy), or can be estimated/guessed by the decision maker. In contrast, the market performance of an entrant is not a decision to be made by the entrant alone. It is the outcome of actions not just by the entrant, but by incumbents; customers; suppliers; and intervening channels, such as distributors and retailers. The context is thus much more open.

A Model of Entrant Market Share

Given the difficulties in specifying a complete and dynamic model of market-share change and the limitations of the available cross-sectional data, I have opted for a static approach based on barriers to entry. Rather than explaining entrant market-share in terms of an ongoing interaction with incumbents, I will try to explain how barriers, and the entrant's ability to overcome them, affect the outcome of the competitive struggle. Essentially, mine is a reduced-form approach, going directly from market structure, competitor characteristics, and overall strategies to long-run market share. My objective is not to predict that share but to understand the extent to which these aggregate variables can influence it.

The share gain of entrants should be affected by:

Market structure and incumbent characteristics,

Entrant characteristics
  parent company characteristics,
  relatedness of other businesses to the entered market,
  motives for entry;

Entrant strategy
  direct or via acquisition,
  actual competitive position relative to incumbents;
Incumbent reaction;

Time since entry.

These sets of explanatory factors are very similar to those used in examining the direct versus acquisition choice. In general, variables that favor direct entry by lowering the effective barrier should favor greater share gain.

Market Structure and Incumbent Characteristics

The market-structure and incumbent-characteristic variables that determine the height of entry barriers for the occurrence of entry should have an identical impact on entrant share gain after entry. Entry is an incremental process: the factors encouraging or discouraging the occurrence of entry at any scale should also apply to the expansion of that scale. These factors have been addressed in chapter 3 and need not be repeated here.

Entrant-Parent Characteristics

Because of the greater resources available, having larger parent companies should allow entrants to gain more market share. These resources allow entry on a larger scale and greater subsidization of the usual losses incurred in building share.

Parent diversity, independent of size, should also be positively associated with entrant share. First, such parents will probably have had more experience with entry, since that activity is a building block of the diversified firm. Second, according to the cross-subsidization hypothesis, diversified firms have a greater ability or willingness to subsidize losses in one business from profits in other businesses. Cross-subsidization is explicitly advocated by corporate portfolio models, such as that of the Boston Consulting Group (although the BCG model is in terms of cash, rather than profit, cross-subsidization). Markham, however, found very little evidence of cross-subsidization in his study of 211 diversified manufacturing companies.[1] Entry certainly entails losses—Biggadike's sample of forty direct entrants had a median ROI of −40 percent in the first two years after entry and −14 percent in the second two years.[2]

Entrant Relatedness

I have argued that relatedness between the entering company's other businesses and the new market lowers the barriers faced by the entrant. Accordingly, market-share gain should be positively associated with the degree of relatedness.

Biggadike has provided the only direct evidence linking relatedness and market-share gain, but he focused on types rather than on degree of relatedness. He found that marketing relatedness was linked with the greatest share gain, forward integration relatedness with the least; technology relatedness was in between these two extremes.

Other studies of relatedness and performance have analyzed relatedness among existing businesses in regard to the performance of the entire firm, rather than the relatedness of a diversification move and the performance of that diversification. Rumenlt conducted the most extensive of these studies.[3] His and similar studies reveal a causality problem that can also apply to studies of individual diversification/entry moves. The problem is that the diversification activities of companies, and hence the companies' degree of diversity or relatedness, are themselves a function of the companies' base businesses. Poor performance of unrelated companies may be the result of unsuccessful, unrelated diversifications, or such companies may be diversifying to escape bad performance in base markets. Ansoff et al. found evidence of diversification, via acquisition, from both weak and strong bases.[4] Also, Caves et al. argued that strategies like Rumelt's need to control for the probability that, given the characteristics of its markets, a firm should have adopted a particular mode of relatedness.[5]

Motives for Entry

Regardless of whether managers are ultimately motivated to maximize profits, growth, their control of the firm, or their personal welfare, there are many immediate motives for pursuing diversification.[6]

The more intense the motives, the greater the entry effort. Also, some motives will encourage faster growth or greater target share than others, given the usual short-term trade-off between growth and profits.

A strong growth motive should result in greater share gain, although this motive may be partially satisfied by entering fast-growing markets and not necessarily by obtaining a large market share. Gort found that companies generally diversify into industries growing faster than their base industries.[7] Thus, the confounding effect of market growth will frequently be present. Biggadike was surprised to find that entrants in fast-growing markets had a poorer share-performance than those in slow-growing markets.[8] He attributed this result to greater resistance from incumbents in the fast-growing markets. An alternative interpretation would be that the entrants in fast-growing markets were less motivated to expand share, because their growth motive was partially or wholly satisfied by the market's growth.

A strong motive to use cash or profits from existing operations should encourage greater share gain. Firms with surplus cash relative to investment opportunities typically apply a lower discount rate than those with a cash shortage. Firms with high profitability from existing operations are more willing and able to incur share-building losses in new ventures, given the common desire to maintain smooth growth in earnings (or given the Baumol hypothesis of growth maximization with a profit constraint).[9] Philip Morris used surplus funds from its base business to expand Miller Brewing's share from 4 percent, when acquired in 1970, to 22 percent in 1981.

Entry made for defensive purposes (to strengthen the entrant's position in its existing businesses) will probably not achieve a large share-gain. Moves made for defensive purposes are primarily forced and therefore not picked for their performance prospects. Vertical integration moves are frequently defensive in purpose—to control supplies or outlets.

Pfeffer and Salancik argued that the desire to control or reduce dependence on external organizations is the major motive for mergers.[10] While their empirical evidence supported this hypothesis, they did not consider the critical alternative motive: to exploit an advantage arising from relatedness.

Entry made to exploit an advantage developed in the entrant's existing businesses should have good share-gain prospects, not only because of the advantage, but also because the move is voluntary (given that there are alternative uses of corporate resources). Both marketing-related and technology-related entrants frequently have this motive (of exploiting an advantage). Gorecki hypothesized that the diversifying firm is motivated by the possession of a specific asset of value in more than one industry.[11] The firm possessing such an asset might have to exploit it through diversification rather than through sale because of various imperfections in the market for that asset: nontransferability, transaction costs, or externalities in the use of the asset by third parties.

Both defensive and offensive motives are probably common. Chandler described how firms respond to both defensive and exploitative motives in an incremental process of diversification.[12] Both these motives are also related to the need to internalize activities as the cost of coordinating them externally rises.[13] Williamson has attributed this latter phenomenon to the failure of market processes, leading to a shift of transactions from market to internal organization.[14]

Entry Mode

There are conflicting arguments as to which entry mode should be associated with greater share gain. Acquisition entrants have the advantage of an established position as a base for expansion. On the other hand, the fact of acquisition implies that the entered company may not be well suited to compete in the market. The Philip Morris acquisition of Miller Brewing is perhaps atypical, in that it depended on an exact match between acquirer and acquired. The entry of Heublein into the beer market via acquisition of Hamms may be a more typical example of the share gain associated with acquisition—poor.[15]

Also, acquisition entrants are generally less motivated than direct entrants to gain share after entry. First, they can probably survive with just the acquired share. Second, any acquisition entry is inherently a partial effort in the traditional sense of entry. The acquisition provides part of the entrant's desired scale or target market-share. Some acquisition entrants may thus be entrants only in the sense of being new to the market; others, with plans for share expansion, are full-fledged entrants. The difference can be observed here only after the event.

While direct and acquisition entrants may achieve similar levels of terminal or steady-state share, direct entrants certainly need to increase share more and faster. They are starting from a lower base, zero, and therefore must expand sales to cover fixed costs and pay for their entry investment. In addition, direct entrants need to achieve a share that will allow the exploitation of economies of scale enjoyed by competitors. Even an acquisition entrant may need to do this if the acquired business has a scale sufficient only to support the strategy of a minor, but not a major, competitor.

Entrant Competitiveness

A stronger competitive position relative to incumbents will obviously result in greater share-gain. Strength or weakness along a particular dimension (for instance, advertising effectiveness) will have a greater impact where that dimension is more salient.

Incumbent Reaction

The severity of incumbent reaction will obviously affect the share gain of entrants. Conversely, incumbents may react more severely to greater threats of share gain by entrants. However, the severity of the reaction may be more closely related to market structure than to entrant strategy. Porter suggests a contingency framework whereby the extent of incumbent retaliation depends on aspects of market structure.[16] Retaliation will be greatest when

The industry growth-rate is slow;

The product is a commodity or is commodity-like;

Firms have high fixed-costs;

There are long-established incumbents, particularly if these are also single-business companies.

The general evidence is that incumbent reactions are much less severe than might be expected. Biggadike judged that the forty entrants he studied faced little direct reaction. However, these entries were primarily in growth markets, where reaction should be milder. The fear of reaction may be greater than the reality. My regressions on the occurrence of entry (chapter 3) found incumbent-parent size, a primary measure of retaliation potential, to be one of the variables with the greatest negative association with the occurrence of entry.

Retaliation may be minimal because incumbents fail to perceive the entry as a direct threat. This seems to occur when the initial customers or needs served by the entrant are somewhat different from those of incumbent firms. Entrants are often allowed to build up a base from which to attack incumbents' traditional business.

Time since Entry

The market share achieved by entrants clearly depends a great deal on how long they have been in the market. However, there is no definitive cutoff point for measuring entrant market performance. Biggadike did find that the greatest share increase occurred in the first two years: his sample's median share was 7 percent after two years and 8 percent in the third and fourth years, and a comparable group of PIMS "adolescent" businesses had a median share-increase of only 9 percent in their fifth to eighth years in the market.

Summary

I have developed above a model of entrant share-gain based on both the structure of the entered market and the characteristics and strategy of the entrant. These factors are closely related to those explaining the occurrence of entry and the choice of entry mode. I turn now to the data collected and analyzed in studying entrant share gain. The data relevant to the model presented here have been described in chapter 4, with the exception of entrant share behavior and incumbent reactions. Share data were available for sixty-nine entrants (into the thirty-one markets) and incumbent-reaction data were available for thirty-six of the sixty-nine entrants.

The Combined Impact of Entrants

The combined share increase of all direct entrants, per market, into the thirty-one markets has already been reported and analyzed in chapter 3. This was done to allow comparison of total entrant share with the number of direct entrants as alternative measures of the incidence of entry. The regressions on TOTAL DIRECT ENTRANT SHARE were less fruitful than those on NUMBER OF DIRECT ENTRANTS in terms of significant coefficients or high R^2. This led to the conclusion that market-share changes depend significantly on entrant characteristics and entry strategy. Market structure alone appears inadequate to explain entrant-share performance—not a surprising result.

Further attempts to explain entrant share are reserved for the analysis using the individual entrant as the unit of observation. However, it is worthwhile at this point to examine the impact of entrants at the market level by reporting the share experience of both direct and acquisition entrants. Also, the impact of entrants on market share is closely related to their impacts on market size and profitability.

The impact data presented here should be viewed as measures of the markets' vulnerability to entrants over a given time period (eight years). Thus, the length of time since each entry is not relevant here. Instead, these data provide a measure of how the markets were affected by all entrants over the eight-year period. Managers of existing businesses expecting entries into their markets may view the data as indications of the possible impact of such entries over an eight-year period.

Impact of Entrants on Market Share

The average market-share impact of entrants was surprisingly small (see table 5-1). The mean impact of all direct entrants per market was the taking of only ten points in share from incumbents, that is, over eight years these markets lost an average of ten share points to all direct entrants. The median share-impact was even less, at six points. However, there was a wide

Table 5-1
Share Gain of Total Entrants

	Mean	Standard Deviation	Median	Minimum	Maximum
Total Direct Entrants[a]	9.8	11.1	6.0	0	42.0
Total Acquisition Entrants[b]	1.8	4.1	0	0	21.0
Total Entrants	11.7	12.1	6.0	0	42.0
Total Acquired Share[c]	5.0	7.1	2.0	0	25.0

N = 31 markets

[a]Sum of maximum share of each direct entrant into a market.

[b]Sum of maximum share change since acquisition of each acquisition entrant.

[c]Sum of share at time of acquisition for each acquisition entrant.

spread in this measure: the maximum combined share gain was forty-two points. Acquisition entrants had an even smaller impact. They acquired an average of five share points per market, but increased their share after acquisition by an average of only two points per market.

When direct and acquisition entrants were combined, the total mean-share increase was twelve percentage points, and the total mean change in share ownership was seventeen percentage points, that is, including the share acquired by acquisition entrants. Despite the relatively small combined share gains of entrants, it should be noted that these gains were unlikely to have come uniformly from existing competitors. The average total gain of 12 percent probably had much more than a 12 percent impact on some existing competitors.

Impact of Entrants on Market Size

While entrants' share gains represented a negative impact on incumbents, entrants had a positive impact on market size. This positive impact may have been due to a demand response to price reductions (or product improvements) or to supply effects (for example, increased category penetration of distribution outlets.)

The mean impact of the entries on the dollar size of the market was an increase of 11 percent. No markets reported a decrease as a result of the entries. The median increase was 5 percent (see table 5-2). Surprisingly, the mean positive impact increased as the entrants took more market share (see table 5-3), suggesting that vigorous efforts by entrants have benefits as well as penalties for incumbents. The mean overall market-size increase of 11 percent almost exactly offset the mean share gain of 12 percent for entrants.

The mean impact on market size was also slightly more positive (12 percent versus 10 percent) in mature/decline markets than in growth markets. This result suggests that entrants in growth markets can do little to add to demand-led growth forces, while in mature/decline markets entrants can

Table 5-2
Impact of All Entrants on Market Size and Incumbent Profitability

	Percentage Change				
Mean Impact	*Mean*	*Standard Deviation*	*Median*	*Minimum*	*Maximum*
On Dollar Size of Market	+11	20	+5	0	+100
On Profit Margins	− 7	18	−5	−70	+ 16

(Percentage not point change)

N = 31 markets

Table 5-3
Share Gain and Impact of Entrants on Market Size and Incumbent Profitability
(percentage)

Share Gain for All Entrants	Mean Impact on Market Size	Mean Impact on Profit Margins
(1) up to 2.5 ($N = 7$)	1.4	.9
(2) 2.5 to 12.5 ($N = 13$)	16.3	−10.4
(3) 12.5 and over ($N = 11$)	11.2	−16.4

$N = 31$ markets

help revive growth, perhaps by engaging in demand-stimulating activities such as price cutting and product innovations.

Impact of Entrants on Profit Margins

The positive impact of entrants on market size was offset by their negative impact on incumbents' profit margins. The mean impact on profit margins was −7 percent (percent, not point change; see table 5-2), and the median was −5 percent. When all three types of market impact were combined, the entrants had a negative estimated overall impact on the combined absolute profits of incumbents:

$$\text{Total Profit Impact} = (1 + \Delta) \text{ Market Size}$$
$$\text{(ratio of postentry} \quad \times (1 + \Delta) \text{ Incumbent Profit Margins}$$
$$\text{to preentry profits)} \quad \times (1 + \Delta) \text{ Incumbent Share}$$
$$= 1.1 \times .93 \times .88 = .90$$

In other words, total profit was estimated to be .9 of what it would have been without the entries, or a 10 percent reduction.

In contrast to the positive impact of entrant share-gain on market size, there was an increasingly negative impact on profit margins as entrants gained more share (see table 5-3). At the lowest level of share gain (up to 2.5 percentage points), the estimated impact on profit margins was actually positive, while at the highest level (12.5 percentage points or more), the impact had a mean of −16 percent.

Individual-Entrant Share Gain

I turn now from a market/incumbent to an entrant viewpoint and analyze the share gain of individual entrants. Before reporting the regression analyses to explain entrant share, I present, in this section, summary statistics on the initial and maximum shares of the sixty-nine entrants. The other variables used to explain entrant share-gain have been described in chapter 4.

Market Share Achieved

Direct entrants had a mean entry-year share of 2.3 percent, while acquisition entrants had a mean acquired share of 6.3 percent, the difference being statistically significant at the 99 percent level (see table B-13 in appendix B). This difference is not surprising, since a major purpose for choosing acquisition is to achieve immediate scale.

Although direct entrants started with much lower initial shares than acquisition entrants (2.3 versus 6.3 percent), their maximum share during the observed period (1972 to 1979) was much closer (6.8 versus 8.8 percent) (see table B-13). Thus, direct entrants increased their initial share by a mean of 4.5 percent for a total share gain of 6.8 percent, while acquisition entrants managed only 2.5 percent, which was also their total share gain. Nor was this difference due to length of time since entry—the mean and median entry year was the same for both groups (1975). Table 5-4 summarizes the patterns of share behavior.

The share gain by acquisition entrants did not vary much with their initial, acquired share (see table B-15). When divided into three categories by acquired share (0 to 3.0 percent, 4.0 to 6.0 percent, and 6.5 to 20.0 percent), the mean share-gain was greatest at 2.9 percent for the middle category. In contrast, theory might suggest that the gain would be greatest either for the lowest category of acquired share, because it presents the greatest scope for expansion, or for the highest category, which has the largest absolute base.

Table 5-4
Market Share of Entrants

		All Entrants	Direct Entrants	Acquisition Entrants
		N = 69	N = 45	N = 24
Year one or acquired share	Mean	3.7	2.3	6.3
	(Median)	(1.5)	(1.0)	(4.0)
Share gain after	Mean	3.8	4.5	2.5[a]
year one	(Median)	(4.5)	(4.0)	(2.5)
Maximum share	Mean	7.5	6.8[a]	8.8
	(Median)	(6.0)	(5.0)	(6.5)

[a]The maximum share gain of direct and acquisition entrants.

Minimum Required Share

The share achieved by entrants might usefully be compared to the level required in each market to be a viable competitor or to adopt a particular strategy. A crucial distinction is the one between the share levels necessary to be a major and a minor competitor. One minimum share level may be required to function as a major competitor, to be able to adopt strategies similar to those of other major competitors, for example, to be able to offer a full product line or adopt a policy of vertical integration. The required minimum share needed to be a minor (for example, a specialist) competitor may be lower. Accordingly, I developed a measure of these two levels (line 108 of the entry forms, see Appendix E):

Minimum Share for Major and Minor Competitors

(1a & 1b)
Estimate the minimum market share that a direct entrant would require if it were seeking to survive with a business strategy similar to those of *major* competitors in this market in 1972 and 1979.

(2a & 2b)
Estimate the minimum market share that a direct entrant would require if it were seeking to survive with a business strategy similar to those of *minor* competitors in this market in 1972 and 1979.

Clearly, the choice of *major* and *minor* as the only classifications of competitors is arbitrary and does not reflect the many possible classifications. However, it seemed that these would be the most readily understood and generally applicable ones.

Table B-16 in appendix B shows that respondents did see a definite and large difference between the two share-levels, with a mean ratio of 3.2 for the major share relative to the minor. The absolute levels are also interesting—11 and 12 percent in 1972 and 1979 for the major share, and 4 and 5 percent for the minor. The existing PIMS measure on entry occurrence reported only entrants achieving 5 percent or more share. (This measure was the dependent variable in the regressions reported in chapter 3). The increase between 1972 and 1979 for both minimum shares suggests that some consolidation was taking place, and that barriers were rising, perhaps as a result of the entries. Table B-17 suggests that, for the minimum major-share, the increase over time occurs only in mature or declining markets, not in growth markets. This result is consistent with Abernathy and Utterback's hypothesis that competition becomes more process-oriented as the product life-cycle progresses.[17] The increasing minimum for a major share may well be the result of increasing production economies-of-scale that arise from competitors' investment in more cost-efficient plants.

Table B-16 also shows that the minimum major share was not simply defined by respondents as the share of the largest competitor. The minimum required major share in 1972 was .35 of the share of the largest competitor, and .40 in 1979.

The sixty-nine entrants into the thirty-one markets did not all achieve viable major, or even minor, competitor status by the minimum-share criterion. Table B-18 shows the percentage of entrants that achieved the major and minor minimums for the markets they entered. Since entrant's shares appear on average to have peaked around the sixth year after entry, I split entrants according to whether they had been in six or more years.

Of those entrants that had been in the market for six or more years, 36 percent of direct entrants ($n = 11$) and 50 percent of acquisition entrants ($n = 4$) had a maximum share greater than that required to be a major competitor. In contrast, 64 percent of direct entrants and 100 percent of acquisition entrants made it to minor-competitor status. Of those in the market fewer than six years, only 15 percent of direct entrants ($n = 34$) and 35 percent of acquisition entrants ($n = 20$) achieved major-competitor status; 35 and 45 percent, respectively, achieved minor-competitor status.

All acquisition entrants did better than direct entrants. Of course, acquisition entrants had the advantage of buying instant share. However, only 33 percent acquired a share that allowed major-competitor status, and 46 percent minor. These proportions support a view that many sales to acquirers are prompted by the poor viability of the sold business. The proportions also imply that most acquirers have to invest and increase share to render their new businesses viable. With many bargain acquisitions of struggling businesses, the acquirer fails to make the necessary investment or share increase and suffers the consequences. Heublein's failure with Hamms Brewing is one example, in contrast to Philip Morris's success with Miller.[18]

Incumbents' Reactions

Incumbents' reactions were reported in my data base for only the thirty-six most important of the sixty-nine entrants. These thirty-six were chosen on the basis of their having achieved the greatest share gain of any entrant in the market; for an acquisition entrant this gain was the difference between the acquired share and subsequent maximum share. Reaction data were obtained for the most important entrants, since these should elicit the strongest incumbent response. Five respondents elected to report data for both the most important direct and the most important acquisition entrants, resulting in a total of thirty-six observations: twenty-one direct entrants, of which twenty were the single-most-important entrant in their market, and fifteen acquisition entrants, of which eleven were the single-most-important entrant.

Before incumbents could react, they had to be aware of the entry. Respondents were asked to report when they became aware that the entry had occurred. Respondents claimed to have been aware of seventeen of the twenty-one direct entries immediately, and of the remaining four within one year (see table B-19). It should be noted that these were the most important direct entrants in eight years. The fact that four of them (19 percent) were not noticed immediately confirms that entry-deterring activities, such as limit pricing, and entry-reactions, such as collusive price-reductions, can be limited by imperfect information (for instance, as suggested by Phillips and Stern[19]).

Phillips and Stern also suggested that incumbents may underreact because they assign the entry a minor role in their decisions. Respondents claimed that, at the time of entry, 29 percent of the entries were considered insignificant threats, 43 percent moderate threats, and 29 percent serious threats. By 1979 these proportions had worsened: 5 percent were considered insignificant, 62 percent moderate threats, 29 percent serious, and 5 percent serious enough to threaten the survival of the respondent. This altered perception is dramatic, even when allowing for the regression effect that, while in the latter period, the specific entrants had become the single-most-important entrant, they may not have been so in the initial-entry period.

Measurement

For each of the thirty-six single most important entrants, respondents (incumbents) were asked to report changes they and other incumbents made as a response along the eight relative-position dimensions. A potential measurement problem was that respondents may not have been able to distinguish between moves by themselves and other incumbents in response to the entries, and moves they would have made anyway. There was also a pattern of reporting incumbents showing more positive response than other incumbents—selective perception must play a part in this difference, as well as the objective difference that the reporting incumbents had, on average, larger market shares than other incumbents, and might, therefore, have taken leadership roles.

Reaction Pattern

The response to entrants was virtually nonexistent for acquisition entrants and generally low (about 10 to 20 percent responding competitively) for direct entrants. The exception was for relative product quality and relative price (about 30 percent responding competitively). This pattern of response has two implications. First, acquisition entry does appear to be an excellent way of avoiding reaction barriers to entry—even when the acquirers made competitive changes there was virtually no response from incumbents. The Philip Morris experience is an excellent example of this phenomenon: for many years after Philip Morris's acquisition of Miller Brewing, and despite extensive and intensive competitive changes, the other brewers failed to react. A direct entry, even on a smaller scale, would surely have provoked a strong reaction. The second implication of the pattern of response is that incumbents' reactions to direct entrants are much weaker and less universal than might be expected.

One reason for the lack of response may be that it is difficult to tell which entrants will pose the greatest threats. Although these were the most successful entrants in terms of market-share gain, the initial position of these thirty-six entrants was not superior, on average, for any dimension relative all sixty-nine entrants as a group.

Thus a view of extensive reaction to entry is not well supported by this limited evidence. In contrast, the evidence is more consistent with my earlier arguments from a corporate-strategy perspective: that incumbent reactions are constrained by the strategic costs of altering existing strategies to meet those of entrants and by organizational barriers to change.

Regressions on Individual-Entrant Share Gain

Estimation Procedures

I turn now to the explanation of entrant share gain. I defined the variable to be explained, ENTRANT SHARE GAIN, as the maximum share ever achieved by direct entrants or the maximum share ever achieved since acquisition, minus the acquired share, by acquisition entrants (up to the end of the observation period, 1979). The time since entry was used as an explanatory variable. The alternative would have been to use as the dependent variable *share gain per year since entry*, but this measure would not have suited my objective of explaining the equilibrium share of entrants. The use of actual maximum share gain as an indicator of equilibrium share seemed justified in that most entrants had passed their period of maximum share growth. The average number of years since entry was four to five, and, on average, entrants' share had grown fastest over the first four years (see table B-21 for the twenty-one most-important direct entrants. Less important entrants should have reached their maximum share even sooner).

Based on the theoretical model developed earlier in this chapter, a model with the following sets of variables was estimated:

$$Y_{\Delta\,MS} = f(\text{Market Share and Incumbent Characteristics;}$$

> Entrant Characteristics:
> Parent Characteristics,
> Relatedness—Type of Move
> —Activities Shared with Parent,
> Motivation for Entry;
>
> Entrant Strategy:
> Direct or Acquisition,
> Competitive Position Relative to Incumbents;
>
> Other:
> Time Since Entry,
> Acquired Share, if acquisition entrant)

Incumbent reactions were part of the theoretical model but could not be included because of the limited sample for which reaction data were available. Also, since incumbent reactions were minimal, they would probably not have had a significant impact in the regressions. Furthermore, the bivariate correlations between entrant share-gain and incumbent reactions were primarily positive (see table B-22) suggesting that the direction of causation was from entrant share gain to incumbent reaction.

Various specifications of the model were tested on the combined data base of sixty-nine direct and acquisition entrants. Dummy interaction terms were also used to test if direct and acquisition entrants revealed different intercept and slope coefficients; that is, did the market-share gain of the two types of entrants respond differently to the explanatory variables? Table 5-5 presents the best single equations, in terms of highest R^2 and largest number of significant variables. Equation 1 is without interaction terms, that is, forcing the same slope coefficients for all sixty-nine entrants as a group. Equation 2 includes interaction terms. These terms (ACQ* _____) show the change in the estimated coefficient for the group of twenty-four acquisition entrants relative to direct entrants. The main terms in equation 2 provide the slope coefficients for direct entrants, while the sums of the main terms and the interaction terms provide the slope coefficients for acquisition entrants (see Net Standardized Coefficient). A statistically significant coefficient for an interaction term (and the intercept dummy, DUMMY FOR ACQUISITION) means that the coefficient on the variable is different for acquisition entrants for that for direct entrants. Two of the eleven interaction terms had significant coefficients: UNRELATED BUSINESS PARENT and AVERAGE SHARING. Table 5-6 presents the correlation matrix of variables.

An F-test for homogeneity was conducted comparing equations 1 and 2. The F-statistic was highly significant, indicating that share gain is explained

Table 5-5
Regressions on Market-Share Gain

	Equation 1			Equation 2			Hypothesized Sign
	Natural Coefficient	Standardized Coefficient	Significance	Natural Coefficient	Standardized Coefficient	Significance	
Constant	793	n.a.	(.87)	871	n.a.	(.84)	
Dummy for acquisition	n.a.	n.a.	n.a.	-183	.00	(.55)	—
Exit of competitors	4.906	.21	(.94)*	7.576	.31	(.97)*	+
Incumbent-parent size	-.002	-.44	(.99)*	-.004	-.71	(.99)*	—
Four-firm share	.026	.11	(.80)	.025	.10	(.75)	?
Real-market growth	-.027	-.06	(.68)	-.041	-.09	(.73)	+
Year of entry	-.399	-.13	(.86)	-.438	-.15	(.83)	—
Entrant-parent size	-.000	-.01	(.52)	-.000	-.03	(.60)	—
Unrelated-business parent	1.343	.28	(.99)*	8.432	.68	(.99)*	+
Unrelated diversification	2.834	-.14	(.87)	-7.984	-.39	(.98)*	+
Average sharing	.008	.00	(.51)	1.088	.22	(.94)*	—
Relative prices	1.060	.17	(.92)*	.789	.13	(.84)	+
Relative costs	-1.560	-.25	(.98)*	-1.578	-.26	(.95)*	—

	Natural Coefficient	Standardized Coefficient	Significance	Net Standardized Coefficient
ACQ*Exit of Competitors	-5.550	-.16	(.75)	.15
ACQ*Incumbent Parent Size	.002	.37	(.87)	-.34
ACQ*Four Firm Share	-.080	-.47	(.87)	-.37
ACQ*Real Mkt Growth	.056	.06	(.65)	-.03
ACQ*Year of Entry	.096	.00	(.55)	-.15
ACQ*Entrant Parent Size	.000	.08	(.66)	.05
ACQ*Unrel. Bus. Parent	-7.012	-.43	(.98)*	.25
ACQ*Unrel. Diversification	4.359	.18	(.80)	-.21
ACQ*Average Sharing	-2.095	-.40	(.90)*	-.18
ACQ*Relative Prices	-1.608	-.35	(.76)	-.22
ACQ*Relative Costs	1.027	.29	(.71)	.03

Table 5-6
Correlation Matrix: Regressions on Market-Share Gain

	(1)	(2)	(3)	(4)	(5)	(6)	(7)	(8)	(9)	(10)	(11)	(12)	(13)
Market-share gain	(1) 1.00												
Dummy for acquisition	(2) -.36	1.00											
Exit of competitors	(3) .12	.08	1.00										
Incumbent-parent size	(4) -.34	.19	.26	1.00									
Four-firm share	(5) .17	-.19	-.04	-.28	1.00								
Real-market growth	(6) -.13	-.12	.12	.34	.03	1.00							
Year of entry	(7) -.30	.05	-.14	.23	.01	.16	1.00						
Entrant-parent size	(8) -.13	.05	-.06	.24	-.03	.28	.07	1.00					
Unrelated-business parent	(9) .16	.18	-.16	.10	-.02	.14	-.12	.07	1.00				
Unrelated diversification	(10) -.13	.21	-.08	.08	-.33	-.06	-.04	.12	.24	1.00			
Average sharing	(11) -.09	.03	-.14	.17	.10	.19	.27	.13	-.07	-.20	1.00		
Relative prices	(12) .10	-.11	.18	.12	-.20	.22	-.02	.22	.09	.14	.16	1.00	
Relative costs	(13) -.05	-.03	-.12	-.35	.23	.05	.02	.07	.13	-.01	-.06	.11	1.00

N = sixty-nine entrants
Correlations above |.23| are statistically significant at the 95 percent level, two-tail.

differently for direct and acquisition entrants, even though there were significant differences for only two of the eleven explanatory variables, and only one variable revealed significant opposite signs for the two groups. It was hypothesized at the beginning of this book that direct and acquisition entrants might behave similarly. These results suggest that this is not the case for their market-share behavior. The results are also consistent with the findings on choice of entry mode: market structure and entrant characteristics discriminated strongly between acquisition and direct entry. It is therefore not surprising that the two modes result in two different patterns of share gain associated with market structure and entrant characteristics.

Detailed Results

Market Structure. In view of collinearity problems arising from the small sample sizes, only four structure/incumbent variables were included in the final equation: measures of market growth, concentration, exit of competitors, and incumbent-parent size. Apart from testing for the significance of each variable, it was also necessary to include them to control for market conditions when testing the effect of the entrant-characteristic and strategy variables.

Market-growth rate has been hypothesized to be a major source of disequilibrium, easing entry, and was found to be highly significant in the regressions on the occurrence and choice of entry. Its impact is not significant in either equation here. (The regressions on the combined-share gain of all direct entrants per market, reported in chapter 3, showed similar results.)

The other major measure of disequilibrium, EXIT OF COMPETITORS, was the most important single explanatory variable for the occurrence of entry. It was also highly significant here in explaining entrant share gain, with a positive sign as hypothesized. (There is some simultaneity problem with the exit variable and the entrant-share-gain variable. Such simultaneity would increase their observed positive association.) Although the interaction term in equation 2 was not sigificant, its sign was negative, and the significant coefficient for the main term was much larger in equation 2 than in equation 1 (.31 versus .21). This suggests that exits helped direct entrants more than they did acquisition entrants.

It was not clear what should be the direction of association between entrant share-gain and market concentration. High levels of concentration usually mean that new competitors have less market power relative to incumbents (for example, to bargain for distribution). Conversely, the smaller the number of existing competitors, the larger the proportion of sales that an additional competitor should be able to obtain. Schmalensee has argued that one purpose of brand proliferation in concentrated markets is to prevent such proportionality effects from benefitting entrants.[20] Again, as in the other regressions, FOUR FIRM SHARE did not prove to be statistically significant in either equation. However, the interaction term's coefficient was negative and almost significant (p-value .87).

INCUMBENT-PARENT SIZE showed a strong negative association with the occurrence of entry, and a strong positive association with the acquisition choice, supporting its hypothesized barrier effect. It was also significant and negative here. Although the interaction term was not significant, it was positive, and the coefficient for the main term (for direct entrants) in equation 2 was much larger than in equation 1 ($-.71$ versus $-.44$). Thus, incumbent-parent size appears to have a strong negative impact on the share gain of both types of entrants, and perhaps a less negative impact on acquisition entrants. These results are consistent with the finding that acquisition entrants evoked very little reaction. Incumbent-parent size should be particularly relevant to the ability of incumbents to react.

Entrant-Parent Characteristics. It was hypothesized that entrants with existing parents, that is, not newborn entrants, would be aided in their share gain. This hypothesis was not supported—the EXISTING COMPANY variable (dummy) was not significant (not shown in table 5-5). ENTRANT-PARENT SIZE was not significant either. The results for these two variables suggest that share gain is not closely tied to the existence of general corporate resources. One problem is that I did not observe whether these resources were applied. However, the relative-position variables indicate the results of the application of specific resources.

It was hypothesized that the more diversified firms would have a better share-gain performance because of their greater experience in diversification. The main term for the the UNRELATED BUSINESS PARENT variable (dummy versus all other parent types) was significant and positive in both equations, supporting the hypothesis. The interaction term's coefficient was also significant, but negative, indicating that the variable had a weaker positive association with share gain for acquisition entrants. The net coefficient was $+.25$ for acquisition entrants, compared with $+.68$ for direct entrants and $+.28$ for the combined sample (see table 5-5). A possible interpretation of these results is that diversified entrants are more likely to run acquisition entries as status quo operations, but are more likely to expand direct entries.

Type of Move. It was hypothesized that share gain would be less as relatedness to the parent's existing businesses decreased. One measure of relatedness was the overall nature of the entry move. In the combined sample (without the interaction terms), the UNRELATED DIVERSIFICATION variable (dummy versus all other types of move) had a higher significance level than the other variables (GEOGRAPHIC EXPANSION and so forth), although not quite statistically significant. However, in Equation 2 with the interaction term, the main term was significant and negative, as hypothesized, while the interaction term was not significant. This suggests that unrelated diversification hurts the share gain of both direct and acquisition entrants.

Shared Activities. The overall degree of sharing between entrant and parent, as measured by AVERAGE SHARING, was not significant for the combined sample in Equation 1 but was significant for both terms in Equation 2. The coefficient was $+.22$ for the main direct-entry term and $-.40$ for the interaction term, for a net coefficient of $-.18$ for acquisition entrants, suggesting that sharing helps the share gain of direct entrants and hurts that of acquisition entrants. This was the only variable with significant opposite signs for the two groups. It is not surprising that shared activities and customers help direct more than acquisition entrants. The benefits, or synergy, from sharing should be much easier to realize for direct than for acquisition entrants. The direct entrant is built up internally—there is every opportunity to build links with other parts of the parent. Managers of such internally developed entrants will also know the best procedures for operating those links. In contrast, it is well known and documented that the achievement of synergy in acquisitions is extremely difficult.

Motives for Entry. It was hypothesized that stronger motives for entry would result in greater share gain. Two motivations tested were MOTIVATION-OFFENSE (to exploit an advantage) and MOTIVATION—DEFENSE (to strengthen an existing position). Neither of these variables was significant.

Position Relative to Incumbents. Entrants' average relative position (on all competitive dimensions except prices and costs) was found to be significant in the regressions on the direct versus acquisition choice. That variable, AVERAGE RELATIVE POSITION, was not significant here. However, the RELATIVE PRICES and RELATIVE COSTS variables were significant in some of the equations. RELATIVE PRICES was significant and positive for the combined sample (equation 1). The positive association between relative price and share gain is, of course, counter to theory. However, RELATIVE PRICES was highly correlated with RELATIVE PRODUCT QUALITY (.63 in the combined sample). Thus, relative price was largely a proxy for relative product quality. However, entrants had lower prices on average than incumbents (see chapter 4 and table B-9), so the observed beneficial effect of higher relative price does not necessarily apply when entrants' prices are much higher than incumbents'.

RELATIVE COSTS, in contrast, behaved as expected. Share gains were smaller for those entrants with higher relative costs. This was true for both direct and acquisition entrants.

Time since Entry. The number of years since entry should affect the total share gained. The variable used was the calendar year of entry, since share gain was reported as the maximum gain up to 1979. The variable, YEAR OF ENTRY, was not significant in either equation. This result helps justify use of total rather than annual share gain as the dependent variable.

Summary of Results

Five variables were found to be significant in explaining share gain for the combined sample of sixty-nine entrants. The significant positive variables were EXIT OF COMPETITORS, UNRELATED BUSINESS PARENT, and RELATIVE PRICE. The significant negative variables were INCUM-BENT PARENT SIZE and RELATIVE COSTS. All these associations were of the hypothesized sign. The one exception was RELATIVE PRICE, which had a positive sign but was highly correlated with RELATIVE PRO-DUCT QUALITY, which should have a positive association with share gain.

Also tested was whether direct and acquisition entrants' share gains were explained differently by market structure and entrant characteristics. An overall test strongly suggested that direct and acquisition entrants did not form a homogeneous sample in relation to share gain. This was not surprising in view of the large difference in maximum share gain between direct and acquisition entrants (average of 6.8 percentage points for direct versus 2.5 for acquisition). There were, however, few individual variables for which the hypothesis was rejected that their regression slopes were the same for the two groups, and only one variable (degree of sharing) for which the two coefficients had significant opposite signs. Also, all those variables showing significant differences were entrant rather than market-structure variables; that is, market structure appeared to have the same impact on share gain for both types of entrants.

Three entrant differences were significant. First, having a diversified parent was more help for direct than for acquisition entrants. Second, sharing activities with the parent hurt the share gain of acquisition entrants but helped that of direct entrants. Third, unrelated diversification also appeared to hurt the share gain of direct entrants more than that of acquisition entrants.

Notes

1. Jesse W. Markham, *Conglomerate Enterprise and Public Policy* (Boston: Division of Research, Harvard Business School, 1973).

2. E. Ralph Biggadike, *Corporate Diversification: Entry Strategy and Performance* (Boston: Division of Research, Harvard Business School 1979), and also in "The Risky Business of Diversification," *Harvard Business Review* 57, no. 3 (May-June 1979):103-111.

3. Richard P. Rumelt, *Strategy, Structure, and Economic Performance* (Boston: Division of Research, Harvard Business School, 1974).

4. H. Igor Ansoff, Richard G. Brandenburg, Fred E. Portner, and Raymond Radosevich, *Acquisition Behavior of U.S. Manufacturing Firms, 1946-1965* (Nashville, Tenn.: Vanderbilt University Press, 1971).

5. Richard E. Caves, Michael E. Porter, A. Michael Spence, and John T. Scott, *Competition in the Open Economy* (Cambridge, Mass.: Harvard University Press, 1980).

6. See Malcolm S. Salter and Wolf A. Weinhold, *Diversification through Acquisition: Strategies for Creating Economic Value* (New York: The Free Press, 1979) p. 3 for a comprehensive list.

7. Michael Gort, *Diversification and Integration in American Industry* (Princeton, N.J.: Princeton University Press, 1962). Gort's sample was 111 of the largest U.S. manufacturing corporations and their product structures, for each of the years 1929, 1939, 1947, 1950 and 1954.

8. Biggadike, *Corporate Diversification.*

9. W.J. Baumol, *Business Behavior, Value and Growth,* rev. ed, (New York: Harcourt, 1967).

10. Jeffrey Pfeffer and Gerald R. Salancik, *The External Control of Organizations: A Resource Dependence Perspective* (New York: Harper & Row, 1978). Their source was Federal Trade Commission data (FTC 1970) on 854 mergers from 1948 to 1969. Pfeffer and Salancik used the amount of transactions between two industries as the measure of dependence.

11. Paul K. Gorecki, "An Inter-industry Analysis of Diversification in the U.K. Manufacturing Sector," *The Journal of Industrial Economics* 24, no. 2 (December 1975):131-146.

12. Alfred D. Chandler, Jr., *Strategy and Structure,* (Cambridge, Mass.: M.I.T. Press 1962).

13. Alfred D. Chandler, Jr., *The Visible Hand: The Managerial Revolution in American Business* (Cambridge, Mass.: The Belknap Press of Harvard University Press, 1977).

14. Oliver E. Williamson, "Markets and Hierarchies: Some Elementary Considerations," *American Economic Review* 63 (May 1973):316-325.

15. For a comparison of the two acquisitions, see William K. Hall, "A

Tale of Two Acquisitions," *University of Michigan Business Review* (May 1977) pp. 1-8.

16. Michael E. Porter, *Competitive Strategy: Techniques for Analyzing Industries and Competitors* (New York: The Free Press, 1980).

17. William J. Abernathy and James M. Utterback, "Innovation and the Evolving Structure of the Firm," *Harvard Business School*. Research paper no. 8-676-003, June 1975.

18. Hall, "A Tale."

19. Lynn W. Phillips and Louis W. Stern, "Limit Pricing Theory as a Basis for Anti-Merger Policy," *Journal of Marketing* 41, no.2, (April 1977):91-97.

20. Richard Schmalensee, "Entry Deterrence in the Ready-to-Eat Breakfast Cereal Industry," *Bell Journal of Economics* 9, no. 2 (Autumn 1978):305-327.

6 Summary and Implications

This study sought to integrate the industrial-organization-economics theory of barriers to entry with a corporate-strategy perspective of markets, firms, and competition. As originally developed, the theory of entry barriers hypothesized many ways in which market structure could impose disadvantages on entrants relative to incumbents. Market structure rather than firm characteristics was the key. Therefore, if examined without reference to the characteristics of potential entrants or, if entrants are viewed implicitly as newborn firms (as Bain did explicitly), many markets might appear well protected by their barriers. This view of market structure's dominant role in determining entry barriers was consistent with industrial organization's emphasis on market-wide characteristics as determinants of the nature of competition. The original theory has been significantly modified by recent theoretical developments emphasizing the uniqueness of competitors and competitive strategies—a viewpoint more akin to corporate strategy.

Taking a corporate-strategy perspective, I have focused on two factors that can reduce or eliminate the entry barriers imposed by market structure. First, the assets and skills of potential entrants can offset barriers. I have expanded Caves and Porter's formulation of this process. Second, the availability of unique competitive strategies allows entrants to avoid direct confrontation with barriers. This second factor does not appear to have been proposed in previous research.

These two factors can be so effective in offsetting or avoiding barriers that, in some situations, market structure will have a weak role in preventing entry. The market-structure variables giving rise to barriers may even proxy the existence of gateway effects such that entrants can obtain advantages by virtue of being entrants. The same sources of barriers, such as heavy advertising or R&D expenditures, can provide opportunities for skilled (or lucky) entrants to develop superior competitive strategies, and incumbents may be unable to alter their ex post inferior strategies.

Thus, I have proposed a third stage to the development of the theory of entry barriers. The first stage was Bain's formulation of the concept in relation to newborn firms. The second stage was the inclusion of existing firms as potential entrants. The third stage is the role of competitive strategies in providing opportunities for negative barriers or gateways.

The Occurrence of Entry

Previous empirical tests of entry barriers supported the existence of significant barriers without exposing the more complex view suggested here. These earlier studies used industry profitability rather than the occurrence of entry as the dependent variable, a small set of explanatory variables, and a sample of broadly defined industries. This was partly due to limitations on available data.

I tested the existence of entry barriers against the occurrence of entry—an arguably better test, and decidedly more relevant to corporate strategy. My unique data set allowed the use of a large set of explanatory variables for a narrowly defined market. The results offer strong support for the view that barriers, as represented by market structure alone, are much weaker in preventing entry than predicted by traditional theory. Few of the structure variables hypothesized to pose barriers to entry were significantly and negatively associated with the occurrence of entry. In contrast, many more variables had significant positive associations. A caveat is that the tests were conducted on narrowly defined markets: many entrants may have come from markets closely related to the entered one.

The significant positive variables were market-growth rate in all except the introductory stages of the product life-cycle, incumbent profitability, price spread, exit of competitors, and new product activity. Capacity utilization was the only variable that did not reveal the hypothesized positive association and its significant negative association may well have been due to simultaneity with the dependent variable.

The significant negative variables were incumbent-parent size, advertising intensity in consumer-durable markets, and selling intensity (sales-force expenses/revenues). Nonsignificant variables included concentration, investment intensity, advertising intensity in consumer-nondurable and in industrial markets, R&D intensity, and incumbent-parent diversity.

How can these results be reconciled with previous tests using industry profitability as the dependent variable? The differences may be attributed to my use of entry occurrence as the dependent variable. I have presented several arguments as to why industry profitability is not a perfect test of the existence of barriers, although occurrence as a measure has its limitations too. Also, the two measures are likely to have opposite biases in their conclusions about the height of barriers, since high profitability can coexist with frequent entry into fringe strategic groups. Occurrence as a measure probably results in an underestimate of the height of barriers, since it does not capture the costs of entry.

In respect to previous tests also using entry occurrence as the dependent variable, there are two possible explanations for the different results. One is that these previous tests used a measure of entry that was net of exit, that is, gross entry and gross exit were combined in one measure. I used a yes/no measure of recent major entry (5 percent or more market share). The other explanation is that I used a narrow, demand-oriented definition of the entered market rather than a broad, supply-oriented definition. With markets defined narrowly, many entrants may have come from closely related markets, and therefore faced relatively low barriers. The sample of 793 U.S. and Canadian consumer- and industrial-products markets that I used came from a data base that appears to be highly representative of such markets. Indeed, the data base covers at least 60 percent of the four-digit—manufacturing industries in the Standard Industrial Classification scheme.

Direct versus Acquisition Entry

I proposed that entry via acquisition and direct entry (via internal development) should be analyzed in the same framework, and that the presence of entry barriers has systematic implications for choosing between the two modes. This choice is usually analyzed in terms of financial and managerial considerations. Additional considerations should be the extent of entry barriers, and entrants' ability to overcome barriers. It was proposed that high barriers and low ability encourage acquisition rather than direct entry, because the cost of direct entry depends more than does that of acquisition entry on the entrant's ability to overcome barriers. In addition, high barriers create more uncertainty about outcome and a longer entry period for direct entrants. Managers may choose acquisition entry to avoid this long period of uncertainty and its possible negative effect on their careers. A company's organization and evaluation procedures therefore affect the seriousness of this potential bias against direct entry.

This view of the direct versus acquisition choice was tested on the special subsample of thirty-one markets for which data on entrants and entry behavior were collected. The results supported the hypothesis. The combination of market structure and entrant characteristics explained a large percentage of the variance in the choice of entry mode of fifty-nine entrants into the thirty-one markets. In addition, several individual variables had significant coefficients with the predicted signs. Given the small sample size and the subjectiveness of some of the data, only tentative conclusions can be drawn. However, these findings provide the first known evidence on this issue.

Six variables had significant signs of the predicted direction. Those negatively associated with acquisition as the chosen entry mode were market-growth rate, market-investment intensity, market growth as an entrant motive, and the average position of the entrant relative to incumbents.

Those positively associated with the acquisition choice were incumbent-parent size and entrants with diversified parents.

Market concentration did not prove significant as an explanation of entry choice, just as it had not been significant in explaining the occurrence of entry. Other nonsignificant variables were the type of diversification move (horizontal, vertical, and so on) and the degree of relatedness as measured by the average of activities shared between entrant and parent (although some individual types of sharing had significant but opposite effects). The size of entrants' parents was positively associated with the acquisition choice and was nearly significant statistically.

These results provide some evidence that entrants may use acquisition entry to avoid barriers. Acquisition entry was favored as a vehicle into low-growth markets or into those with incumbents having large parent companies. It also appeared that acquisition was second best (to direct entry) in terms of obtaining a strong initial position relative to incumbents, because the average initial competitive position of direct entrants was better than that of acquisition entrants. By inference, the acquisition route was chosen partly because a strong relative position could not be established via direct entry.

There was also some evidence that parent company characteristics independently affect the choice of entry mode. The more diversified parent companies preferred acquisition. However, larger companies did not reveal a significant preference for either mode.

Surprisingly, the two measures of relatedness (the type of diversification move and average degree of sharing of activities with parent) did not significantly discriminate between the two entry modes. A possible explanation is that the degree of relatedness determines the strength of the entrant's relative position. The latter is more important for entry performance, and therefore it is more important in influencing the choice of entry mode.

Market-Share Gain of Entrants

Share gain should be a function of the market-structure variables giving rise to barriers, the entrant's size (as an indicator of its general resources for overcoming barriers), the entrant's degree of relatedness to the new market (as an indicator of its specific ability to overcome barriers), and the entry mode and entry strategy.

The determinants of entrant-share gain were tested on a sample of sixty-nine entrants into the thirty-one markets for which original data were collected. As expected, the analysis was less successful in explaining entrants' market-share gain than in explaining their entry mode. Market-share gain is determined in a more complex process that involves actions by third parties—incumbents, customers, suppliers, and retailers. Nevertheless, some structural and entrant-characteristic variables had significant coefficients of the predicted sign.

Five variables were found to be significant in explaining share gain for the combined sample of sixty-nine entrants. Share gain was positively associated with the exit of competitors, entrants with diversified parents, and entrants with a higher price than incumbents. Share gain was negatively associated with the size of incumbents' parent companies and entrants with higher costs than incumbents. All these associations were of the hypothesized sign, except for the positive association of share gain with high relative price. The relative-price variable was, however, highly correlated with a variable representing relative product quality, which should, of course, have a positive association with share gain. Thus, the combination of high relative prices and high relative product-quality probably favored share gain.

Also tested was whether direct and acquisition entrants' share gains were explained differently by market structure and entrant characteristics. A statistical test strongly suggested that direct and acquisition entrants did not form a homogeneous sample in relation to share gain. This was not surprising in view of the large difference in maximum share gain between direct and acquisition entrants (average of 6.8 percentage points for direct versus 2.5 for acquisition). There were, however, few individual variables for which the hypothesis was rejected that their regression slopes were the same for the two groups, and only one variable (degree of sharing) for which the two coefficients had significant opposite signs. Also, all those variables showing significant differences were entrant rather than market-structure variables; that is, market structure appeared to have the same impact on share gain for both types of entrants.

Significant individual differences were (1) having a diversified parent was more help for direct than acquisition entrants, and (2) sharing activities with the parent hurt acquisition entrants' share gain but helped that of direct entrants. It also appeared that unrelated diversification hurt the share gain of direct entrants more than that of acquisition entrants.

One of the key issues in this study was the extent to which acquisition entrants behaved like true (direct) entrants. The much smaller average share gain of acquisition entrants, compared to direct entrants, implies that the former are entrants only in a partial sense. Acquisition entry is, after all, an inherently partial-entry effort. The acquisition itself provides part of the entrant's desired scale or target market share. Some acquisition entrants may even be satisfied with their acquired share. The data did not permit an analysis of entrant's motives to expand share. Only actual behavior was reported.

The results suggest that acquisition entrants are also different from direct entrants in terms of how their share gain is affected overall by market structure and by their own characteristics and strategy. Market-structure variables appeared to affect market-share gain in much the same way for direct and acquisition entrants. However, certain entrant variables affected the two types of entrants differently in terms of share gain. The overall implication is that market structure may indeed have the same effect on the share gains of both types of entrants, while entrant characteristics and strategies differentiate between the two types.

A third implication of the results is that lack of relatedness hurts entrant market-share performance. This evidence lends support to the emphasis in diversification research on the importance of relatedness for business performance.

Implications for Researchers

These findings suggest directions for further research on the topic of entry and for strategy research in general.

Research on Entry

The results I have reported here open up three avenues for further research on entry. First, the coverage of entrants and markets can be extended. I study observed markets and all their entrants (in a given time period) cross-sectionally, focusing on initial entry strategy. Biggadike observed one entrant per market longitudinally. The next step would be a study combining my breadth and Biggadike's depth. All the entrants in a given time period in a market could be observed longitudinally. An extremely useful further extension would be to observe the characteristics of potential entrants that did not enter. (Appendix A includes a discussion of some of the difficulties in observing nonentrants.)

Second, further research can use other measures of entry. By using the occurrence of entry as the dependent variable, I was able to consider some new questions that could not be studied with profitability as the dependent variable. However, neither my measure of the occurrence of entry nor those formulated by other researchers is perfect. In fact, there probably is no single perfect measure of entry, but other measures that might be explored are

A count of the number of entrants (not net of exit, as in Orr's study);

A measure of the combined scale of entrants;

A ratio of successful to unsuccessful entry attempts;

The costs of entry imposed by barriers, beyond those required to create the ongoing business.

A third avenue for further research would be a nonstatistical, clinical approach. Research inside companies would allow a more detailed analysis of how entry decisions are made. Two key issues could be studied: (1) whether potential entrants evaluate possible barriers to entry, and if so, how; and (2) how entrants make the choice between direct and acquisition entry. This clinical approach should help reveal the extent to which managers are able to perceive, and willing to follow, the messages of market structure and competitor strengths and weaknesses.

Research on Strategy

This study also suggests directions for future research in the field of strategy, particularly the emerging subfield of strategy research using quantitative methods to investigate the link between market structure and business-level strategy. Perhaps the major theoretical thrust in this area is the integration of industrial-organization and corporate-strategy concepts.

The research reported here can be distinguished from most previous studies in the subfield in three respects: the type of sample analyzed, the source of data, and the scope of the issues covered.

Most previous studies have used either a multi-industry sample with a limited number of industry wide variables or single-industry samples that include competitor-specific variables. The PIMS Program is the pathbreaking exception—a multimarket data base with market as well as competitor variables. Other PIMS-based studies have focused on the business as the unit of analysis, whereas I have used both the market and individual businesses (entrants) as units of analysis. This approach offers a clearer view of the close link between a market's structure and competitor performance. The PIMS data base also has a major gap in coverage: most business-unit data are available about only one competitor, the reporting business. To close this gap, I collected data on competitors (the entrants) other than the reporting business.

Following the PIMS methodology, I obtained the data directly from businesses rather than use third-party compilations of published data collected for other purposes. Both the larger PIMS experience and this study's more limited one suggest that the questionnaire techniques developed by marketing research can be used to gather valuable data from executives about strategic issues. In addition, this study has used one business to report extensive data about its competitors. Among the weaknesses of such an approach is the obvious problem of whether the reporting business can really answer for its competitors (see the more extensive discussion in appendix A). To minimize that problem, I posed only questions whose answers should be known to the reporting business. The need for data about all competitors per market, rather than just one, is too great to ignore this collection method.

This study is also significant in the scope of its coverage. It provides a further example of the integration of the market-structure focus of industrial organization and the competitor focus of corporate strategy. The results confirm that this integration is necessary. Also, the focus on competitors is very broad, including characteristics of the parent company, as well as of the competitor itself. Most previous studies have combined only two of the three variables, market structure, business, and corporate characteristics. This study covers all three.

Implications for Public Policy

Maintaining easy entry conditions is a major goal of U.S. antitrust policy. The theory of entry barriers has frequently been invoked to argue that the structure of some markets hinders entry. A recent example is the FTC investigation of the market for ready-to-eat breakfast cereals, and the argument that the combination of brand proliferation and high concentration creates insurmountable entry barriers. In January 1982, however, the FTC, under new leadership, reversed its position and dropped this case after ten years of effort. Public policy has therefore moved toward the same view as this study's, that market structure per se does not determine barriers.

While intervening to alter market structure is one way in which public policy seeks to promote entry, discouragement of acquisition entry is another. Acquisition entries have been prevented or reversed (through forced sale) in order to keep the acquirer only a potential direct entrant. In addition to the prevention of monopoly per se, the policy of limiting acquisition entry is based on one of at least three assumptions in regard to entry:

1. That the presence of potential entrants affects the behavior of incumbents, and therefore constrains their prices and profits;
2. That potential entrants might enter directly if denied the acquisition route;
3. That direct entry is more likely than acquisition to promote competition.

This study questions the assumption about the impact of potential entrants. First, it suggests that barriers have a complex role in deterring major entry attempts, and their operation depends on entrant characteristics. For example, high advertising-intensity provides a high differentiation barrier. Entrant characteristics, however, determine the effective barrier for a particular entrant. First, the need for differentiation may be partially met by the entrant's existing reputation or brand identity. Second, the high advertising-intensity may provide a gateway, or negative barrier, for an entrant with superior advertising skills or a stronger reputation or brand identity.

The presence of potential entrants should therefore affect incumbent behavior only if the entrants have the characteristics needed to lower barriers. It seems, however, that acquisition entrants may often not have such characteristics (because if they did, direct entry would be more profitable).

The second assumption, that potential entrants would enter directly if denied the acquisition route, is questioned by the finding that market structure and entrant characteristics appear to discriminate very clearly between the two entry modes. In particular, entrants with low relatedness to high-barrier markets appear unlikely to enter except via acquisition. The finding is not conclusive; a complete test would require two matched groups of potential entrants and markets, and one group would have to be denied the acquisition route.

The public-policy premise against acquisition entry rests on the third assumption, that direct entry is more likely to promote competition. The evidence reported here supports that assumption. With entrants' share gain used as a proxy for their impact on market competitiveness, direct entrants were found to have a much larger average impact. Few of the acquisition entrants in the sample transformed the market as Philip Morris did the beer market.

A broader public-policy issue is also affected by the role of acquisition entry in bringing new competitors to markets. There are intermittent efforts in the U.S. Congress to pass antimerger legislation that would prevent acquisitions by large companies. The rationale for such legislation is not solely antitrust issues of market concentration, but a broader sociopolitical issue concerning the concentration of corporate power. Without addressing the sociopolitical issue, I have suggested a market argument against the bill. It appears that slow-growth, concentrated markets are unlikely to be entered except via acquisition, and this legislation would effectively prevent the introduction of new competitors into such markets—which are those most in need of new competition, whatever the entry route.

Implications for Managers

Entry is a major strategic issue for both entrants and incumbents. Some of the statistical regularities revealed by this study of entry behavior may suggest guidelines for managers concerned with this issue.

Implications for Incumbents

For incumbents the major finding may well be that while many aspects of market structure appear to encourage entry, the factors that discourage it must be viewed only in the context of the strengths and resources available to potential entrants. As expected, high profitability and rapid market growth were major inducements to entry: the one representing immediate reward and the other future reward. If a market is attractive, it appears that some potential entrants will have suitable assets to offset barriers, or will be able to develop strategies to avoid direct confrontation with barriers. The source of a crucial barrier may even become a gateway for the entrant with superior skills or resources in that particular area. Incumbents are then at a disadvantage.

Many of the factors encouraging entry appeared to be difficult for incumbents to control, or costly or dangerous to reduce. Market-growth rate and the exit of competitors are difficult to control; reducing profitability is costly; and reducing new-product activity is dangerous. The only inducement to entry that incumbents may be able to control is price spread. A wide spread in price among incumbents may provide a price umbrella for entrants.

Only three variables of those tested appeared to contribute to barriers in my sample: a high ratio of sales-force expenditures to revenues (probably indicating the presence of economies of scale in serving large geographic areas); a high ratio of advertising to sales, but only for consumer-durable products; and a large corporate parent. Incumbents can do little about the size of their parent company. They may not be able to do much about the other two variables either.

The overall lesson for incumbents appears to be that market-structure characteristics may not be very effective in protecting them from the entry of new competitors. In many markets, relying on market barriers to entry may be like relying on the Maginot Line. Perhaps the best protection for incumbents is to develop a distinctive competence that can withstand the entry of new competitors. This study did not address that issue—large-sample statistical analysis, by its nature, cannot identify the sources of unique competitive strengths and weaknesses.

Implications for Entrants

This study suggests that an entrant can minimize the costs of entry—by choosing the most suitable market, the more suitable of the two modes, and the most suitable overall strategy.

Choice of Market. A common wisdom is that companies should enter fast-growth markets. The evidence on the occurrence of entry suggests that this belief is widely followed. Unfortunately, fast-growth markets frequently attract many entrants with the same idea. Some markets in the special sample reported as many as eight direct entries within a few years. Several fast-growth markets have been turned into loss makers by an excess of entrants: recreational boats, mobile homes, snowmobiles, and pocket calculators are recent examples. This study suggests that a way to avoid such problems is for a company to enter a market where barriers are high for everyone except itself. Doubtless most companies try to apply this rule, but perhaps implicitly rather than explicitly. An explicit analysis of barriers should improve the company's ability to choose the right markets for entry.

The analysis should attempt to establish:

Which markets are inherently attractive,

The extent to which these markets are protected from other entrants, and

The extent to which the entrant is particularly suited for a given market.

Choice of Entry Mode. Barriers and the entrant's ability to overcome them should also be considered when choosing between the direct- and acquisition-entry modes. An acquisition purchase price should be evaluated in terms of the barriers surrounding a market and the cost of breaching them, given the entrant's skills and resources. Does the price demanded by the seller, or offered by other bidders, incorporate a higher barrier than would be faced via direct entry? Despite apparently high barriers, the entrant's relatedness may suggest a lower cost for direct entry than for acquisition (or a better return for different-sized investments). Entrants should, of course, consider other factors affecting the choice of entry mode, particularly the impact of each mode on the balance sheet and cash flow, the urgency for growth through diversification, and management preference.

Entrants need to analyze the precise nature of barriers and the precise way in which relatedness might offset them. Often an entrant can greatly reduce all barriers except one crucial one; acquisition entry may then be the logical choice. The entrants in this sample of markets preferred acquisition in low-growth, low-investment markets, against incumbents with large parent companies, or when their own parents were more diversified companies. Initially acquisition entrants also had worse positions relative to incumbents than did direct entrants.

Some expected preferences were not statistically significant: less-related entries did not reveal a preference for acquisition, although, when not controlling for other variables, the unrelated-diversification category did have the highest proportion of acquisitions, compared to other types of moves (geographic expansion, segment expansion, related expansion). Another notable result was that the level of market concentration did not affect the choice. The conflicting influences of concentration appeared to cancel one another out: a highly concentrated market should encourage ac-

quisition to avoid barriers, but it usually offers fewer candidates for acquisition and may pose more antitrust problems for an acquirer.

Choice of Entry Strategy. This study did not analyze entry strategies in sufficient detail to propose the most effective strategies. However, some
evidence was provided on the influence of market structure, entrant
characteristics, and entry strategy on share gain after entry.

Although acquisition entrants increased share much less than direct entrants, market structure appeared to have the same influence on their
respective ability to increase share. Acquisition entrants may be insuffi-
ciently aggressive. They should perhaps exploit the corporate focus on them
immediately after acquisition to obtain resources for expansion. This
appears to be particularly important in view of the finding that large incumbent parents had the greatest negative association with entrant-share expansion. Neither rapid market growth nor a high level of concentration
appeared to help entrant-share gain. Exit of competitors was the only structural variable that did help.

Several entrant and entry-strategy variables appeared to help share gain.
Diversified firms were more successful, suggesting that experience does
count. Paradoxically, unrelated diversification moves were less successful,
yet firms become diversified by making somewhat unrelated diversification
moves. The results also suggest that direct entrants should try to share activities and customers with their parents. Also, high costs relative to incumbents should be avoided, but high relative prices need not be a problem
and may actually help.

An overall guideline suggested by the study is that firms considering entry into a high-barrier market must do at least one of the following:

Use their existing assets and skills in ways that reduce the barriers they
have to confront;

Develop a differentiated strategy that allows them to avoid direct confrontation with barriers;

Develop a strategy that constrains effective incumbent retaliation;

Exploit disequilibrium, which diminishes or eliminates barriers.

Appendix A:
Data Base
and Data Collection

As described in the text, existing data on markets, their structure, and their incumbents were used to analyze the occurrence of entry; and additional new data on entrants and entry behavior were collected. This appendix describes the existing data base, PIMS, and its external and internal validity. It also describes the data-collection procedures and validity of the special sample of thirty-one PIMS markets, for which entrant and entry behavior data were obtained. These new data were merged with existing structure- and incumbent-data on the same markets.

The Existing Data

The PIMS Program

The PIMS Program of the Strategic Planning Institute (SPI) collects strategic and operating data from participant companies, develops general (cross-sectional) models from these data, and uses the models to provide strategic diagnoses of individual businesses belonging to participant companies.

Data are collected at the business level. The core program currently collects data on about 180 concepts per business. About seventy of these concepts are reported for several time periods (typically each of the previous five years). Thus, a total of almost 500 individual data items are reported by businesses when they first join the program. In addition, participating businesses are asked to update annually about thirty of the data items.

The data collected cover these categories:

Characteristics of the business environment,

Competitive position of the business,

Structure of the production process,

Discretionary budget allocations,

Strategic moves,

Operating results.

The data are reported on a standard questionnaire—the PIMS Data Forms—by executives usually in consultation with other executives and with a PIMS service coordinator, who explains PIMS concepts to participants. Appendix F provides excerpts from the data forms.

The data are used to estimate the parameters of the PAR ROI model, which predicts what the ROI of each business should be, given its strategic characteristics (that is, its "par" ROI). The model is a single-equation cross-sectional regression on forty-three terms (twenty-nine variables, plus interactions, on 1,500 observations—the businesses. An individual business's PAR ROI is obtained by plugging in the values for that business on each term in the model. This model has been described in several articles.[1]

My research used only the PIMS-research data base, not the PAR ROI model. Therefore, I will not address the validity of the model, only the validity of the data base.

The PIMS-Research Data Base

The PIMS-research data base contains all the variables reported by participating businesses, plus a number of corporate variables obtained from annual reports and entered directly by PIMS staff.

Definition of Business Unit. Businesses are defined in the PIMS Program Data Manual as follows:

> The unit of observation in PIMS is a business. Each business is a division, product line, or other profit center within its parent company, selling a distinct set of products and/or services to an identifiable group of customers, in competition with a well-defined set of competitors, and for which meaningful separation can be made of revenues, operating costs, investments and strategic plans.

The 1,500 businesses belong to approximately 200 companies. Most businesses are located in the United States and are part of *Fortune* 500 companies.

A special feature of this data base is that the businesses, their parent companies, and their industries are not identified by name, only by their statistical characteristics. The size of the business is disguised, but the size of the parent company is not. Although the industries are not identified, they are broadly classified as follows:

Consumer-Durable Products

Consumer-Non-Durable Products

Capital Goods

Raw or Semi-Finished Materials

Components for Incorporation into Finished Products

Supplies or Other Consumable Products

Services

Retail and Wholesale Distribution

Except for "Services" and "Retail and Wholesale Distribution," there are over 100 businesses in each category. In addition, about half the businesses are identified by the four-digit SIC code of their market. (The PAR ROI model treats the 1,500 businesses as a homogeneous set rather than segmenting the data base by business type.)

Definition of Served Market. The "business" is one definition on which many data items are based (for example, R&D expenses). The other key definition is the "served market" of the business. In essence, the PIMS served market is equivalent to a market segment rather than a total market. If a number of segments are sold to, they are combined into one served market. Segments not sold to are excluded from the definition. Since the served market is a crucial PIMS concept, I quote the full definition provided in the PIMS Data Manual:

> A served market is a segment of a total market where a set of customers have similar requirements for a product or service. A business elects to serve a unique set of customer requirements by designing products, structuring and establishing prices to cover the costs of these requirements in line with the prices charged by competitors. Data used to measure the served-market size and growth rate should cover only the specific products or services, customer types, and geographic areas in which a business actually competes.
>
> The process of defining the served market of a business normally begins with defining the total market for the general types of products or services offered by the business. Specific characteristics of the particular products or services offered (basic design, quality, etc.) narrow the appeal of the products or services to a smaller group of customers within the total market. Finally, management, through selective advertising and selling, and perhaps also through adjustments in the auxiliary services provided, targets its efforts to a more precise portion of the broad market segment to which the products or services would appeal. This final subsegment of the total market is the served market of the business. Two examples of this process follow.
>
> Adolph Coors Company produces a beer aimed at the premium segment of the total beer market within a limited geographic area. All its marketing and distribution efforts are concentrated on this market segment. For Coors, the total market is all beer sales in the U.S. The segment to which its product appeals is the U.S. market for premium beers. The served market is the sales of premium beers within a limited geographic area.

Timex watches are targeted at the economy segment of the watch market, and are sold through mass-merchandising channels of distribution. The total market for Timex is the U.S. market for watches. Their products appeal to the economy segment of that market, and their served market is that portion of the economy segment reached through mass-merchandising channels of distribution.

Is the served market correctly defined? The served market definition is certainly very narrow. It includes only those product categories, geographic areas, and customer groups that the reporting business serves, and excludes categories, areas, and groups that may be served by its competitors.

There are various arguments about the suitability of this narrow market-definition for a study of barriers to entry. An argument in favor of the narrow definition is that most firms enter a narrow market-segment, at least initially. Against the narrow definition is that many entrants redefine the entered market in some way—even a broad market-definition would fail to capture fully that effect, but it would probably fail less than a narrow definition.

The correctness of the definition should affect seriously only those explanatory variables measured on a market base (for instance, growth rate, concentration, exit). The many other variables measured on the business (for instance, investment intensity, profitability) should be much less affected by the market definition.

External Validity of the PIMS Data

What is the external validity, or generalizability, of the markets comprising the PIMS data base? The issue revolves around "nonresponse error," or the extent to which PIMS participants are a biased sample of a universe to which we would like to generalize. Sampling error is not relevant since PIMS does not attempt to draw a sample from its universe of interest. That universe, business corporations in the United States and other countries, is sufficiently small that it is treated as the sample. Thus, PIMS attempts to recruit any business corporation above some minimum size. For example, the *Fortune* 500 is one universe and is also the sample that PIMS seeks to recruit. For this study of entry, the relevant universe is the U.S. markets in which *Fortune* 500 companies compete. Nonresponse, or nonparticipation, bias can arise from two sources: (a) the companies that join the program, and (b) the business units/markets for which they elect to report data.

Company Representativeness. For the purposes of this study of entry into markets, company representativeness is not particularly important in itself. Our concern is with the representativeness of the 793 markets used in explaining the occurrence of entry, and as the universe from which thirty-one markets were chosen for the more detailed data on entry.

It would, however, be useful to know whether these markets have among their competitors a representative variety of companies. We know the nature of only one competitor per market—the PIMS participant.

The primary corporate characteristics are perhaps nationality, size, and degree of diversification. In terms of nationality, the sample is predominantly (over 90 percent) American. In terms of size, the sample is heavily biased toward very large corporations: the mean size of parent companies is about $1,500 million, the median about $750 million. The median-sized corporation would rank about 275th in the *Fortune* 500, making the size distribution very similar to the *Fortune* 500. Size and other parent characteristics are measured at the time data are submitted; the median year for the 793 businesses is 1976. The comparison is therefore with the *Fortune* 500 for 1976. In terms of degree of diversification, the sample of business units is heavily biased toward more diversified parent-companies.

Thus, corporate ownership of the business units in the sample appears to be fairly representative of the *Fortune* 500. Since I used parent size and degree of diversity as explanatory variables in my analyses, any bias was controlled for.

Market Representativeness. Since market structure characteristics were used as explanatory variables in my study, it is not necessary to analyze the data base's representativeness with respect to these characteristics. In any case there was a very wide spread in the values of each key structure variable.

Industry type is not a market-structure characteristic and was not used as an explanatory variable (except in the interaction terms for advertising intensity). Both the overall PIMS data base of 1,500 markets and the subset of 793 used for analyzing the occurrence of entry represent several types of manufacturing industries:

	Total Data Base (1,500 Markets; percentage)	793 Markets Used for Occurrence of Entry (percentage)
Consumer Durable-Products	9	12
Consumer Non-Durable-Products	13	12
Capital Goods	22	24
Raw or Semi-Finished Materials	12	8
Components for Finished Products	26	30
Supplies or Consumable Products	13	15
Services	2	—
Retail/Wholesale Distribution	2	—
Total	100	100

The data base also represents at least 60 percent of four-digit industries in the manufacturing division of the Standard Industrial Classification system, although only about half of the PIMS markets identify their SIC code. A PIMS market is also usually much smaller than a four-digit industry.

Internal Validity of the PIMS Data

Internal validity concerns the extent to which a measure reflects the characteristic of interest. A potential source of distortion is the definition of the served market—this issue has been discussed. Two other sources of validity problems are (a) the accuracy of the data reported by PIMS participants, and (b) the use in this study (of entry) of the characteristics of reporting businesses to represent some market-structure characteristics (for instance, advertising intensity).

Data Accuracy. Many of the PIMS measures involve complex concepts. There may be inaccuracy arising from the concepts not being well understood, the data not being available, or difficulties in assigning revenues and expenditures to appropriate categories. Moreover, some of the measures, such as the business unit's position relative to competitors on various dimensions, are subjective; they rely on the opinion of the respondent. As mentioned earlier, the PIMS Program provides service coordinators to help members complete the questionnaire. There are also extensive checks of completed questionnaires. However, there is no specific evidence of the accuracy of the PIMS data.

Business Representativeness. PIMS collects data on only one competitor per market—the reporting business unit. Measures of business characteristics (for instance, profitability, advertising intensity), as opposed to market characteristics, (for instance, concentration, growth rate), are therefore based on one competitor representing all competitors. Fortunately, most PIMS businesses are major competitors in their markets (median market-share rank of second), and entry barriers are more a function of the characteristics of major than of minor competitors.

Collection of the New Data

Although the existing PIMS data were adequate for the study of the occurrence of entry, the other research issues (direct versus acquisition entry and market-share gain) required additional data:

Entrants' characteristics,

Entry strategy,

Incumbent reactions,

Outcome for entrants and incumbents.

The most economical approach was to collect new data from existing PIMS members, that is, the data on the structure of the entered markets and their incumbents already existed, and could be merged with the new data on entrants.

Choice of Respondent

The new data could have been collected from either entrants or incumbents. Entrants should, in general, be more suitable respondents, since the data concern their entries. However, there were several compelling reasons for choosing incumbents. First, the focus of the study was on markets and the barriers around them. Thus observations were needed on all entries into a given market during a given time period. Incumbents would be in a much better position to report on all entrants. (In contrast, a study on diversification would ideally require observations on all entered markets for a given company.) Second, the required information was not particularly detailed and should be known to incumbents. Most of the data were either external to the entrants (for example, market share) or relative to incumbents (for example, quality of entrants' products relative to incumbents'). The sets of internal data on motives for entry and activities shared with parent were sufficiently general that incumbents should be able to provide answers. The main type of information not considered reportable by incumbents was that on financial performance of entrants. Again, these data were not crucial to the study. Third, the PIMS data base included many more incumbents than recent entrants—30 percent of all PIMS businesses had experienced the recent entry of a new competitor, but only a very small percentage were themselves recent entrants.

Implications of Choosing PIMS

Some general restrictions and advantages arose from the strategy of collecting new data from PIMS members to merge with existing data. The key restrictions were that:

Respondents were limited to businesses already in the data base.

The question format had to match the existing PIMS format.

Many concepts were already defined, especially the market.

The key advantages were that:

Recruiting was greatly simplified; in particular, the confidentiality issue had been resolved.

Communication was simplified because many concepts and definitions were already understood.

There was ongoing access to the executives who completed my data forms.

Questionnaire Design

The information requirements led to a five-part questionnaire designed to obtain both breadth and depth of data, while minimizing the number of items and the space they occupied.

Form 1 asked a minimum of information about all entries and their impact on the market.

The items included:

Number of direct entrants,

Number of acquisition entrants,

Number of exits,

An estimate of the strength of eleven specific types of entry barriers,

Impact of all recent entrants on the current size and profitability of the market.

Form 1 was also used to obtain information not specifically related to entry, but required for analysis, and not provided in the existing data base:

Size of the largest incumbent company,

The minimum share to be a major or minor competitor.

Forms 2 and 3 provided more depth on each of up to three direct entrants (Form 2) and three acquisition entrants (Form 3). Their focus was on the initial nature and strategy of the entrants. The items included:

Year of entry,

Market shares,

Whether new or existing company,

Size of parent company,

Nature of parent company,

Motivation for entry (ten categories),

Activities shared with parent (seven categories),

Entrant's position relative to incumbents (eight categories),

Importance of entry into this market as motive for acquisition (Form 3 only).

Forms 4 (direct entrant) and 5 (acquisition entrant) provided further depth on the single-most-importance entrant (defined by greatest change in market share since entry). Their focus was on the response by, and the impact on, incumbents. The items included:

Incumbent's response to the entrants' served-market and product-line changes,

Incumbent's awareness of the entry,

Incumbent's evaluation of the seriousness of the threat,

Incumbent's responses along each of the "relative position" dimensions in Forms 2 and 3,

Capacity additions and response,

Which incumbent was hurt most,

Market-share history of entrant,

Estimate of share loss by reporting business.

Figure A-1 shows the components of the questionnaire.

Field Tests

Six field tests were conducted with member-company executives to check their comprehension of the questions and ability to answer them. Various questions were modified as a result of the tests. Several questions and concepts were adapted from Biggadike's questionaire and had therefore been "tested" by the forty businesses participating in that study.

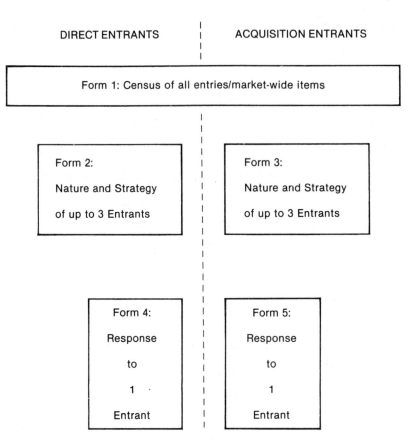

DIRECT ENTRANTS   ACQUISITION ENTRANTS

Form 1: Census of all entries/market-wide items

Form 2:

Nature and Strategy

of up to 3 Entrants

Form 3:

Nature and Strategy

of up to 3 Entrants

Form 4:

Response

to

1

Entrant

Form 5:

Response

to

1

Entrant

Figure A-1. Components of the Questionnaire

Recruiting

Participants were recruited over the summer of 1979. Two methods were used. One was a mailing to all PIMS member companies inviting participation and providing a return form. In addition I also contacted by telephone all companies owning any of the 377 businessess that had indicated in the existing data base that they had experienced the recent entry of a major competitor. This latter method proved to be the more effective recruiting procedure.

Ultimately, thirty-one data forms were completed for thirty-one markets and sixty-nine entrants. The thirty-one reporting businesses belonged to twenty different companies.

External Validity of the Special Sample

Proportion Recruited

Although only thirty-one markets were recruited, their generalization to all U.S. manufacturing markets is increased by their having been recruited from the PIMS data base, rather than directly. A direct recruiting effort would have been unlikely to provide an equal chance of participation for each of the thousands of qualified markets. Recruiting from the PIMS data base involved a two-stage-sampling procedure.

The first stage was the initial recruitment of the total data base, which is highly representative of U.S. manufactured product markets. This high degree of representativeness was achieved through many years of effort and extensive publicity. Probably the vast majority of *Fortune* 500 companies have had the opportunity to join the PIMS program.

The second stage, my recruiting effort, reached all PIMS members. Thus both stages effectively reached all of their sampling frame. A single-stage-recruiting method for my study would not have reached all *Fortune* 500 companies and their markets.

The generalizability of the special sample to all U.S. manufactured-products markets therefore depends on its generalizability to the PIMS data base as a whole. The analysis below suggests that the recruited sample is reasonably representative of the data base as a whole, comprising perhaps 18 percent of all qualified markets.

During the recruiting period there were 1,300 businesses/markets in the PIMS data base, of which 377 had previously indicated the recent entry of a major new competitor. The standard Data Form asks: "During the past 5 years, have any competitors with at least 5 percent market share entered the served market? (yes/no)." These 377 markets are the core comparison group, or universe, from which my sample of thirty-one was obtained. However, only twenty-one of the thirty-one came from the group of 377, for the following reasons:

My sample included acquisition entrants. The recent entry question for the total data base is ambiguous as to whether it included acquisition entrants.

My sample had a qualifying cutoff for entrants of 1 percent instead of the 5 percent for the total data base.

The recent-entry question is asked only once, when the business/market is first submitted for the PIMS Program. My qualifying period was the last seven years, not the last five.

Thus my recruitable universe was larger than the 377 markets. However, a direct comparison can be made only between the twenty-one recruited markets that had answered "yes" to the recent entry question and the 377. Only about 120 of the 377 qualified for recruitment. Reasons for not qualifying included: the member company was no longer an active participant, the businesses had not reported data for two or more years, or the businesses were not in U.S. markets. Thus, the twenty-one recruited markets represent about 18 percent of the 120—which seems a reasonable proportion from which to generalize to the entire data base. (In the absence of information about the universe for the other ten recruited markets, I have to assume a similar proportion.) In turn, the total data base can be reasonably generalized to all U.S. markets. This is the advantage of the two-stage design inherent in recruiting from PIMS.

Thus, it appears that each entered market was given an approximately equal chance for participation. Did the reported entry behavior reflect this apparent representativeness? There are, of course, no comparison data in PIMS, since the object of this research was to obtain such data. However, the market-share gain of entrants is perhaps a good indicator of representativeness. Table 5-1 in chapter 5 shows that the thirty-one markets did not suffer greatly from the entries (median share-loss of 6.0 percent and mean share-loss of 11.7 percent over eight years to all entrants). Thus, one expected bias did not materialize—that participants would be in markets that had particularly suffered from new competitors. Table 5-2 further suggests this lack of bias—the median impact of all entrants on the markets was to increase the market-dollar size by 5 percent and reduce profit margins by only 5 percent (not five points).

Nonstructural Characteristics of Sample

The sample comprised six consumer nondurable and twenty-five industrial manufacturing markets. All were U.S. national or regional markets. Thus, the generalizability of the sample is clearly limited to these types of markets. Tables A-1 and A-2 compare the sample, on industrial and geographic dimensions, with the total PIMS data base of all entered markets (the 29 percent of respondents who replied "yes" to the question on entry). The sample did not include any markets in the introduction stage of the product life-cycle (see table A-3).

Most of the businesses reporting data for these markets are market leaders in terms of share. As table A-4 shows, thirteen of the thirty-one are ranked first, and twenty-seven are ranked in the first four. The mean rank of the thirty-one is 2.65, which is somewhat higher than the total PIMS mean of 3.04. (The relative narrowness of the PIMS market definition results in relatively high reported-share ranks.)

Table A-1
Sample Characteristics: Industry Type

	Recruited Sample		Control Group
	(N = 31)		(N = 152)
	Number	Percent	Percent
Consumer Manufacturing			
Durables	0	0	0
Non-Durables	6	19	11
Industrial Manufacturing			
Capital Goods	11	35	34
Raw or Semi-Finished			
Materials	3	10	14
Components	4	13	31
Supplies or Consumable			
Products	7	23	11
Services	0	0	0
Retail and Wholesale			
Distribution	0	0	0
Total	31	100	100

Structural Characteristics of Sample

Since each entered PIMS market had an equal chance of participation in the special sample, the latter ended up with structural characteristics very similar to the data base as a whole, when controlling for the nonstructural characteristics.

Table A-2
Sample Characteristics: Location of Served Markets

	Sample of Thirty-One Entered Markets	
	Number	Percent
Entire United States	12	39
United States and Canada	13	42
Regional within		
United States and/or Canada	6	19
Total	31	100

Table A-3
Sample Characteristics: Stage of Product Life-Cycle

| | Recruited Sample (N = 31) | | Control Group (N = 152) |
	Number	Percent	Percent
Introductory	0	0	0
Growth	12	39	31
Maturity	17	55	66
Decline	2	6	3
Total	31	100	100

Table A-5 compares the structural characteristics of the special sample of thirty-one markets with a control group from the total data base, defined as follows:

Entered markets;

Time period 1972-1975; the special sample covered the period 1972-1979. Our concern is with the structural conditions before, or at the time that, entries occurred. Therefore, the conditions in the earlier part of the observed period, 1972-1975, are most relevant.

United States, or United States and Canada, national or regional;

Consumer nondurables and industrial manufacturing;

Growth, maturity, or decline stages of product life-cycle.

This control group totaled 152 markets as of February 10, 1980. (The PIMS research data base is continually being enlarged.)

Table A-4
Sample Characteristics: Share Rank of Reporting Business

Rank	Number
1	13
2	5
3	6
4	3
5	1
6	1
7	1
11	1
	31

Mean = 2.65; Median = 2

Mean rank for total PIMS data base is 3.04, and median rank is 2.

Table A-5 shows that the recruited sample and the control have very similar structural characteristics. The ratio between their means (column 4) was within ±20 percent, except for four characteristics:

Table A-5
Sample Characteristics: Structure and Incumbent Variables

	(1) Recruited Sample	(2) 31 Markets	(3) PIMS	(4) Control
	Mean (N = 31)	Median (N = 31)	Mean (N = 152)	Ratio of Sample to Control (1) ÷ (3)
Market (Percentage)				
Real-market growth	3.4	– .6	2.7	1.26
Industry LT growth 1	10.7	9.0	10.5	1.02
Four-firm share	70	78	74	.95
*Patents product	39	n.a.	29	1.34
*Patents process	26	n.a.	24	1.08
*Technological change	42	n.a.	37	1.14
*Exit of competitors	7	n.a.	36	.19
Business (Incumbent) (Percentage)				
Net income/investment	20	22	23	.87
Investment/revenues	59	49	56	1.05
Manufacturing/revenues	23	25	28	.82
R&D/revenues	3.1	2.2	2.7	1.15
Sales force/revenues	6.8	5.0	5.8	1.17
Advertising and Promotion/ revenues	2.1	1.2	1.5	1.40
New products as percentage of sales	13	8	11.5	1.13
Competitors' new products as percent of sales	9	4	10.2	.88
Business Parent				
Revenues $million	1150	638	1325	.87
Diversity	1.2	1.2	1.4	.86

See appendix C for a description of each variable.

*These are 0, 1 dummy variables—values show percent answering 1 = yes.

1. All variables are from the regular PIMS data base, not the new data collected for this study.
2. The PIMS control sample consists of 152 markets selected to include only American consumer nondurable or industrial manufacturing, and only the growth, maturity, or decline stages of the product life cycle, that is, the same characteristics as the recruited sample.
3. The observation period for the "Business" variables and Four-Firm Share is the annual average for the first two years of data available for the recruited sample (mostly 1972-1973 and 1973-1974), that is, before or soon after the reported entries occurred, and for 1972-1973 exclusively for the PIMS control sample. Real-Market Growth is the four-year annual average for the first four years of data. Industry LT Growth is a ten-year annual average mainly for the period 1966-1975.
4. None of the other variables have a time dimension; they are reported once only and up-dated as necessary.

1. The sample has a somewhat lower mean real-market-growth rate of 3.4 percent compared to 2.7 percent for the entered control (ratio of 1.26). This may be due to the slight difference in proportions of growth, maturity, and decline-stage markets, as shown in table A-3. However, the long-term industry-growth rate (nominal rather than real-growth rate) shows almost no difference between the two groups (ratio 1.02). (The industry is typically larger than the market, and is usually measured at the four-digit SIC level.)

2. The sample has a much higher proportion than the control, of markets where product patents are significant (39 versus 29 percent). However, the proportion is almost the same for process patents (26 versus 24 percent).

3. The sample has a much lower proportion than the control, of markets from which major (5 percent share) competitors have recently exited (7 versus 36 percent).

4. The sample has a much higher level of advertising-and-promotion/revenues than the control (2.1 versus 1.5 percent).

Overall, one can probably generalize with some confidence from the recruited sample to the PIMS data base as a whole, for U.S. consumer-nondurable and industrial-manufacturing markets in other than the introductory stage of the product life-cycle.

Internal Validity of the Special Sample

A final issue is internal validity or accuracy. Since the same data-collection format was used for the ENTRY data as for PIMS, the same potential sources of lack of internal validity apply, as discussed earlier. Since the EN-TRY data were primarily about competitors rather than about the reporting businesses themselves, an additional potential problem is the accuracy of responses. With this in mind, I designed as many questions as possible to ask for nominal or ordinal (rank) rather than ratio (numerical) responses. Finally, every incoming data form was checked for errors and inconsistencies, and comparison checks were run across all the thirty-one forms for improbable values. Errors and queries were raised with the respondents.

Note

1. See Sidney Schoeffler, Robert D. Buzzell, and Donald F. Heany, "Impact of Strategic Planning on Profit Performance," *Harvard Business Review* 52, no. 2 (March-April 1974):137-145; Robert D. Buzzell, Bradley T. Gale, and Ralph G.M. Sultan, "Market Share—A Key to Profitability,"

Harvard Business Review 53, no. 1 (January-February 1975):97-106; Bradley T. Gale, "Planning for Profit," *Planning Review* 6, no. 1 (January 1978):4-32; and "Cross-Sectional Analysis: The New Frontier in Planning," *Planning Review* 6, no. 1 (March 1978):17-20; and Thomas H. Naylor, "PIMS: Through a Different Looking Glass," *Planning Review* 6, no. 2, (March 1978):15-34.

Appendix B:
Supplementary Tables

Table B-1
Activities and Customers Shared with Parent: All Entrants

	(1) No Existing Parent 0 Number	(2) Up to 10 percent 1 Number	(3) 10 to 50 percent 2 Number	(4) 50 to 90 percent 3 Number	(5) 90 to 100 percent 4 Number	(6) Mean of Codes 0 to 4
(a) Manufacturing/production	8	33	12	4	12	1.7
(b) R&D	8	24	14	6	17	2.0
(c) Distribution/service	8	27	9	11	14	1.9
(d) Sales	8	28	13	14	16	2.0
(e) Advertising and promotion	8	25	11	15	10	1.9
(f) Immediate customers	8	25	9	12	15	2.0
(g) End users	8	25	14	13	17	2.0
Average						1.9

Table B-2
Activities and Customers Shared with Parent: Direct versus Acquisition

	Direct N = 45 mean	Acquisition N = 24 mean
(a) Manufacturing/production	1.8	1.5
(b) R&D	2.1	1.9
(c) Distribution/service	2.0	1.9
(d) Sales	2.0	2.0
(e) Advertising and promotion	1.8	2.1
(f) Immediate customers	1.9	2.2
(g) End users	1.9	2.3

Note: See table B-1 for units.

Table B-3
Activities and Customers Shared with Parent: Correlation Matrix
(69 entrants)

	(a)	*(b)*	*(c)*	*(d)*	*(e)*	*(f)*	*(g)*
(a) Manufacturing/production	1.00						
	1.00						
(b) R&D	.85	1.00					
	.71	1.00					
(c) Distribution/service	.61	.69	1.00				
	.27	.32	1.00				
(d) Sales	.59	.71	.91	1.00			
	.20	.22	.96	1.00			
(e) Advertising and promotion	.59	.62	.83	.85	1.00		
	.38	.40	.84	.85	1.00		
(f) Immediate customers	.46	.56	.81	.85	.81	1.00	
	.42	.40	.66	.57	.67	1.00	
(g) End users	.50	.60	.80	.89	.81	.95	1.00
	.31	.27	.62	.71	.82	.71	1.00

Upper number is for forty-five direct entrants, lower for twenty-four acquisition entrants
Correlations above |.30| are significant at 95 percent level, two tail, for direct entrants, and
above |.40| for acquisition entrants.

Table B-4
Motivation for Entry: All Entrants

	(1) Not Relevant[a] 0 Number	*(2)* Little/No Importance 1 Number	*(3)* Some Importance 2 Number	*(4)* Major Importance 3 Number	*(5)* Mean of Codes 0 to 3
(a) Profitability	2	2	32	33	2.4
(b) Growth	2	6	7	54	2.6
(c) Share costs	2	42	12	13	1.5
(d) Exploit advantage	2	33	10	24	1.8
(e) Strengthen position	2	26	14	27	2.0
(f) Access to suppliers	2	65	2	0	1.0
(g) Access to outlets	2	37	17	13	1.6
(h) Counter-cyclical sales	2	63	4	0	1.0
(i) Generate cash	2	53	13	1	1.2
(j) Use cash	2	49	13	5	1.3
Average					1.64

[a] Applies to the two acquisition entrants for whom entry into the served market was reported as
not relevant or incidental to the acquisition.

Table B-5
Motivation for Entry: Direct versus Acquisition

	Direct N = 45 mean	Acquisition N = 24 mean
(a) Profitability	2.6	2.1
(b) Growth	2.9	2.2
(c) Share costs	1.4	1.7
(d) Exploit advantage	1.8	1.8
(e) Strengthen position	1.8	2.2
(f) Access to suppliers	1.0	1.0
(g) Access to outlets	1.5	1.8
(h) Counter-cyclical sales	1.0	1.0
(i) Generate cash	1.2	1.1
(j) Use cash	1.2	1.4

Note: See table B-3 for units.

Table B-6
Motivation for Entry: Correlation Matrix
(69 entrants)

	(a)	(b)	(c)	(d)	(e)	(f)	(g)	(h)	(i)	(j)
(a) Profitability	1.00 1.00									
(b) Growth	−.12 .71	1.00 1.00								
(c) Share costs	−.24 .40	.02 .31	1.00 1.00							
(d) Exploit advantage	−.04 .29	−.32 .43	.10 .30	1.00 1.00						
(e) Strengthen position	−.24 .48	.13 .30	.40 .22	.39 .20	1.00 1.00					
(f) Access to suppliers	−.16 .66	.04 .46	.33 .35	.03 .41	.03 .54	1.00 1.00				
(g) Access to outlets	−.21 .53	.18 .55	.20 .41	.24 .43	.64 .44	.30 .39	1.00 1.00			
(h) Counter-cyclical sales	−.02 .57	.06 .29	.02 .25	−.18 .28	−.09 .55	−.03 .90	.14 .27	1.00 1.00		
(i) Generate cash	−.25 .58	.14 .46	.41 .35	.17 .18	.22 .24	.28 .57	.28 .58	−.12 .48	1.00 1.00	
(j) Use cash	−.25 .35	.02 .49	.13 .12	.32 .36	.28 .52	−.07 .49	.08 .42	.11 .61	.16 .24	1.00 1.00

Upper number is for forty-five direct entrants, lower for twenty-four acquisition entrants.

Correlations above |.30| are significant at 95 percent level, two tail, for direct entrants, and above |.40| for acquisition entrants.

Table B-7
Shared Activities versus Motivation for Entry: Correlation Matrix
(69 entrants)

	Shared Activities						
Motivations	*Manufacturing/ Production*	*R&D*	*Distribution/ Service*	*Sales*	*Advertising and Promotion*	*Immediate Customers*	*End Users*
Profitability	-.25 .36	-.21 .25	-.25 .06	-.28 .04	-.37 -.01	-.34 .25	-.32 .19
Growth	.29 .16	.32 .10	.27 .42	.24 .48	.25 .38	.23 .35	.23 .46
Share costs	.39 .48	.35 .43	.30 .62	.30 .52	.26 .34	.19 .56	.24 .31
Exploit advantage	.19 .01	.30 .38	.22 .28	.29 .32	.21 .26	.34 .34	.38 .44
Strengthen position	.58 .36	.59 .24	.49 .09	.49 .13	.60 .03	.54 .19	.55 .27
Access to suppliers	.02 .11	.09 -.02	-.10 -.02	-.10 .00	-.08 -.18	-.09 .25	-.09 .12
Access to outlets	.35 .55	.45 .38	.18 .20	.30 .22	.35 .19	.31 .39	.38 .38
Counter-cyclical sales	.03 .05	.06 -.09	.08 -.09	.14 -.07	.11 -.25	-.06 .15	-.06 .02
Generate cash	.20 .10	.19 -.04	-.06 .08	-.01 .06	-.06 -.15	-.10 .18	.00 .00
Use cash	.04 .29	.09 .20	.10 .23	.24 .29	.20 .25	.40 .24	.36 .31

Upper number is for forty-five direct entrants, lower for twenty-four acquisition entrants.
Correlations above |.30| are significant at 95 percent level, two tail, for direct entrants, and above |.40| for acquisition entrants.

Table B-8
Position Relative to Incumbents: All Entrants
(69 entrants)

	(1) Much Lower 1 Number	(2) Somewhat Lower 2 Number	(3) About the Same 3 Number	(4) Somewhat Higher 4 Number	(5) Much Higher 5 Number	(6) Mean of Codes 1 to 5
(a) Product quality	8	18	30	10	3	2.7
(b) Prices	8	23	29	7	2	2.6
(c) Costs	1	15	28	19	6	3.2
(d) Production effectiveness	6	21	28	14	0	2.7
(e) Sales-force effectiveness	11	22	26	10	0	2.5
(f) Distribution effectiveness	12	28	32	7	0	2.5
(g) Advertising and promotion expenditures	10	25	23	10	2	2.6
(h) Reputation/ brand name	12	19	22	11	5	2.7
Average						2.6

Average excludes (b) and (c).

Table B-9
Position Relative to Incumbents: Direct versus Acquisition
(69 entrants)

	Direct N = 45 mean	Acquisition N = 24 mean
(a) Product quality	2.8	2.5
(b) Prices	2.7	2.5
(c) Costs	3.2	3.2
(d) Production effectiveness	2.8	2.7
(e) Sales-force effectiveness	2.5	2.5
(f) Distribution effectiveness	2.5	2.5
(g) Advertising and promotion expenditures	2.6	2.5
(h) Reputation/brand name	2.8	2.5

Note: See table B-5 for units.

Table B-10
Position Relative to Incumbents: Correlation Matrix
(69 entrants)

	(a)	*(b)*	*(c)*	*(d)*	*(e)*	*(f)*	*(g)*	*(h)*
(a) Product quality	1.00							
	1.00							
(b) Prices	.65	1,00						
	.55	1.00						
(c) Costs	−.16	.12	1.00					
	−.28	.09	1.00					
(d) Production effectiveness	.31	.18	−.31	1.00				
	.60	.53	−.41	1.00				
(e) Sales-force effectiveness	.01	.13	−.38	.25	1.00			
	.79	.44	−.06	.57	1.00			
(f) Distribution effectiveness	.10	.23	−.42	.20	.81	1.00		
	.73	.37	−.24	.62	.78	1.00		
(g) Advertising and promotion expenditures	.26	.36	−.23	.42	.32	.35	1.00	
	.66	.53	−.15	.38	.55	.51	1.00	
(h) Reputation/brand name	.60	.57	−.19	.46	.54	.54	.43	1.00
	.69	.34	.06	.55	.72	.72	.48	1.00

Upper number is for forty-five direct entrants; lower for twenty-four acquisition entrants.

Correlations above |.30| are significant at 95 percent level, two tail, for direct entrants, and above |.40| for acquisition entrants.

Table B-11
Shared Activities versus Relative Position: Correlation Matrix
(69 entrants)

Relative Position	Shared Activities						
	Manufacturing/ Production	R&D	Distribution/ Service	Sales	Advertising and Promotion	Immediate Customers	End Users
Product quality	.25	.23	.09	.15	.12	.26	.25
	−.28	−.12	−.30	−.27	−.11	−.25	−.09
Prices	.06	.12	.16	.13	.04	.14	.16
	.00	−.03	.17	.19	.33	.35	.47
Costs	−.21	−.25	−.15	−.17	−.17	−.12	−.15
	.10	−.02	.34	.34	.23	.43	.46
Production effectiveness	.44	.46	.52	.52	.48	.44	.42
	−.23	−.22	−.34	−.20	−.06	−.35	.06
Sales-force effectiveness	.20	.27	.30	.28	.24	.20	.27
	−.26	−.15	−.23	−.16	−.09	−.14	.03
Distribution effectiveness	.23	.32	.38	.31	.27	.26	.33
	−.31	−.15	−.31	−.28	−.09	−.25	−.10
Advertising and promotion expenditures	.12	.21	.06	.11	.08	.09	.11
	.09	−.14	−.31	−.37	−.27	−.09	−.22
Reputation/ brand name	.42	.47	.39	.37	.36	.37	.39
	−.40	−.28	−.33	−.23	−.26	−.43	−.13

Upper number is for forty-five direct entrants, lower for twenty-four acquisition entrants

☐ = correlations between closely related Shared Activities categories and Relative Position dimensions.

Correlations above |.30| are significant at 95 percent level, two tail, for direct entrants, and above |.40| for acquisition entrants.

Table B-12
Relative Position versus Motivation for Entry: Correlation Matrix
(69 entrants)

Motivations	Product Quality	Prices	Costs	Production Effectiveness	Sales-Force Effectiveness	Distribution Effectiveness	Advertising and Promotion Expenditures	Reputation/ Brand Name
Profitability	-.08	.05	.02	.05	-.25	-.33	-.15	-.21
	-.34	-.14	.30	-.44	-.36	-.36	-.15	-.29
Growth	-.08	-.03	.01	-.01	.40	.36	-.05	.39
	-.40	-.17	.18	-.43	-.39	-.44	-.50	-.40
Share costs	.00	.02	-.05	.13	.09	.14	.17	.05
	-.48	.04	.39	-.53	-.54	-.63	-.14	-.42
Exploit advantage	.32	.14	-.26	.18	-.06	.06	.04	.12
	-.16	.11	.20	-.12	-.15	-.31	-.49	-.22
Strengthen position	.21	.17	-.17	.41	.20	.32	.06	.40
	-.12	-.05	.32	-.03	.19	.05	.05	.12
Access to suppliers	.02	-.10	-.03	.04	.08	.08	.06	-.10
	-.26	-.01	.30	-.20	-.12	-.24	-.11	-.11
Access to outlets	.24	.20	.12	.25	.26	.29	.20	.42
	-.34	-.02	.11	-.27	-.26	-.57	-.10	-.44
Counter-cyclical sales	-.17	.07	.28	.18	.00	-.12	.08	.04
	-.06	.19	.25	-.04	.05	-.05	.14	.13
Generate cash	.18	.23	-.34	-.15	.38	.42	.31	.23
	-.24	-.14	.22	-.41	-.12	-.52	-.03	-.29
Use cash	.38	.28	-.19	.17	.02	.03	.09	.33
	.04	.18	-.04	.02	.12	-.06	-.08	-.03

Position Relative to Incumbents

Upper number is for forty-five direct entrants, lower for twenty-four acquisition entrants.
Correlations above |.30| are significant at 95 percent level, two tail, for direct entrants, and above |.40| for acquisition entrants.

Table B-13
Year-One Share or Acquired Share
(69 entrants)

	(1) *All* *Entrants* *N = 69*	*(2)* *Direct* *Entrants* *N = 45*	*(3)* *Acquisition* *Entrants* *N = 24*
Mean	3.7	2.3	6.3
Standard Deviation	5.6	4.9	6.0
Median	1.5	1.0	4.0
Minimum	0	0	.3
Maximum	31.0	31.0	25.0

Table B-14
Maximum Share
(69 entrants)

	(1) *All* *Entrants* *N = 69*	*(2)* *Direct* *Entrants* *N = 45*	*(3)* *Acquisition* *Entrants* *N = 24*
Mean	7.5	6.8	8.8
Standard Deviation	6.6	6.3	7.0
Median	6.0	5.0	6.5
Minimum	.5	1.0	.5
Maximum	31.0	31.0	25.0

Table B-15
Share Gain versus Acquired Share
(24 acquisition entrants)

	Share Gain		
Acquired Share *(Percent)*	*Mean* *(Percent)*	*Median* *(Percent)*	*Number of* *Observations*
0 to 3.0	2.1	1.5	9
4.0 to 6.0	2.9	1.5	7
6.5 to 20.0	2.5	1.0	8
Total	2.5	1.5	24

Table B-16
Minimum-Required Shares
(31 markets)

	Mean	Standard Deviation	Median	Minimum	Maximum
Major in 1972 (Percent)	11.0	9.4	8.0	1.0	35.0
Minor in 1972 (Percent)	4.0	3.3	4.0	.1	12.0
Ratio major/minor 1972	3.5	2.0	3.0	1.0	10.0
Major in 1979 (Percent)	12.3	10.2	10.0	2.0	50.0
Minor in 1979 (Percent)	5.0	4.1	5.0	.2	18.0
Ratio major/minor 1979	3.2	1.9	3.0	1.0	10.0
Ratio major 72/share of No. 1 incumbent[a]	.35	.30	.25	.08	1.15
Ratio major 79/share of No. 1 incumbent	.40	.29	.31	.08	1.15

[a]Four-year-average share, approximately 1972 to 1975, of incumbent ranked No. 1 in share.

Table B-17
Life-Cycle Stage and Change in Minimum Shares
(31 markets)

	Growth Stage N = 12	Maturity/Decline Stage N = 19
Major share percent		
1972	11.5	10.7
1979	11.3	12.9
(percent change)	(−2)	(21)
Minor share percent		
1972	3.1	4.6
1979	3.8	5.7
(percent change)	(23)	(24)

Table B-18
Comparison Minimum Share and Achieved Share

	Direct Entrants N = 45 (Percentage)	Acquisition Entrants N = 24 (Percentage)
Maximum Achieved >Major 79		
Entered < 6 yrs.	15 (N = 34)	35 (N = 20)
Entered ≥ 6 yrs.	36 (N = 11)	50 (N = 4)
Maximum Achieved >Minor 79		
Entered < 6 yrs.	35	45
Entered ≥ 6 yrs.	64	100
Entry Year 1 or Acquired Share > Major 79	4	33
Entry Year 1 or Acquired Share > Minor 79	9	46

Table B-19
Twenty-One Most Important Direct Entrants

Awareness of Entry	Number	Percent
Immediately upon start-up	17	81
Within one year after start-up	4	19
More than one year after start-up	0	0
Total	21	100

	At Time of Entry		1979	
Seriousness of Threat	Number	Percent	Number	Percent
Insignificant	6	29	1	5
Moderate	9	43	13	62
Serious	6	29	6	29
Threatens survival	0	0	1	5
Total	21	100	21	100

Table B-20
Thirty-Six Most Important Entrants: Relative Position, Change, and Response—Correlation Coefficients

Relative Position	Acquired versus Change (15 acquisition entrants)	21 Direct Entrants Response versus Initial			15 Acquisition Entrants Response versus Change		
		Reporting Incumbent	Other Incumbents	Reporting versus Other	Reporting Incumbent	Other Incumbents	Reporting versus Other
(a) Product quality	.14	.04	−.14	−.04	.42	.42	−.07
(b) Prices	.00	.29	.12	.45	.42	.42	1.00
(c) Costs	−.14	−.51	−.40	.52	.32	.50	.73
(d) Production effectiveness	.07	.07	−.30	.50	.00	.33	.00
(e) Sales-force effectiveness	−.19	.07	.01	.82	−.16	.00	.00
(f) Distribution effectiveness	−.51	−.21	−.15	.71	.00	.00	.00
(g) Advertising and promotion expenditures	−.50	.34	.41	.87	.23	.00	.00
(h) Reputation/ brand name	−.03	.30	.10	.57	−.20	.00	.00

Note: Correlations above |.43| are statistically significant at 95 percent level, two tail, for direct entrants, and |.51| for acquisition entrants.

Table B-21
Thirty-Six Most Important Entrants: Pattern of Share Increase

	Mean			Median		
	Direct Entrants N = 21	Acquisition Entrants N = 15	Total Entrants N = 36	Direct Entrants N = 21	Acquisition Entrants N = 15	Total Entrants N = 36
Number of years since entry						
1	3.9 (20)	7.1 (15)	5.3 (35)	1.0	7.0	3.5
2	3.4 (19)	8.3 (14)	5.5 (33)	2.0	8.0	3.7
3	4.7 (17)	7.9 (12)	6.0 (29)	3.0	6.0	5.0
4	6.3 (16)	9.0 (11)	7.4 (27)	6.0	7.0	7.0
5	7.9 (14)	8.9 (8)	8.2 (22)	8.0	7.0	8.0
6	9.3 (10)	8.6 (7)	9.0 (17)	9.0	7.0	9.0
7	9.7 (7)	9.3 (3)	9.6 (10)	10.0	4.0	9.0
8	6.5 (2)	13.0 (2)	9.8 (4)	1.0	3.0	3.0

Note: Number in parentheses = number of observations.

Table B-22
Incumbent Reactions versus Entrant-Share-Gain Correlations

Reaction Dimension	Direct Entrants[a]		Acquisition Entrants[b]	
	Reporting[c]	Other[d]	Reporting	Other[d]
Product quality	.29	.07	−.13	.70
Prices	.03	−.03	.06	.06
Costs	−.02	.18	.57	.70
Production effectiveness	−.09	.01	.00	.70
Sales-force effectiveness	.14	.15	−.54	.00
Distribution effectiveness	−.10	−.24	.00	.00
Advertising and promotion expenditures	.21	.21	−.42	.00
Reputation/ brand name	.00	.24	−.70	.00

[a]For twenty-one most important direct entrants.
[b]For fifteen most important acquisition entrants.
[c]For the incumbent reporting data for entrants.
[d]Other incumbents on average.
Note: Correlations above |.43| are statistically significant at 95 percent level, two tail, for direct entrants, and |.51| for acquisition entrants.

Appendix C:
Description of
Variables

The regressions on the occurrence of entry (see chapter 3) used existing PIMS data on 793 markets. The other regressions used combined data from the existing PIMS data base and the new ENTRY data. This section provides a key to all PIMS variables and to ENTRY variables that are constructions of more than one item. All other ENTRY variables are fully described by the ENTRY DATA FORMS and DATA MANUAL (see appendixes D and E).

Variable	Base	Time Dimension	Source[a]	Comments
Active acquisition year	Entrant	Year of entry	Dummy from FTC data	1972 and 1973 coded 1, other years 0
Advertising/revenues	Incumbent	4-year average	P212/P201	Media advertising only
Advertising*durables	Incumbent and market	4-year average	P212/P201 and P101	Advertising/revenues times dummy for consumer durable products
Advertising*nondurables	Incumbent and market	4-year average	P212/P201 and P101	Advertising/revenues times dummy for consumer nondurable products
Advertising*industrial	Incumbent and market	4-year average	P212/P201 and P101	Advertising/revenues times dummy for industrial products
Advertising & promotion/revenues	Incumbent	2-year average	P212/P201	Advertising and promotion expenditures
Average relative position	Entrant	Time of entry	E211	Average of all relative position dimensions except Relative Prices and Relative Costs
Average sharing	Entrant	Time of entry	E210	Average of all categories of sharing
Percentage capacity addition	Incumbent	Constant	P512 and P235	Minimum efficient scale for capacity addition
Capacity utilization	Incumbent	4-year average	P236	
Competitors' percentage new products	Incumbent	4-year average	P334	New products as percentage of sales for competitors of reporting incumbent
Percentage direct entrants	Market	72 to 79 total	E101 and E102	Direct entrants as percentage of all entrants into market
Four-firm share	Market	4-year average	P306 to P310	
Incumbent-parent diversity	Incumbent	Constant		A 0 to 3 continuous scale applied subjectively by PIMS. Higher values indicate greater diversity

	Level	Time	Line number[a]	Description
Incumbent-parent size	Incumbent	Constant		Size of corporate parent in $ million
Investment/revenues	Incumbent	4-year average	P228/P201	
Life-cycle stage	Market	Constant	P103	Dummy, coded 1 for Introductory, 2 for Growth, 3 for Maturity, 4 for Decline
Manufacturing/revenues	Incumbent	2-year average	P206/201	
Market growth *PLC1 *PLC2 *PLC3 *PLC4	Market	4-year average	P301, P312 and P103	Interaction of Real Market Growth Rate and dummies for each stage of product life cycle
New products as percentage sales	Incumbent	4-year average	P323	
Price spread	Incumbent	4-year average	P319	P319 is an index of the incumbent's prices relative to competitors. This variable is constructed as follows: $$X = \sqrt{(P319\text{-}100)^2}$$ This gives an absolute measure of price spread between incumbents and their competitors.
Real-market growth rate	Market	4-year average	P301 and P312	
R&D/revenues	Incumbent	4-year average	P207 + P208/P201	
ROI	Incumbent	4-year average	P217/P228	
Sales force/revenues	Incumbent	4-year average	P210/P201	
Technological change	Market	Constant	P110	
Total direct-entrant share	Entrant	1972 to 1979	E203	Sum of largest market share ever of up to three direct entrants per market

[a]Refers to line numbers from (P)IMS and (E)NTRY DATA FORMS. ENTRY DATA FORMS and DATA MANUAL are reproduced in appendixes D and E. Relevant portions of the PIMS Data Forms are reproduced in appendix F.

Appendix D:
Entry Project Data
Forms

177

ENTRY PROJECT DATA FORMS 1, 2, 3, 4, & 5

PIMS Identifying Number
(write in your existing PIMS number)

Return To: The PIMS Program–Data Control
             The Strategic Planning Institute
             955 Massachusetts Avenue
             Cambridge, Ma. 02139

ENTRY DATA FORM 1   Do not complete without
referring to Entry Data
Manual.

□□□□□

GENERAL

	1972	1973	1974	1975	1976	1977	1978	1979
101: No. of Direct Entrants	□	□	□	□	□	□	□	□
102: No. of Acquisition Entrants	□	□	□	□	□	□	□	□
103: No. of Exits - Closed Down	□	□	□	□	□	□	□	□
104: No. of Exits - Sold to Competitors	□	□	□	□	□	□	□	□
105: No. of Exits - Sold to Outsider	□	□	□	□	□	□	□	□

106: Difficulties in Entering this Served Market

   (a) Capital □   (b) Product Design □   (c) Production □   (d) R&D □

   (e) Distribution □   (f) Sales Force □   (g) Advertising & Promotion □   (h) Sales Volume □

   (i) Raw Materials, Labor □   (j) Outlets Penetration □   (k) Patents, Licenses □

107: Size of Largest Incumbent Company $ __ , __ , 000 , 000

108: Minimum Share Required to Compete with

   1a: Major in 1972 [%]   2a: Minor in 1972 [%]

   1b: Major in 1979 [%]   2b: Minor in 1979 [%]

109: Industry Capacity Utilization for this Market

1972	1973	1974	1975	1976	1977	1978
[%]	[%]	[%]	[%]	[%]	[%]	[%]

110: Impact of Entrants   (a) on $ Size of Served Market [%]

   (b) on Profit Margins (ROS) [%]

111: Total Market   (a) Ratio to Served Market Sales [times]

   (b) Price Increase for 10% Sales Switch [%]

THE STRATEGIC PLANNING INSTITUTE, 1979

PIMS Identifying Number   **ENTRY DATA FORM 2**   Do not complete without
☐☐☐☐☐   Page 1   referring to Entry Data
                                                        Manual

THREE LARGEST <u>DIRECT</u> ENTRANTS

	Largest Direct Entrant	2nd Largest Direct Entrant	3rd Largest Direct Entrant
201: Year of Entry			
202: Market Share 1st Year	%	%	%
203: Largest Market Share Ever	%	%	%
204: Estimated Market Share 1979	%	%	%
205: New ("0") or Existing ("1") Company			
206: Size (revenues) of Parent Company	$ Million	$ Million	$ Million
207: Nature of Parent Company	☐	☐	☐
208: Nature of Entry Move	☐	☐	☐
209: Motivation for Entry			
(a) Profitability	☐	☐	☐
(b) Growth	☐	☐	☐
(c) Share Costs	☐	☐	☐
(d) Exploit Advantage	☐	☐	☐
(e) Strengthen Position	☐	☐	☐
(f) Improve access to Suppliers	☐	☐	☐
(g) Improve access to Outlets	☐	☐	☐
(h) Counter Cyclical Sales	☐	☐	☐
(i) Generate Cash	☐	☐	☐
(j) Use Cash	☐	☐	☐

THE STRATEGIC PLANNING INSTITUTE, 1979

Complete other side first **ENTRY DATA FORM 2** Do not complete without referring to Entry Data Manual

Page 2

	Largest Direct Entrant	2nd Largest Direct Entrant	3rd Largest Direct Entrant
210: Activities & Customers Shared with Parent			
(a) Manufacturing/Production	☐	☐	☐
(b) R&D	☐	☐	☐
(c) Distribution	☐	☐	☐
(d) Sales	☐	☐	☐
(e) Advertising & Promotion	☐	☐	☐
(f) Immediate Customers	☐	☐	☐
(g) End Users	☐	☐	☐
211: Entrant's Position Relative to Incumbents			
(a) Product Quality	☐	☐	☐
(b) Prices	☐	☐	☐
(c) Costs	☐	☐	☐
(d) Production Effectiveness	☐	☐	☐
(e) Sales Force Effectiveness	☐	☐	☐
(f) Distribution Effectiveness	☐	☐	☐
(g) Ad & Promotion Expenditures	☐	☐	☐
(h) Reputation/Brand Name	☐	☐	☐

PIMS Identifying Number   **ENTRY DATA FORM 3**   Do not complete without referring to Entry Data Manual

☐☐☐☐☐

Page 1

THREE LARGEST ACQUISITION ENTRANTS

	Largest Acquisition Entrant	2nd Largest Acquisition Entrant	3rd Largest Acquisition Entrant
301: Year of Acquisition	☐	☐	☐
302: Market Share when Acquired	%	%	%
303: Largest Share since Acquisition	%	%	%
304: Estimated Market Share 1979	%	%	%
305: Size (revenues) of Acquiring Parent Company	$ Million	$ Million	$ Million
306: Nature of Acquiring Parent	☐	☐	☐
307: Nature of Acquisition Move	☐	☐	☐
308: Importance of this Market	☐	☐	☐
309: Motivation for Entry			
(a) Profitability	☐	☐	☐
(b) Growth	☐	☐	☐
(c) Share Costs	☐	☐	☐
(d) Exploit Advantage	☐	☐	☐
(e) Strengthen Position	☐	☐	☐
(f) Improve access to Suppliers	☐	☐	☐
(g) Improve access to Outlets	☐	☐	☐
(h) Counter Cyclical Sales	☐	☐	☐
(i) Generate Cash	☐	☐	☐
(j) Use Cash	☐	☐	☐

ENTRY DATA FORM 3

Complete other side first

Do not complete without
referring to Entry Data
Manual

Page 2

	Largest Acquisition Entrant	2nd Largest Acquisition Entrant	3rd Largest Acquisition Entrant
310: Activities & Customers Shared with Parent			
(a) Manufacturing/Production	☐	☐	☐
(b) R&D	☐	☐	☐
(c) Distribution	☐	☐	☐
(d) Sales	☐	☐	☐
(e) Advertising & Promotion	☐	☐	☐
(f) Immediate Customers	☐	☐	☐
(g) End Users	☐	☐	☐
311: Acquired Business' Position Relative to Competitors			
(a) Product Quality	☐	☐	☐
(b) Prices	☐	☐	☐
(c) Costs	☐	☐	☐
(d) Production Effectiveness	☐	☐	☐
(e) Sales Force Effectiveness	☐	☐	☐
(f) Distribution Effectiveness	☐	☐	☐
(g) Ad & Promotion Expenditures	☐	☐	☐
(h) Reputation/Brand Name	☐	☐	☐

PIMS Identifying Number   **ENTRY DATA FORM 4**   Do not complete without
referring to Entry Data
☐☐☐☐☐   Manual.

SINGLE MOST IMPORTANT

ENTRANT - <u>DIRECT</u>

401: Relative Breadth Served Market ☐   408: Entrant's Capacity Addition [%]

402: Relative Breadth Product Line ☐   409: Capacity Response

403: Seriousness of Threat (a) then ☐   (a) You   added/reduced [%]

                          (b) now ☐   (b) Other   added/reduced [%]
                                                 Incumbents
404: Awareness of Entry ☐
                                          410: Hardest Hit Incumbent
405: Served Market Response
                                             (a) Who lost   (b) Who lost
    (a) You ☐   (b) Other ☐   most share ☐   greatest ☐
                    Incumbents   points   proportion
                                                                   of sales
406: Product Line Response
                                          411: Market Shares
    (a) You ☐   (b) Other ☐
                    Incumbents   (a)   (b)
                                                    Entrant   Lost by You
407: Relative Position Response
                                          1972   [%]   [%]
                          Other   1973   [%]   [%]
                 You   Incumbents   1974   [%]   [%]
    (a) Product ☐   ☐   1975   [%]   [%]
        Quality
                                          1976   [%]   [%]
    (b) Prices   ☐   ☐   1977   [%]   [%]

    (c) Costs   ☐   ☐   1978   [%]   [%]

    (d) Production ☐   ☐   1979   [%]   [%]
        Effectiveness

    (e) Sales Force ☐   ☐
        Effectiveness

    (f) Distribution ☐   ☐

    (g) Ad & Promotion ☐   ☐
        Expenditures

    (h) Reputation/ ☐   ☐
        Brand Name

PIMS Identifying Number

ENTRY DATA FORM 5

Do not complete without
referring to Entry Data
Manual.

☐☐☐☐☐

SINGLE MOST IMPORTANT

ENTRANT - <u>ACQUISITION</u>

501: Relative Breadth of Served Market

(a) At time of ☐   (b) Change ☐
    Acquisition

(c) Your ☐   (d) Others' ☐
    Response   Response

502: Relative Breadth of Product Line

(a) At time of ☐   (b) Change ☐
    Acquisition

(c) Your ☐   (d) Others' ☐
    Response   Response

503: Relative Position

	Change	Your Response	Others' Response
(a) Product Quality	☐	☐	☐
(b) Prices	☐	☐	☐
(c) Costs	☐	☐	☐
(d) Production Effectiveness	☐	☐	☐
(e) Sales Force Effectiveness	☐	☐	☐
(f) Distribution	☐	☐	☐
(g) Ad & Promotion Expenditures	☐	☐	☐
(h) Reputation/ Brand Name	☐	☐	☐

504: Capacity

(a) At time of
    Acquisition   ☐ %

(b) Change   added/reduced   ☐ %

(c) Your Response
    added/reduced   ☐ %

(d) Others' Response
    added/reduced   ☐ %

505: Hardest Hit Competitor

(a) Who lost   (b) Who lost
    most ☐   greatest
    share   proportion ☐
    points   of sales

506: Market Shares

	(a) Entrant	(b) Lost by You
1972	☐ %	☐ %
1973	☐ %	☐ %
1974	☐ %	☐ %
1975	☐ %	☐ %
1976	☐ %	☐ %
1977	☐ %	☐ %
1978	☐ %	☐ %
1979	☐ %	☐ %

Appendix E:
Entry Project Data
Manual

P I M S

ENTRY PROJECT

DATA MANUAL

© **SPI** The Strategic Planning Institute 1979

PREFACE

Thank you for agreeing to participate in the Entry Project.

This manual provides instructions on how to complete the attached data forms of the Entry Project. Please note that these data forms cannot be completed without close reference to this manual.

The forms should take you about an hour to complete. The questions relate to the served market of this reporting business. They are about other competitors who have recently entered this served market. The served market is the one defined for this business in the regular data forms of the PIMS Program and in the regular Data Manual.

Since the object of this project is to collect data about entrants from the viewpoint of those already in the market, project participants must have been operating in their served markets before the start of the period for which we are collecting data, i.e., this business unit should not participate if it started operations in 1972 or later, or if it was acquired in 1972 or later by a company not previously competing in this served market.

If you have any problems in completing the forms, contact George Yip at (617) 491-9200.

When you have completed the forms please return them to Data Control. Please do not include this manual.

ABOUT THE DATA FORMS

There are five data forms that relate to the Entry Project. You have been sent all of these forms, but you need to complete only some of them:

<u>FORM 1</u> should be completed by all participants. It contains questions about all types of entry into the served market of the reporting business unit.

<u>FORM 2</u> is about the up to three largest <u>Direct Entrants</u> (if any) who have entered this served market within the last seven years (1972 to 1979). A <u>Direct Entrant</u> is a competitor who has started operations in this served market without first acquiring a business that was already competing in this served market. You should complete Form 2 only if there have been Direct Entrants into this served market. Form 2 has space for responses on up to three Direct Entrants: "Largest Direct Entrant", "2nd Largest Direct Entrant" and "3rd Largest Direct Entrant." Rank the entrants according to the greatest annual share of this served market achieved <u>at any time</u> since the entry, <u>not</u> according to their present share.

<u>FORM 3</u> is about the up to three largest <u>Acquisition Entrants</u> (if any) who have entered this served market within the past seven years (1972 to 1979), by first acquiring an existing competitor. Do not count as an Acquisition Entrant a company already competing in your served market who acquires another competitor in the served market. You should complete Form 3 only if there have been Acquisition Entrants into this served market.

An example of an acquisition entry is Philip Morris' entry into the beer market through acquisition of the Miller Brewing Co.

Form 3 has space for responses on up to three Acquisition Entrants: "Largest Acquisition Entrant", "2nd Largest Acquisition Entrant", and "3rd Largest Acquisition Entrant".

Rank these three (or fewer) acquisition entrants by the amount of market share <u>increase</u> since the acquisition. Do <u>not</u> rank by absolute market share at the time of acquisition, i.e. this project is not concerned with acquisitions as such but with acquisitions used as an entry base for expansion.

<u>FORM 4</u>
or   is about the single most important entrant. Complete Form 4 if the single
<u>FORM 5</u> most important entrant was a Direct Entrant and Form 5 if an Acquisition Entrant. The single most important entrant is the one who has gained the <u>most percentage points of this served market since entry.</u> For example, a Direct Entrant who starts from zero and reaches 7% annual share in any year should be chosen over an Acquisition Entrant who acquired a 10% share company and increased that share to a maximum of 15%, in any year, for a net maximum increase of 5%.

DO NOT WRITE ANSWERS ON THIS DATA MANUAL, BUT ON THE SEPARATE ENTRY DATA FORMS.

REMEMBER TO WRITE IN YOUR BUSINESS' PIMS IDENTIFYING NUMBER IN THE SPACES PROVIDED ON EACH PAGE.

FORM 1 QUESTIONS

Write in answers on separate ENTRY DATA FORM 1.

101 - 105: NUMBER OF ENTRIES AND EXITS

For each of the last seven years, estimate for the served market of this reporting business the number of

(In each case below count only businesses that had 1% or more share of this served market at any time.)

101:   Direct Entrants   (as defined above in description of FORM 2)

102:   Acquisition Entrants   (as defined above in description of FORM 3)

103:   Exits - Closed Down (businesses that ceased operations in this served
                            market, and were not sold as ongoing businesses)

104:   Exits - Sold to Competitor (businesses that were sold to another competitor
                            in this served market)

105:   Exits - Sold to Outsider (businesses that were sold to a company not
                            previously competing in this served market)

106:   DIFFICULTIES IN ENTERING THIS MARKET

For a new competitor that is an established company but that has not previously competed in this served market or industry, estimate the level of difficulty in meeting the requirements in this served market for

(a) Sufficient Financial Capital
(b) Competitive Product Design
(c) Adequate Production Quality/Efficiency
(d) Successful R&D
(e) Extensive enough Distribution Network
(f) Competitive Sales Force
(g) Advertising and Promotion to develop Product Image/Identity
(h) Sales Volume necessary to support overhead costs
(i) Getting Raw Materials or Labor
(j) Getting penetration of Distribution Outlets e.g. wholesalers or retailers
(k) Obtaining Patents/Licenses

In each box for this question, write one of the following:

   "1" (if your estimate is "Little Difficulty")
   "2" (if your estimate is "Moderate Difficulty")
   "3" (if your estimate is "High Difficulty")

107:   SIZE OF LARGEST INCUMBENT COMPANY

Estimate the approximate corporate annual revenues in 1978 of the largest parent company of any business competing in this served market throughout 1972 to now i.e, not an entrant since 1972. The largest company is not necessarily the same as the company with the largest market share, as its corporate revenues may include revenues from markets other than this one.

-3-

108:   MINIMUM SHARE FOR MAJOR & MINOR COMPETITORS

(1a & 1b)
Estimate the minimum market share that a direct entrant would require if it
were seeking to survive with a business strategy similar to those of major
competitors in this market in 1972 and 1979.

(2a & 2b)
Estimate the minimum market share that a direct entrant would require if it
were seeking to survive with a business strategy similar to those of minor
competitors in this market in 1972 and 1979.

109:   INDUSTRY CAPACITY UTILIZATION FOR THIS MARKET

Estimate for each year since 1972 combined sales for all competitors
(including entrants into this served market) as a percent of combined
industry capacity (an approximate estimate to the nearest 10% is adequate).

110a: IMPACT OF ENTRANTS ON SIZE OF SERVED MARKET

Estimate the impact of all entries (within last seven years) on the current
dollar size of this served market.

Write in your estimate of the percent by which the current size is larger
or smaller than otherwise. You may round out your estimate to within 10%.

        e.g., +50% if current size 50% larger than otherwise
        e.g., -10% if current size 10% smaller than otherwise
        e.g.,   0% if no effect

110b: IMPACT OF ENTRANTS ON PROFIT MARGINS

Estimate the impact of all entries (within last seven years) on the average
current level of profit margins for all competitors as measured by net return
on sales. Write in the estimated percent change (not percentage points change).

111:   TOTAL MARKET

The standard Data Manual asks PIMS businesses to define their served market
as narrowly as possible. Please provide here information about a broader
"Total Market" of which this Served Market is a part.

The Total Market should include

- all types of customers and all geographic areas, to which the products/
  services of the business unit could (practically speaking) be sold;

- all versions, sizes, etc., of products which could (practically speaking)
  be included in the offering of the business unit.

Please estimate

(a) the ratio of the dollar size of this Total Market to the dollar size of the
Served Market. Use the average ratio for the past seven years. e.g. 3.5 times

(b) how much the average price level in the Served Market would have to rise,
in percentage terms, before 10% or more of Served Market sales would be lost to
other parts of the Total Market. Allow whatever time is needed for demand
to adjust to the price change. For example, "compact new passenger automobiles
sold in the U.S." may be the Served Market and "all new passenger automobiles
sold in the U.S." may be the Total Market. An estimate might be that the price
of compact automobiles would have to rise by 5% before 10% or more compact sales
were lost to other types of automobiles.

-4-

FORM 2 QUESTIONS

THREE LARGEST DIRECT ENTRANTS (if any)

Write in answers on separate ENTRY DATA FORM 2.

As described earlier FORM 2 is about the three (or fewer) largest DIRECT
ENTRANTS, as defined by "largest annual market share ever achieved since entry,"
if entry within the last seven years. Do not count entrants who never reached
at least 1% annual market share. There is a column on DATA FORM 2 for each of up
to three Direct Entrants. (If there have been no Direct Entrants, go to page 9.)
For each answer the following:

201:    YEAR OF ENTRY

Calendar year in which entry occurred.

202-204: MARKET SHARES

202:    Share of this served market in first year after entry.

203:    The largest annual share _ever_ achieved since entry.

204:    The expected market share for 1979

NEW OR EXISTING COMPANY

205:    State whether the Direct Entrant was

.. a newly started company, not owned by an existing company (write "0" in box)

.. an existing company already competing in other markets (write "1" in box)

206:    SIZE OF PARENT COMPANY OF DIRECT ENTRANTS

At the time of entry what were the approximate annual revenues of the parent
company of the entrant? (If the entrant is a new company without a parent,
the answer is zero.)

207:    NATURE OF PARENT COMPANY OF DIRECT ENTRANTS

Characterize the parent company of each entrant, prior to the entry, as _one_
of the following:

SINGLE BUSINESS (write "1" in box)

a company that manufactures and distributes a single product, a line
of products with variations in size and style, or a set of closely related
products linked by technology or market structure. Examples are Peabody
Coal, American Motors and Anheuser-Busch.

DOMINANT BUSINESS (write "2" in box)

a company that derives 70%-95% of sales from a single business (as
defined above) or a vertically integrated chain of businesses. Examples
are General Motors, IBM, Texaco, Scott Paper, U.S. Steel and Xerox.

(continued on page 6)

-5-

RELATED BUSINESS (write "3" in box)

a company that has diversified into related areas, where no single business accounts for more than 70% of sales. Examples are DuPont, Eastman Kodak, General Electric, General Foods and Philip Morris.

UNRELATED BUSINESS OR CONGLOMERATE (write "4" in box)

a company that has diversified without necessarily relating new businesses to old, and where no single business accounts for as much as 70% of sales. Examples are Litton, LTV, North American Rockwell, Olin and Textron.

NO PARENT COMPANY (write "0" in box)

.. if you answered "New ("0")" for line 205, the entrant has no previous parent company.

208:   NATURE OF DIRECT ENTRY MOVE

Characterize each direct entry as one of the following in relation to the pre-existing businesses of the entering company:

GEOGRAPHIC EXPANSION (write "1" in box)

.. the new entry is the expansion of an existing product or
   service to a previously unserved geographic area.

SEGMENT EXPANSION (write "2" in box)

.. the entering company was already competing in the Total Market of
   which this Served Market is a segment.

RELATED EXPANSION (write "3" in box)

.. the entering company was not already competing in the Total
   Market, but the entry is closely related horizontally to its
   pre-existing businesses.

FORWARD VERTICAL INTEGRATION (write "4" in box)

.. the new entry is related to pre-existing businesses and is at a
   stage closer to the end user.

BACKWARD VERTICAL INTEGRATION (write in "5" in box)

.. the new entry is related to pre-existing businesses and is at a
   stage closer to sources of supply.

UNRELATED DIVERSIFICATION (write "6" in box)

.. the new entry is not closely related to its pre-existing business.

NO PRE-EXISTING BUSINESSES (write "0" in box)

.. if you answered "new ("0")" for Line 205, the entrant has no pre-
   existing businesses.

-6-

209: <u>MOTIVATION FOR DIRECT ENTRY</u>

Estimate for each entrant the importance of each of the following in motivating entry:

(a) Served market profitability at time of entry

(b) Served market growth prospects

(c) To share costs with entrant's other activities

(d) To exploit an advantage arising from entrant's other activities (basically an offensive move)

(e) To strengthen entrant's market position in other activities (basically a defensive move)

(f) To improve access to suppliers for entrant's other activities

(g) To improve access to outlets for entrant's other activities

(h) Served market sales are counter-cyclical to entrant's other sales

(i) Served market would generate surplus cash for entrant's other activities

(j) Served market would use surplus cash from entrant's other activities

In each box for this question, write one of the following:

                "1" (if your estimate is "Little/No Importance")
                "2" (if your estimate is "Some Importance")
                "3" (if your estimate is "Major Importance")

210:    <u>SHARED ACTIVITIES AND CUSTOMERS</u>

What was the maximum proportion of each entrant's activities or customers
that were shared, at any time, with other components of its parent company?

(a) Manufacturing/Production

(b) R & D

(c) Distribution/After Sales Service

(d) Sales

(e) Advertising and Promotion

(f) Immediate Customers

(g) End Users

In each box for this question, write one of the following:

"0" (if a new company without an existing parent)
"1" (if up to 10% of activities were shared with parent)
"2" (if 10% to 50% of activities were shared with parent)
"3" (if 50% to 90% of activities were shared with parent)
"4" (if 90% to 100% of activities were shared with parent)

211:    <u>ENTRANT'S POSITION RELATIVE TO INCUMBENTS</u>

For each direct entrant, estimate the level relative to leading incumbents
at the time of entry, for:

(a) Product Quality (include after sales service)

(b) Prices

(c) Costs

(d) Production Effectiveness

(e) Sales Force Effectiveness

(f) Distribution Effectiveness

(g) Advertising and Promotion Expenditures

(h) Reputation of Company/Strength of Brand Name

In each box for this question, write one of the following:

"1" (if your estimate is "much lower")
"2" (if your estimate is "somewhat lower")
"3" (if your estimate is "about the same")
"4" (if your estimate is "somwhat higher")
"5" (if your estimate is "much higher")

-8-

FORM 3 QUESTIONS

<u>THREE LARGEST ACQUISITION ENTRANTS</u> (if any)

Write in answers on separate ENTRY DATA FORM 3.

As described earlier, FORM 3 is about the three (or fewer) largest ACQUISITION ENTRANTS, as defined by "greatest increase in annual market shares since acquisition," if acquired within the last seven years. Do not count Acquisition Entrants who never reached at least 1% annual market share. There is a column on DATA FORM 3 for each of up to three ACQUISITION ENTRANTS. (If there have been no Acquisition Entrants, go to page 13.) For each answer the following:

301:    YEAR OF ACQUISITION

Calendar year in which acquisition occurred

302-304   MARKET SHARES

302:    Annual share of the Served Market at time of acquisition

303:    Largest annual market share at any time since acquisition

304:    The expected market share for 1979

305:    SIZE OF ACQUIRING PARENT COMPANY

At the time of acquisition what were the approximate corporate revenues of the parent company making the acquisition?

306:    NATURE OF ACQUIRING PARENT COMPANY

Characterize the acquiring parent company, prior to the acquisition, as one of the following:

SINGLE BUSINESS (write "1" in box)

a company that manufactures and distributes a single product, a line of products with variations in size and style, or a set of closely related products linked by technology or market structure. Examples are Peabody Coal, American Motors and Anheuser-Busch.

DOMINANT BUSINESS (write "2" in box)

a company that derives 70%-95% of sales from a single business (as defined above) or a vertically integrated chain of businesses. Examples are General Motors, IBM, Texaco, Scott Paper, U.S. Steel and Xerox.

RELATED BUSINESS (write "3" in box)

a company that has diversified into related areas, where no single business accounts for more than 70% of sales. Examples are DuPont, Eastman Kodak, General Electric, General Foods, and Philip Morris.

UNRELATED BUSINESS OR CONGLOMERATE (write "4" in box)

a company that has diversified without necessarily relating new businesses to old, and where no single business accounts for as much as 70% of sales. Examples are Litton, LTV, North American Rockwell, Olin and Textron.

-9-

307:     <u>NATURE OF ACQUISITION ENTRY MOVE</u>

Characterize each acquisition entry as one of the following in relation to the
pre-existing businesses of the acquiring company (ignore businesses not
competing in this served market and which may have been acquired at the
same time as the one competing in this served market).

GEOGRAPHIC EXPANSION (write in "1" in box)
.. the new entry is the expansion of an existing product or service
to a previously unserved geographic area.

SEGMENT EXPANSION (write "2" in box)
.. the entering company was already competing in the Total Market of
which this Served Market is a segment.

RELATED EXPANSION (write "3" in box)
.. the entering company was not already competing in the Total Market
but the entry is closely related horizontally to its pre-existing
businesses.

FORWARD VERTICAL INTEGRATION (write "4" in Box)
.. the new entry is related to pre-existing businesses and is at a
stage closer to the end user.

BACKWARD VERTICAL INTEGRATION (write "5" in box)
.. the new entry is related to pre-existing businesses and is at stage
closer to sources of supply.

UNRELATED DIVERSIFICATION (write "6" in box)
.. the new entry is not closely related to pre-existing businesses.

308:     <u>IMPORTANCE OF THIS MARKET FOR ACQUISITION</u>

Entry into this served market may have been an incidental reason for the
acquisition, e.g., the business competing in this served market was acquired
as part of a larger company. Indicate which one of the following best
describes the importance of entry into this market as a reason for the
acquisition:

Entry not relevant or incidental (write "0" in box)

Entry of minor importance (write "1" in box)

Entry of major importance (write "2" in box)

309: <u>MOTIVATION FOR ACQUISITION ENTRY</u>

For each acquisition entrant for whom the answers above were "1 minor importance" or "2 major importance," estimate the importance of each of the following in motivating the acquisition entry:

(a) Served market profitability

(b) Served market growth

(c) To share costs with acquiror's other activities

(d) To exploit an advantage arising from acquiror's other activities (basically an offensive move)

(e) To strengthen acquiror's market position in other activities (basically a defensive move)

(f) To improve access to suppliers for acquiror's other activities

(g) To improve access to outlets for acquiror's other activities

(h) Served market sales are counter-cyclical to acquiror's other sales

(i) Served market would generate surplus cash for acquiror's other activities

(j) Served market would use surplus cash from acquiror's other activities

In each box for this question, write one of the following:

"0" (if question does not apply, because you answered "0"
     "Entry not Relevant" to line 308)
"1" (If your estimate is "Little/No Importance")
"2" (if your estimate is "Some Importance")
"3" (if your estimate is "Major Importance")

310: <u>SHARED ACTIVITIES AND CUSTOMERS</u>

For each acquired business unit, estimate the proportion of the following activities or customers <u>in this served market</u> which were potentially capable of being shared with other components of the acquiring company:

(a) Manufacturing/Production

(b) R & D

(c) Distribution/After sales service

(d) Sales

(e) Advertising and Promotion

(f) Immediate Customers

(g) End Users

-11-

In each box for this question, write one of the following:

"1" (if 0% to 10% was potentially capable of being shared with parent)
"2" (if 10% to 50% was potentially capable of being shared with parent)
"3" (if 50% to 90% was potentially capable of being shared with parent)
"4" (if 90% to 100% was potentially capable of being shared with parent)

311:     NATURE OF ACQUIRED BUSINESS' POSITION RELATIVE TO COMPETITORS

For each acquired business, estimate the level relative to the major
competitors in this served market at the time of its acquisition, for:

(a) Product Quality (include after sales service)

(b) Prices

(c) Costs

(d) Production Effectiveness

(e) Sales Force Effectiveness

(f) Distribution Effectiveness

(g) Advertising and Promotion Expenditures

(h) Reputation of Company/Strength of Brand Name

In each box for this question, write one of the following:

"1" (if your estimate is "Much Lower")
"2" (if your estimate is "Somewhat Lower")
"3" (if your estimate is "About the Same")
"4" (if your estimate is "Somewhat Higher")
"5" (if your estimate is "Much Higher")

FORM 4 QUESTIONS

SINGLE MOST IMPORTANT ENTRANT - DIRECT

Write in answers on separate ENTRY DATA FORM 4.

This section applies only to the single most important entrant, as defined at the beginning of this data form, if a DIRECT ENTRANT. If the single most important entrant is an ACQUISITION ENTRANT complete FORM 5 instead. (Go to page 16.) (The Direct Entrant for which you record data here should be the same as the one for which you completed the "Largest Entrant" boxes in FORM 2.)

401:    RELATIVE BREADTH OF SERVED MARKET

Estimate the breadth of the new entrant's <u>target</u> served market, relative to the weighted average of the three largest existing competitors (including yourself)

Write in box:

    "1" if much narrower
    "2" if somewhat narrower
    "3" if same
    "4" if somewhat broader
    "5" if much broader

402:    RELATIVE BREADTH OF PRODUCT LINE

Relative to the weighted average of the product lines of the three largest incumbents (including yourself if one of three largest) already established in this market, estimate the breadth of the product line of the entrant business during the first two years of entry.

Write in box:

    "1" if much narrower
    "2" if somewhat narrower
    "3" if same
    "4" if somewhat broader
    "5" if much broader

403:    SERIOUSNESS OF THREAT

(a) At the time of entry how serious a threat did you (the reporting business) consider the new competitor?

(b) How serious do you consider the threat now?

Write in box:

    "1" if insignificant threat
    "2" if moderate threat
    "3" if serious threat
    "4" if threatens survival

-13-

404:     AWARENESS OF ENTRY

When did you (the reporting business) decide that the new entrant was competing in this served market, relative to the start-up of the entrant's activities?

Write in box:
    "1" if immediately upon start-up
    "2" if within one year after start-up
    "3" if more than one year after start-up

405:     SERVED MARKET RESPONSE

(a) Indicate the maximum change made in the relative breadth of <u>your</u> served market as a response to this entry.

(b) Indicate the maximum change made in the relative breadth of <u>their</u> served markets by other incumbent competitors (on average).

Write in box:
    "1" if responded by greatly narrowing served market
    "2" if responded by somewhat narrowing served market
    "3" if responded with no change
    "4" if responded by somewhat broadening served market
    "5" if responded by greatly broadening served market

406:     PRODUCT LINE RESPONSE

(a) Indicate the maximum change made in the breadth of <u>your</u> product line as a response to this entry

(b) Indicate the maximum change made in the breadth of <u>their</u> product lines by other incumbent competitors (on average).

Write in box:
    "1" if responded by greatly narrowing product line
    "2" if responded by somewhat narrowing product line
    "3" if responded with no change
    "4" if responded by somewhat broadening product line
    "5" if responded by greatly broadening product line

407:     RELATIVE POSITION RESPONSE

Indicate the maximum change you and other incumbent competitors (on average) have made since the entry to affect your position <u>relative to this entrant,</u> for:

(a) Product Quality (include after sales service)

(b) Prices

(c) Costs

(d) Production Effectiveness

(e) Sales Force Effectiveness

(continued on next page)

-14-

(f) Distribution Effectiveness

(g) Advertising and Promotion Expenditures

(h) Reputation of Company/Strength of Brand Name

Write in box:

"1" if greatly lowered relative position
"2" if somewhat lowered relative position
"3" if relative position kept the same
"4" if somewhat raised relative position
"5" if greatly raised relative position

408: <u>CAPACITY ADDITION</u>

How much production capacity has the entrant added since its entry, as a percent of industry capacity for this market before the entry?

409: <u>CAPACITY RESPONSE</u>

How much production capacity have (a) you, and (b) all other incumbents as a group, added or reduced since the entry, as a percent of industry capacity for this market before the entry?

410: <u>HARDEST HIT INCUMBENT</u>

Which incumbent competitor has lost to this entrant the greatest
(a) number of absolute share points (b) proportion of its sales

Write in box:

"0" if this reporting business
"1" if largest other incumbent competitor
"2" if second largest other incumbent competitor
"3" if third largest other incumbent competitor
"4" if another incumbent competitor

411: <u>MARKET SHARES</u>

Estimate for each year since entry

(a) the market share achieved by the entrant

(b) the number of percentage points market share that this reporting business has less of, as a direct or indirect result of the entry, i.e. report the estimated <u>cumulative</u> share points loss for each year.

FORM 5 QUESTIONS

SINGLE MOST IMPORTANT ENTRANT - ACQUISITION

Write in answers on separate ENTRY DATA FORM 5

This section applies only to the single most important entrant, as defined at the begining of this data form, if an ACQUISITION ENTRANT. If the single most important entrant is a DIRECT ENTRANT, complete FORM 4 instead. (The Acquisition Entrant for which you record data here should be the same as the one for which you completed the "Largest Entrant" boxes in FORM 3.)

501:     RELATIVE BREADTH OF SERVED MARKET

(a) estimate the breadth of the acquired business' served market, at the time of acquisition, relative to the weighted average of the three largest other competitors (including yourself if one of three largest).

Write in box:

        "1" if much narrower
        "2" if somewhat narrower
        "3" if same
        "4" if somewhat broader
        "5" if much broader

(b) Estimate the maximum change in the breadth of the acquired business' served market at any time since acquisition.

Write in box:

        "1" if greatly narrowed
        "2" if somewhat narrowed
        "3" if no change
        "4" if somewhat broadened
        "5" if greatly broadened

(c) Indicate any changes made in the relative breadth of your served market as a response to moves by the acquired business (use same response codes as for (b)).

(d) Indicate any changes made in the relative breadth of their served market by other competitors (on average) as a response to moves by the acquired business (use same response codes as for (b)).

-16-

502:   ## RELATIVE BREADTH OF PRODUCT LINE

(a) Estimate the breadth of the acquired business' product line, at the time of acquisition, relative to the weighted average of the three largest other competitors (including yourself if one of three largest).

Write in box:

"1" if much narrower
"2" if somewhat narrower
"3" if same
"4" if somewhat broader
"5" if much broader

(b) Estimate the maximum <u>change</u> in the breadth of the acquired business' product line at any time <u>since</u> its acquisition.

Write in box:

"1" if greatly narrowed
"2" if somewhat narrowed
"3" if no change
"4" if somewhat broadened
"5" if greatly broadened

(c) Indicate any changes made in the relative breadth of <u>your</u> product line as a response to moves by the acquired business (use the same response codes as for (b)).

(d) Indicate any changes made in the relative breadth of <u>their</u> product lines by other competitors (on average) as a response to moves by the acquired business (use the same response codes as for (b)).

503:   ## RELATIVE POSITION CHANGES & RESPONSES

For each of the categories (a) to (h) below,

(1) indicate the maximum changes in level made by the acquired business at any time since its acquisition.

(2) indicate the maximum change made by <u>you</u> in response to the acquired business.

(3) Indicate the maximum change made by other competitors (on average) in response to the acquired business.

(a) Product Quality (include after sales service)

(b) Prices

(c) Costs

(d) Production Effectiveness

(e) Sales Force Effectiveness

(f) Distribution Effectiveness

(g) Advertising and Promotion Expenditures

(h) Reputation of Company/Strength of Brand Name

-17-

Write in box:

      "1" if greatly lowered relative position
      "2" if somewhat lowered relative position
      "3" if relative position kept the same
      "4" if somewhat raised relative position
      "5" if greatly raised relative position

504:    CAPACITY

Estimate as a percent of industry capacity for this market at the time of acquisition

(a) the acquired business' capacity

(b) the maximum change, at any time since the acquisition, for the acquired business' capacity

(c) the maximum change in your capacity as a direct or indirect response to the acquired business

(d) the maximum change in their combined capacity, by other competitors as a group, as a direct or indirect response to the acquired business

505:    HARDEST HIT COMPETITORS

Which competitor has lost to the acquired business since acquisition the greatest

(a) number of absolute share points (b) proportion of its sales

Write in box:

      "0" if this reporting business
      "1" if largest other competitor
      "2" if second largest other competitor
      "3" if third largest other competitor
      "4" if another competitor

506:    MARKET SHARES

Estimate for each year since the acquisition

(a) the market share of the acquired business

(b) the number of percentage points market share that this reporting business has less of, as a direct or indirect result of the entry, i.e., report the estimated cumulative share points lost for each year.

-18-

Appendix F:
Excerpts from PIMS Data Forms of the Strategic Planning Institute

101: TYPE OF BUSINESS

This business is best described as . . . *(Check one of the following eight boxes)*

CONSUMER-PRODUCTS MANUFACTURING:

. . . Durable Products   ☐ 1

. . . Non-Durable Products   ☐ 2

INDUSTRIAL/COMMERCIAL/PROFESSIONAL-PRODUCTS MANUFACTURING:

. . . Capital Goods   CHECK   ☐ 3

. . . Raw or Semi-Finished Materials   ONE   ☐ 4

. . . Components for Incorporation into Finished Products   ONLY   ☐ 5

. . . Supplies or Other Consumable Products   ☐ 6

SERVICES   ☐ 7

RETAIL AND WHOLESALE DISTRIBUTION   ☐ 8

103: "LIFE CYCLE" STAGE OF PRODUCT CATEGORY

How would you describe the stage of development of the types of products or services sold by this business during the last three years? *(Check one)*

. . . Introductory Stage: Primary demand for product just starting to grow; products or services still unfamiliar to many potential users   ☐ 1

. . . Growth Stage: Demand growing at 10% or more annually in real terms; technology or competitive structure still changing   ☐ 2

. . . Maturity Stage: Products or services familiar to vast majority of prospective users; technology and competitive structure reasonably stable   ☐ 3

. . . Decline Stage: Products viewed as commodities; weaker competitors beginning to exit   ☐ 4

106-107: PATENTS AND TRADE SECRETS

Does this business benefit *to a significant degree* from patents, trade secrets, or other proprietary methods of production or operation . . .

106: Pertaining to products or services?   NO ☐ 0   **107:** Pertaining to processes?   NO ☐ 0

                                                    YES ☐ 1   YES ☐ 1

110: TECHNOLOGICAL CHANGE

Have there been *major* technological changes in the products offered by the business or its major competitors, or in methods of production, during the last 8 years? *(If in doubt about whether a change was "major," answer NO.)*

                                                                                          NO ☐ 0

                                                                                          YES ☐ 1

201: NET SALES (REVENUE) (D)

Revenues realized from goods shipped or services rendered net of (1) bad debts, (2) returns, and (3) allowances. Include lease revenues and progress payments applicable to a given year.

206: MANUFACTURING & PHYSICAL-DISTRIBUTION EXPENSES (D)

Indicate direct labor and other costs of converting the purchases into the final product or service, plus all logistical costs (e.g., warehousing, freight, etc.). Exclude depreciation expenses, which belong on Line 215.

207: PRODUCT OR SERVICE R&D EXPENSES (D)

Show all expenses incurred to improve the existing products or services of this business or to develop new products or services. Include improvements in packaging as well as product design, features, and functions. Exclude expenses for process improvement; these belong on Line 208.

208: PROCESS R&D EXPENSES (D)

Indicate all expenses for improving the efficiency of the manufacturing and distribution processes.

210: SALES-FORCE EXPENSES (D)

This includes (1) compensation and expenses incurred by salesmen, (2) commissions paid to brokers or agents, and (3) cost of sales-force administration.

211: ADVERTISING & SALES-PROMOTION EXPENSES (D)

Include all expenditures for (1) media advertising, (2) catalogs, (3) exhibits and displays, (4) premiums, (5) coupons, (6) samples, and (7) *temporary* price reductions for promotional purposes.

212: MEDIA-ADVERTISING EXPENSES (D)

Isolate expenditures for *media* advertising within the total shown on Line 211.

217: PRETAX INCOME (D)

Enter the profit of this business prior to deduction of all federal, state and local taxes.

228: INVESTMENT (D)

Indicate the average investment in this business for each year. Include both fixed and working capital at book value. Exclude corporate investment not specifically required by this business (e.g., corporate aircraft).

235: STANDARD CAPACITY (D)

The sales value in current dollars of the maximum output that this business can sustain with (1) facilities normally in operation and (2) current constraints (e.g., technology, work rules, labor practices, etc.). For most manufacturing businesses, this will consist of 2 shifts, 5 days per week. For process businesses, a 3-shift, 6-day period is typical.

236: CAPACITY UTILIZATION

The percentage of standard capacity utilized on average during the year, including production for inventory. If the business shares production facilities with other businesses, indicate the overall capacity utilization.

301: SIZE OF SERVED MARKET (D)

Indicate the total sales in the market actively served by this business. Your entry should be in current dollars (i.e., including price changes) and reflect the same disguise factor as on Line 201 (Net Sales).

Please note that whenever the largest value entered on Line 301 is less than four or more than five digits, all Form 2 and 3 data designated "(D)" will automatically be rescaled.

302: GEOGRAPHIC LOCATION OF SERVED MARKET

Was the served market for this business, as measured on Line 301, primarily located in . . . *(Check one)*

Entire United States	☐ 1	United Kingdom	☐ 5
All of Canada	☐ 2	Common Market	☐ 6
U.S. and Canada	☐ 3	Regional within Europe	☐ 7
Regional within U.S. and/or Canada	☐ 4	Other	☐ 8

304: ENTRY OF COMPETITORS

During the past 5 years, have any competitors with at least 5% market share entered the served market?

NO ☐ 0   YES ☐ 1

305: EXIT OF COMPETITORS

During the past 5 years, have any competitors with at least 5% market share dropped out of the served market?

NO ☐ 0   YES ☐ 1

306-310: MARKET SHARES

For each year, report the share of the *served* market accounted for by this business and by each of the three largest competing businesses. "Share of market" is defined as being the sales of a business as a percentage of the served market (defined on Line 301). Please report the market shares in prior years of the three competitors with the largest market shares in the most recent year.

306: THIS BUSINESS

307: COMPETITOR "A" (the largest competitor in the most recent year)

308: COMPETITOR "B" (the second largest competitor in the most recent year)

309: COMPETITOR "C" (the third largest competitor in the most recent year)

310: THREE LARGEST COMPETITORS, COMBINED TOTAL (not including this business)

In the calculation of the relative market share of this business, its share is divided by the combined share of its three largest competitors. Lines 307-309 provide the data necessary for calculating relative share in the most recent year. In prior years, however, the sum of Lines 307-309 will understate the combined share of the three largest competitors if a major competitor has dropped out of the top three. Therefore, on Line 310, please enter the combined share of the three competitors with the largest market shares in each year.

311: MARKET-SHARE RANK

Relative to the latest year of data, what was the market-share rank of this business within the served market?

312: INDEX OF PRICES (1973 = 100%)

For each year, estimate the average level of this business's selling prices as a percentage of the level in 1973. This percentage should not reflect changes in the product mix.

319: RELATIVE PRICES (Weighted Average for Three Largest Competitors = 100%)

For each year, estimate the average level of selling prices of this business's products and services, relative to the average price of the three largest competitors. (Example: If this business's prices averaged 5% above those of leading competitors, report 105%.)

323-324: NEW PRODUCTS, PERCENTAGE OF TOTAL SALES

For each year, estimate what percentage of the total sales was accounted for by products introduced during the 3 preceding years first for this business and then for the simple average of the three largest competitors. **NOTE:** For the distinction between new products and product-line extensions, please consult the *PIMS Data Manual*. (Example: for 1974, "New Products" should include those introduced in 1972, 1973 and 1974.)

512: CAPACITY ADDITIONS

What is the *minimum* economically efficient amount by which the standard capacity of this business could be increased, expressed as a percentage of the standard capacity in the last year reported on Line 235, Form 2?

%

Bibliography

Abernathy, William J., and James M. UtterBack. "Innovation and the Evolving Structure of the Firm," *Harvard Business School.* Research paper no. 8-676-003, June 1975.

Alemson, M.A. "Demand, Entry, and the Game of Conflict in Oligopoly Over Time: Recent Australian Experience," *Oxford Economic Papers* 21, no. 2 (July 1969).

Andrews, Kenneth R. *The Concept of Corporate Strategy,* rev. ed. Homewood, Ill.: Irwin, 1980.

Ansoff, H. Igor. *Corporate Strategy.* New York: McGraw-Hill, 1965.

Ansoff, H. Igor, Richard G. Brandenburg, Fred E. Portner, and Raymond Radosevich. *Acquisition Behavior of U.S. Manufacturing Firms, 1946-1965.* Nashville, Tenn.: Vanderbilt University Press, 1971.

Bain, Joe S. *Barriers to New Competition.* Cambridge, Mass.: Harvard University Press, 1956.

Baumol, W.J. *Business Behavior, Value and Growth,* rev. ed. New York: Harcourt Brace, 1967.

Berry, Charles H. "Corporate Growth and Diversification," *The Journal of Law and Economics,* 14, no. 2, (October 1971).

Berry, Charles H. *Corporate Growth and Diversification.* Princeton, N.J.: Princeton University Press, 1975.

Bevan, Alan. "The U.K. Potato Crisp Industry, 1960-72: A Study of New Entry Competition," *Journal of Industrial Economics.* 22, no. 4 (June 1974):281-297.

Biggadike, E. Ralph. *Corporate Diversification: Entry, Strategy and Performance.* Boston: Division of Research, Harvard Business School, 1979.

_____ . "The Risky Business of Diversification," *Harvard Business Review* 57, no. 3 (May-June 1979):103-111.

Boston Consulting Group. "Perspectives on Experience." Boston, 1968; and "The Experience Curve—Reviewed, I, II, III, IV." Boston, 1973, 1974.

Brock, Gerald W. *The U.S. Computer Industry: A Study of Market Power.* Cambridge, Mass.: Ballinger, 1974.

Business Week. "Turmoil among the Brewers: Miller's Fast Growth." November 8, 1976.

Business Week. "Pillsbury's Ambitious Plans to Use Green Giant." July 9, 1978.

Buzzell, Robert D., Bradley T. Gale, and Ralph G.M. Sultan. "Market Share—A Key to Profitability," *Harvard Business Review* 53, no. 1 (January-February 1975):97-106.

213

Caves, Richard E., and Michael E. Porter. "From Entry Barriers to Mobility Barriers: Conjectural Decisions and Continued Deterrence to New Competition," *Quarterly Journal of Economics* 91 (May 1977):241-262.

Caves, Richard E., Michael E. Porter, A. Michael Spence, and John T. Scott. *Competition in the Open Economy.* Cambridge, Mass.: Harvard University Press, 1980.

Chandler, Alfred D., Jr. *Strategy and Structure.* Cambridge, Mass.: The M.I.T. Press, 1962.

Chandler, Alfred D., Jr. *The Visible Hand: The Managerial Revolution in American Business.* Cambridge, Mass.: The Belknap Press of Harvard University Press, 1977.

Comanor, William S., and Thomas A. Wilson. "Advertising, Market Structure and Performance," *Review of Economics and Statistics* 69, no. 4 (November 1967):423-440.

Duetsch, Larry L. "Structure, Performance and the Net Rate of Entry into Manufacturing Industries," *Southern Economic Journal* 41, no. 3 (January 1975):450-456.

Fruhan, William E., Jr. "Pyrrhic Victories in Fights for Market Share," *Harvard Business Review* 50, no. 5 (September-October 1972):100-107.

Gale, Bradley T. "Planning for Profit," *Planning Review* 6, no. 1, (January 1978):4-32.

Gale, Bradley T. "Cross-Sectional Analysis: The New Frontier in Planning," *Planning Review* 6, no. 2 (March 1978):17-20.

Gluck, Frederick, Stephen P. Kaufman, and A. Steven Wallech. "The Evolution of Strategic Management," *McKinsey Staff Paper.* New York: McKinsey & Company, October 1978.

Gorecki, Paul K. "An Inter-industry Analysis of Diversification in the U.K. Manufacturing Sector," *The Journal of Industrial Economics* 24, no. 2 (December 1975):131-146.

Gorecki, Paul K. "The Determinants of Entry by Domestic and Foreign Enterprises in Canadian Manufacturing Industries: Some Comments and Empirical Results," *Review of Economics and Statistics* 58, no. 4 (November 1976):485-488.

Gort, Michael. *Diversification and Integration in American Industry.* Princeton, N.J.: Princeton University Press, 1962.

Hall, William K. "A Tale of Two Acquisitions," *University of Michigan Business Review.* May 1977, pp. 1-8.

Harrigan, Kathryn Rudie. *Strategies for Declining Businesses.* Lexington. Mass.: Lexington Books, D.C. Heath and Company, 1980.

Hayes, Robert H., and Steven G. Wheelwright. "The Dynamics of Process-Product Life Cycles," *Harvard Business Review,* 57, no. 2 (March-April 1979):127-136.

Henderson, Bruce D. *Henderson on Corporate Strategy.* Cambridge, Mass.: Abt Books, 1979.

Hines, Howard H. "Effectiveness of 'Entry' by Already Established Firms," *Quarterly Journal of Economics* 71, no. 1, (1957):132-150.

Hofer, Charles, W. "Toward a Contingency Theory of Business Strategy," *Academy of Management Journal* 18, no. 4 (December 1975):784-810.

Hunt, Michael D. *Competition in the Major Home Appliance Industry.* Unpublished Ph.D. dissertation. Cambridge, Mass.: Harvard University, 1972.

Kitching, John. "Why Do Mergers Miscarry?," *Harvard Business Review* 45, no. 6 (November-December 1967):84-101.

Learned, Edmund P., C. Roland Christensen, Kenneth R. Andrews, and William Guth. *Business Policy.* Homewood, Ill.: Irwin, 1969.

Levitt, Theodore. "Marketing Success through Differentiation—of Anything," *Harvard Business Review* 58, no. 1 (January-February 1980):83-91.

Mann, Michael H. "Seller Concentration, Barriers to Entry, and Rates of Return in Thirty Industries, 1950-1960," *Review of Economics and Statistics* 43, no. 3 (August 1966):296-307.

Mansfield, Edwin. "Entry, Gibrat's Law, Innovation, and the Growth of Firms," *American Economic Review* 52 (December 1962):1023-1051.

Markham, Jesse W. *Conglomerate Enterprise and Public Policy.* Boston, Mass.: Division of Research, Harvard Business School, 1973.

Miller, Richard A. "Market Structure and Industrial Performance: Relation of Profit Rates to Concentration, Advertising Intensity, and Diversity," *Journal of Industrial Economics,* 17, no. 2 (April 1969):104-118.

Modigliani, Franco. "New Developments on the Oligopoly Front," *Journal of Political Economy* 66 (June 1958):215-232.

Morrison, Donald G. "On the Interpretation of Discriminant Analysis." 6, no. 2 (May 1969):156-163.

Morrison, Donald G. "Upper Bounds for Correlations between Binary Outcomes and Probabilistic Predictions," *Journal of the American Statistical Association* 67, no. 3 (March 1972):68-70.

Mueller, D., and Tilton, J. "Research and Development Costs as a Barrier to Entry," *Canadian Journal of Economics* 2 (November 1969):570-579.

Naylor, Thomas H. "PIMS: Through a Different Looking Glass," *Planning Review* 6, no. 2 (March 1978):15-34.

Orr, Dale. "The Determinants of Entry: A Study of the Canadian Manufacturing Industries," *Review of Economics and Statistics* 56, no. 1 (February 1974):58-66.

Pfeffer, Jeffrey, and Gerald R. Salancik. *The External Control of Organizations: A Resource Dependence Perspective.* New York: Harper & Row, 1978.

Phillips, Lynn W., and Louis W. Stern. "Limit Pricing Theory as a Basis for Anti-Merger Policy," *Journal of Marketing* 41, no. 2 (April 1977):91-97.

Porter, Michael E. *Interbrand Choice, Strategy, and Bilateral Market Power,* Cambridge, Mass.: Harvard University Press, 1976.

————. "Consumer Behavior, Retailer Power and Market Performance in Consumer Goods Industries," *Review of Economics and Statistics* 56, no. 4 (November 1974):419-435.

————. "Please Note Location of Nearest Exit: Exit Barriers and Planning," *California Management Review* 19, no. 2 (Winter 1976):21-33.

————. "How Competitive Forces Shape Strategy," *Harvard Business Review* 57, no. 2 (March-April 1979):137-145.

————. *Competitive Strategy: Techniques for analyzing Industries and Competitors.* New York: The Free Press, 1980.

————. "The Contributions of Industrial Organization to Strategic Management," *Academy of Management Review.* 6, no. 4 (October 1981):609-620.

Rhoades, Stephen A. "The Effect of Diversification on Industry Profit Performance in 241 Manufacturing Industries: 1963," *Review of Economics and Statistics* 50, no. 2 (May 1973):146-155.

————. "Notes," *Review of Economics and Statistics* 51, no. 4 (November 1974):557-559.

Roach, John D.C. "From Strategic Planning to Strategic Performance: Closing the Achievement Gap," *Outlook.* New York: Booz-Allen & Hamilton, Incorporated, Spring 1981.

Rumelt, Richard P. *Strategy, Structure, and Economic Performance.* Boston: Division of Research, Harvard Business School, 1974.

Salop, Steven C. "Strategic Entry Deterrence," *American Economic Review* 69, no. 2 (May 1979):335-338.

Salter, Malcolm, S. "Stages of Corporate Development," *Journal of Business Policy* 1, no. 1, (1970):23-37.

Salter, Malcolm S., and Weinhold, Wolf A. *Introduction to Corporate Diversification.* Harvard Business School note 1-377-135, June 1977.

————. *Diversification through Acquisition: Strategies for Creating Economic Value.* New York: The Free Press, 1979.

Schmalensee, Richard. "Entry Deterrence in the Ready-to-Eat Breakfast Cereal Industry," *Bell Journal of Economics* 9, no. 2 (Autumn 1978):305-327.

Schlaifer, Robert. *User's Guide to the AQD Collection,* Seventh ed. (Boston: Harvard Case Services, 1978).

Schelling, Thomas C. *The Strategy of Conflict.* Cambridge, Mass.: Harvard University Press, 1960.

Scherer, F.M. *Industrial Market Structure and Economic Performance.* Chicago: Rand McNally & Co. 1970.

Schoeffler, Sidney, Robert D. Buzzell, and Donald F. Heany. "Impact of Strategic Planning on Profit Performance," *Harvard Business Review* 52, no. 2 (March-April 1974):137-145.

Shepherd, William G. "The Elements of Market Structure," *Review of Economics and Statistics* 54, no. 1 (February 1972):25-32.

Scott, Bruce R. "The Industrial State—Old Myths and New Realities," *Harvard Business Review* 51, no. 2 (March-April 1973):133-148.

Stonebraker, Robert J. "Corporate Profits and the Risk of Entry," *Review of Economics and Statistics* 58, no. 1, (February 1976):33-39.

U.S. Federal Trade Commission. *Statistical Report on Mergers and Acquisitions.* Washington, D.C.: Bureau of Economics, November 1976.

U.S. Federal Trade Commission v. *Procter & Gamble Company,* 386 U.S. 568 (1967).

United States vs. *Penn-Olin Chemical Company,* 378 U.S. 158 (1964).

United States vs. *Falstaff Brewing Corporation,* 410 U.S. 526 (1973).

Wall Street Journal. "Procter & Gamble, via Takeover, to Enter Highly Competitive Soft Drink Industry." May 21, 1980.

Williamson, Oliver E. "Selling Expense as a Barrier to Entry," *Quarterly Journal of Economics* 77 (February 1963):112-128.

Williamson, Oliver E. "Markets and Hierarchies: Some Elementary Considerations," *American Economic Review* 63 (May 1973):316-325.

Yip, George S. "Market Selection and Direction, The Role of Product Portfolio Planning." Boston: Harvard Case Services no. 9-581-107, 1981.

Index

About the Author

George S. Yip is an assistant professor at the Harvard Business School where he teaches marketing. He received the B.A. and M.A. in economics from Magdalene College, Cambridge University; the M.B.A. from the Cranfield School of Management, England; and the M.B.A. and D.B.A. from the Harvard Business School. Dr. Yip specializes in strategic planning and strategic marketing. He has also had extensive business experience, having held advertising and product-management positions with companies of the Unilever group, and sales and business-management positions with Data Resources, Inc.